IMAGES OF BELIEF IN LITERATURE

The National Conference of Literature and Religion was founded to explore the common ground between the study of theology and the study of literature. The essays in this book are drawn from the first meeting of the Conference and they are deliberately diverse; they are united by a common concern to seek in the imaginative and metaphorical world of literature a lively and perhaps radical expression of religious faith and belief.

The topics covered include the modern American writers Joan Didion and Flannery O'Connor, whose "experience of mystery" must be mediated through the manners of a literary artifact; W. H. Auden and George Herbert are examined from the point of view of the border of literature and Christian devotion, spirituality, and the life of prayer; while Simone Weil, who interpreted her own life and death in terms of the sacrifice of Christ, gives rise to a discussion of "sacrificial suffering" in a writer.

Other essays range across a wide expanse of Western literature, from the Book of Job and Greek tragedy to the English Romantic poets and George Eliot. Finally, attention is given to more general problems which are raised when religion and literature attempt to focus on common concerns: the problem of religious commitment in art; of exegesis; and the nature and theory of narrative.

As a whole, the book raises issues which are of deep interest to theologians and churchmen and women, students of literature, and anyone concerned with the matter of exploring a communicating religious belief in the modern world.

The editor

David Jasper is Fellow and Chaplain of Hatfield College, Durham. He graduated in English from Jesus College, Cambridge, and subsequently trained for the Anglican ministry, at St Stephen's House, Oxford, where he also took a degree in theology.

He has published articles on literature and religion in various journals and periodicals.

IMAGES OF BELIEF IN LITERATURE

Edited by

David Jasper

Fellow and Chaplain
Hatfield College, Durham

St. Martin's Press   New York

© David Jasper 1984

Printed in Hong Kong.
Published in the United Kingdom by The Macmillan Press Ltd.
First published in the United States of America in 1984

ISBN 0–312–40920–6

Library of Congress Cataloging in Publication Data
Main entry under title:

Images of belief in literature.

Includes index.
Contents: Introduction/F. W. Dillistone—Religion
and imagination/John Coulson—Mystery and mediation:
reflections on Flannery O'Connor and Joan Didion/
D. Z. Phillips—[etc.]
1. Religion and literature—Addresses, essays,
lectures. I. Jasper, David.
PN49.I54   1984   809 '.93382   83–40170
ISBN 0–312–40920–6

Contents

Notes on the Contributors

DOMINIC BAKER-SMITH is Professor of English, Universiteit van Amsterdam.

JOHN COULSON is Senior Lecturer in the Department of Theology, University of Bristol.

F. W. DILLISTONE is Canon Emeritus of Liverpool Cathedral and Fellow Emeritus of Oriel College, Oxford. He is President of the National Conference on Literature and Religion.

MICHAEL EDWARDS is Reader in Literature, University of Essex.

MARTIN JARRETT-KERR was formerly Associate Lecturer in the Department of Theology and the School of English, University of Leeds. He is now of the Community of the Resurrection, Mirfield.

DAVID JASPER is Chaplain and Harris Fellow of Hatfield College, University of Durham.

ANN L. LOADES is Senior Lecturer in Theology, University of Durham.

D. Z. PHILLIPS is Professor of Philosophy at the University College of Swansea.

STEPHEN PRICKETT is Reader in English at the University of Sussex.

ULRICH E. SIMON is Professor Emeritus of Christian Literature and Dean Emeritus of King's College, London.

PETER WALKER is the Bishop of Ely.

HELEN WILCOX is Lecturer in English at the University of Liverpool, and currently editing Herbert's poems for the Longman Annotated English Poets.

T. R. WRIGHT is Lecturer in English at the University of Newcastle-upon-Tyne.

Acknowledgements

The author and publishers wish to thank the following who have kindly given permission for the use of copyright material:

Faber and Faber Ltd and Random House Inc. for extracts from 'Horae Canonicae' in *W. H. Auden: Collected Poems* edited by Edward Mendelson;
Farrar, Straus & Giroux Inc. and Wallace & Shiel Agency Inc. for extracts from *Slouching Towards Bethlehem* by Joan Didion, copyright © 1965, 1966, 1967, 1968 by Joan Didion;
Farrar, Straus & Giroux Inc. and A. D. Peters & Co. Ltd on behalf of the Estate of Mary Flannery O'Connor for extracts from 'Revelation' in *Everything that Rises Must Converge* by Flannery O'Connor. US copyright © 1961, 1965 by the Executors.

Preface

The papers in this Symposium were read at the first National Conference on Literature and Religion in Durham, 23–25 September 1982. They are evidence of the wide range of interests which were represented at the Conference – theologians and literary critics, philosophers and churchmen. Each paper is individual and self-sufficient, yet the collection as a whole sets in motion a series of cross-currents, as tools of different disciplines engage matter of common interest in sacred and secular literature. A coherent attention, therefore, comes to be given to such key issues for both theology and literature as revelation, imagination, commitment and prophecy.

The joint study of literature and theology has for some years flourished in the United States, and the Conference was honored by the presence of Professor Robert G. Collmer of Baylor University, Texas, the President of the American Conference on Christianity and Literature. It is our hope to begin to draw together the considerable amount of work in this field at present being carried out on this side of the Atlantic, to give it focus and to foster fruitful discussion.

Part of Stephen Prickett's paper was published in *Centrum*, Spring 1981. Michael Edwards' paper is to appear as part of a book, *Towards a Christian Poetics*, to be published by Macmillan in 1984. My editorial duties have been eased immensely by the help of Professor J. R. Watson and Mrs. M. M. Gilley. Thanks are also due to Mrs. Frances Durkin, who typed the final script and to Christopher Helliwell who prepared the index.

Hatfield College   DAVID JASPER
University of Durham

Introduction

F. W. Dillistone

I

Over a considerable period, certainly since the ending of the Second World War, there has been a growing interest in America in the relationship between literature and religion. My own interest was quickened through some twelve years of residence on the North American continent and through the facilities offered by the University Library in Toronto and the Widener Library at Harvard. But since returning to England in 1952 I have realised that there has been hesitation, even suspicion in academic circles in this country when attempts have been made to suggest that theology and English literature have much to contribute to one another and to learn from one another. Traditionally religion and philosophy have interacted fruitfully so that philosophy of religion has been regarded as a respectable discipline. This has not, however, been the case with theology and literature. In general it has been assumed that each should have its own subject matter and methodology and that there should be no straying from one department into the other.

A possible breakthrough came with the publication in England in 1964 of Amos Wilder's book *Early Christian Rhetoric*. Wilder, whose brother Thornton achieved fame through novels and dramas, is himself a poet, and a sensitive literary critic, besides being a distinguished biblical scholar. From 1954 until his retirement he held the Chair of New Testament at the Harvard Divinity School and during that period encouraged , with balance and wisdom, the whole study of the relationship between his two major interests. Yet, so far as I have been able to judge, his book with its fascinating exploration of the modes and genres of New Testament literature – the dialogue, the story, the parable, the poem – made little impact in England. He revealed himself as equally familiar with Bornkamm, Bultmann and Dibelius on the one side, with Eliot,

1

Rilke and Auerbach on the other. It was an approach to the New Testament similar to that to the Hebrew Scriptures which has been gaining marked attention and much appreciative comment in 1982 through Robert Alter's *The Art of Biblical Narrative*.

Between 1952 and 1982 there has indeed been a movement here in England towards recognition of the value of interdisciplinary studies but it has been slow. In the particular area of theology and literature a persistent and dedicated advocate of closer relationship has been John Coulson, whose early university degree was in Philosophy and English Literature and who taught in that field before making a special study of Newman and assessing his contribution both to religion and literature in the nineteenth century. Coulson's opening paper at the Durham Conference, which forms Chapter 2 in this book, shows how he has been able not only through his books and articles but also through his active development of courses in the University of Bristol to promote the relationship of which I have been speaking. The co-operation of the two departments of English and Theology has proved its value not least in the warmth of student response.

Elsewhere in British universities there have been few developments of an organisational kind. At Cambridge the system allows students to read one Tripos in English and another in Theology while in the former Tripos the inclusion of a paper on moral issues means that religious perspectives can also sometimes come into view. But in the main contributions to the religion–literature interrelationship have come from the writings of individuals; for example, Helen Gardner in Oxford, L. C. Knights in Cambridge, John Tinsley when at Leeds, Stephen Prickett at Sussex, Ulrich Simon in London. It has been left to Durham to organise the First National Conference on Literature and Religion. All in any way concerned with it would I think agree that this came about largely through the vision and enthusiasm and organisational labours of David Jasper, who, as Chaplain to Hatfield College, stirred the interest and gained the support of members of the departments of English Literature and of Theology in the University of Durham. The conference itself, meeting from 23–25 September 1982 was an outstanding success. The six major papers given at the conference form Chapters 2–7 in this book: in addition nearly forty shorter papers were presented to four groups meeting simultaneously. These papers ranged over a very wide territory: poetry, fiction, literature of particular historical periods, Biblical imagery, the nature of inspiration, narrative form, tragedy. Only a selection of these can appear in this book though my own judgement was that these contributions were full of valuable insights into the inter-relationship which was the main theme of the conference. The striking thing was that one was scarcely conscious of whether a reader came from a department of literature or from a department of theology. There was a natural and unforced interchange.

II

One of the major papers which produced lively interest and discussion was that by Professor D. Z. Phillips. It is remarkable how, over the past two decades, the stories of Flannery O'Connor have gained steadily growing appreciation and even acclaim. In his book *Craters of the Spirit*, Nathan A. Scott, who has been one of the foremost leaders in America in establishing a legitimate place for *Literae Humaniores* in any curriculum of theological studies, described hers as

> an art that very much wanted to wake the spirit's sleep, to break that somnolence into which we flee from the exactions of the moral life; and it consistently expresses a fierce kind of rage at the feckless, lack-lustre slum to which the human world is reduced when, through indolence of spirit or failure of imagination men have lost all sense of the pressure of glory upon the mundane realities of experience and have thus 'fallen' into the profane.[1]

His chapter is entitled 'The Pressure of Glory', a striking phrase which in a measure summarises what the conference at Durham was all about. Can the pressure of glory be felt through reading great literature as well as through meditating on the biblical narratives?

As far as fiction is concerned Flannery O'Connor in her relatively short life and limited output struggled to express this 'pressure of glory' which is the most mysterious element in human experience. About this she wrote:

> The serious fiction writer will think that any story that can be entirely explained by the adequate motivation of the characters or by a believable imitation of a way of life or by a proper theology will not be a large enough story for him to occupy

himself with. This is not to say that he doesn't have to be
concerned with adequate motivation or accurate reference or a
right theology; he does; but he has to be concerned with them
only because the meaning of his story does not begin except at a
depth where these things have been exhausted. The fiction writer
presents mystery through manners, grace through nature, but
when he finishes, there always has to be left over that sense of
mystery which cannot be accounted for by any human formula. [2]

Whether we call it the sense of mystery or the pressure of glory or, in
the words of Harold Bloom, 'the Sublime. . . . that little beyond
ourselves that reason, nature and society together cannot satisfy' (a
review in the *New York Review of Books*, 15 July 1976) or the sense of
an ending (the title of Frank Kermode's book), this is the ultimate
concern of writers who recoil from the blank *nothing more* of
Wordsworth's 'Peter Bell':

> In vain, through every changeful year
> Did Nature lead him as before;
> A primrose by a river's brim
> A yellow primrose was to him,
> And it was nothing more.

III

It is, I realise, easy to look back nostalgically at periods when
theological writings and creative works of literature seemed to
exercise a beneficial influence on one another. Yet it can scarcely be
denied that to-day there exists what has been described as a
disengagement of theology from imagination.

One hardly expects to appeal to Luther, with his emphasis on
justification by faith and forgiveness of sins, for support in
advocating the essential role of imaginative literature in the
theologian's task and yet we find him declaring:

> I myself am convinced that without the knowledge of the
> [Humanistic] studies, pure theology can by no means exist, as has
> been the case until now: when the [Humanistic] studies were
> miserably ruined and prostrate [theology] declined and lay
> neglected, I realize there has never been a great revelation of

God's Word unless God has first prepared the way by the rise and
the flourishing of languages and learning, as though these were
forerunners, a sort of [John] the Baptist. . . . I certainly wish
there would be a tremendous number of poets and orators, since I
realize that through these studies, as through nothing else, people
are wonderfully equipped for grasping the sacred truths, as well
as for handling them skillfully and successfully. . . . Therefore I
beg also you to urge your young people at my request (should this
have any weight) to study poetry and rhetoric deligently. [3]

What Luther advocated in terms of *languages and letters* has in the
theological curricula of the past two centuries all too often been
interpreted in terms either of philological acquaintance with the
Biblical *languages* of Hebrew and Greek (or beyond to other
languages of the ancient world), or of detailed knowledge of
documents revealing the history of events and their interpretation
within the Jewish and Christian traditions. There has been
comparatively little attention to poetry and rhetoric. Yet the
publishers of Hough's *The Dream and the Task* [4] claimed that: 'For
intelligent people to-day literature has come, consciously or
unconsciously, to supply the patterns of conduct, feeling and
imagination that were formerly within the sphere of organised
religion'.

If this is in any way true, theology should be paying careful
attention to literature. It has at various periods established valuable
links with philosophy, with law, with history, and more recently
with psychology and sociology. Its relations with science have been
more uneasy and hitherto, at least in Britain, it has remained at a
distance from literary works and studies. Partly there has been the
admission that from its side it has little to offer in any prospective
partnership though on either side there are bound to be enquiries
about literary modes, about hermeneutical methods, and about
cultural backgrounds. And it is even possible that the historian of
religion has something to contribute to the creator of literature as
has been modestly claimed by Mircea Eliade. In his Journals of
1957–69 published as *No Souvenirs* he wrote:

I am more and more convinced of the literary value of the
materials available to the historian of religion. If art – and above
all literary art, poetry, the novel – knows a new Renaissance in
our time, it will be called forth by the rediscovery of the function

of myths of religious symbols, and of archaic behaviour. Ultimately what I've been doing for more than fifteen years is not totally foreign to literature. It could be that someday my research will be considered an attempt to re-locate the forgotten sources of literary inspiration. [5]

At any rate the Durham Conference was a welcome and promising beginning of what may become a closer relationship. Many conferences are held to focus attention on developments in individual disciplines: experts and specialists share their discoveries with one another. This can be useful and valuable. The happy, and I believe exceedingly fruitful, feature at Durham was the crossing of boundaries, the withdrawing of blinds, the openness to other perspectives. It was a beginning. Time alone will show whether the enthusiasm will continue and whether each area of concern will benefit by a closer relationship with the other.

NOTES

1. Nathan A. Scott, *Craters of the Spirit* (London, 1969), pp. 272–3.
2. Flannery O'Connor, *Mystery and Manners* (London, 1972), p. 153.
3. *Luther's Works*, Vol. 49. *Letters* II. Edited and translated by Gottfried G. Krodel (Philadelphia, 1972), p. 34. To Eobanus Hesse, 29 March 1523.
4. Graham Hough, *The Dream and the Task* (London, 1963).
5. Mircea Eliade, *No Souvenirs* (New York, 1977), p. 119.

1 Religion and Imagination (Relating Religion and Literature) – a syllabus

John Coulson

This is an attempt to show how the connection between religion and imagination may usefully be approached by studying the relationship between religion and literature. I shall also attempt to provide a methodology, or basis for teaching this relationship, by elucidating the proper questions which should inform the syllabus.

For teaching purposes a chronological exposition is always the easiest to grasp; and it is on this basis that the syllabus for the degree in Religion with Literature at Bristol has been constructed. Over three years our syllabus distinguishes four periods or, more properly, modes of relationship between religion and imagination as this is reflected in major works of literature. They are as follows:

(1) Where imaginative forms and religious beliefs reinforce each other. It is to be seen, of course, in Shakespeare, but this reciprocal relationship extends to Dr Johnson and Jane Austen, but not beyond.

(2) Where imaginative forms testify to the beginnings of a dissociation of faith from belief, and culture from religion. At first, the Romantics – Wordsworth, Coleridge and Newman – attempt to restore this reciprocity on new terms. Later writers, however, despair of a recovery and fall back upon culture. For convenience I refer to such writers as Arnold, Tennyson, George Eliot and Hardy as Modernists.

(3) Where the culture is so violently disrupted that the imagination becomes (in Wordsworth's sense) 'impaired'. The poets

of the First World War afford the most obvious example; but
the topic is most fruitfully studied if it is extended to include
Wordsworth himself, Yeats, and the literature not only of
military but of political violence.

(4) Where the imagination is engaged in a society which is
constitutionally committed to a strict secularity, as in the
United States, for example.

I conclude, however, with what may seem to be an extra curricular
question:

(5) What is the place of the confessional imagination in a secular
culture?

I

In almost all the classics of English or European literature written
before the nineteenth century, their authors assume the truth of the
Christian faith. It does not have to be justified. The onus of disproof
rests with the unbeliever. Our appreciation needs to be theologically well informed. Thus it is necessary to know that the moral
structure of *Macbeth* takes us back through Dante to Aristotle.
Macbeth has been deliberately programmed (if that is the right
word) to commit all the gravest and most mortal sins, of which
treachery to guests and lords is the most damnable. Similarly in
reading Milton's *Paradise Lost*, books 9 and 10, it is necessary to have
some conception of the doctrine of original sin, unless we are
prepared to believe that the Fall was simply Eve's fault.

But our theological attention goes deeper than supplying information. We notice that the response we are required to make to the
text requires us to use our imagination – in the sense of responding to
the work as a whole before we break it down into its component
parts. This is one use of imagination; there are others of course; but
what I have in mind is what Coleridge calls its *adunating* power, that
is, its power to bring many diverse elements into one. We have to
believe in the work before, and as a condition of understanding it.
Here, at once, the theologian becomes aware of a similar claim
made upon him by the act of faith, and to the question which that
raises – How may I believe what I cannot understand or absolutely
prove? We might go further and claim that, since the response

demanded by works of literary imagination is comparable in religion to the act of faith, such exercises of imagination when undertaken by theologians restore self-confidence and give them back their nerve when they are confronted by the ruin which over-rigorous exegesis makes of the Gospels.

But there is more to Macbeth than mortal sin. Although we *know* that the sins of which Macbeth is guilty are the deadliest, our imagination is most strongly engaged in those passages where we feel for him. But that feeling is not at variance with our judgement of his actions: such opposed elements are, for the time being, held in unity. The more general question is what is gained when religion and imagination are thus integrated? In this case religion provides a framework which gives substance and reality to the poet's sym-pathy. For example, references in *Macbeth* to 'sacrament' and 'pity' are not to mere similies which we entertain, they have a performat-ive charge and refer to the very bones of an active morality. They are not to be played with. Instead they lead us to what they derive from – to a reality deeper than the social preferences of a people. Their origins are in the Bible and the liturgy.

In such circumstances the culture is the incarnation of the religion, and the elements of our experience which may now seem to be irreconcilably opposed to each other are not as yet fragmented. Such later distinctions as those between imaginative assent and rational reflection, and between how we feel and how we ought to judge are reconciled in what W. B. Yeats called a unity of being.[1] This was reinforced by a comparable continuity of culture such that (to borrow a picturesque illustration from Yeats) even in the eighteenth century the great Venetian ladies finished their balls on the pavement before their doors 'conscious of an all enfolding sympathy'.

Such sentiments may sound over-idealised. What is indisputable is the existence of a strong conservative and religious imagination which, formed and substantiated by belief, is nevertheless able to protect religious assent from cliché and over-simplification. Conversely, the capacity of religion to provide a framework for imagination is still taken for granted by Jane Austen. When, for example, she refers to 'religion' she means by it all that the theologian Joseph Butler means in the *Analogy* and the *Fifteen Sermons*. When, in *Mansfield Park*, she refers to Fanny's 'heroism of principle' (Chapter 27), to 'her being well principled and religious' (Chapter 30), and, in *Sense and Sensibility*, to Marianne's new life as being regulated by religion, by reason, by constant employment' (Chapter 46), she means exactly what Butler means when he writes that 'Religion is a practical thing'. [2] To live heroically by conscience we must acquire habits and principles, since conscience has less power than it has authority: 'Had it strength, as it has right; had it power as it has manifest authority; it would absolutely govern the world'. [3] For neither writer is the existence and authority of conscience an open question, any more than the term 'sacramental' in Shakespeare is to be understood in less than a fully symbolic sense: for Macbeth to murder Duncan is the same kind of blasphemy as to steal the sacred host: each is sacred in the same way.

Here, in a freeze-dried form, is the substance of almost half of the syllabus for the degree of Religion with Literature. We have seen how religion gives substance to imagination. Does this continue as we approach a change in consciousness? The methods of science become paramount. The machines are born.

II

We now enter the second phase of the course. By about 1840 a new sense of there being a radical discontinuity between the past and present begins to become apparent. The controlling image is that of being between two worlds – one dead, the other powerless to be born. The best introduction to what becomes two opposed tendencies is afforded by Mill's essays on Bentham (1838) and Coleridge (1840). Bentham's attitude to received beliefs is to question their truth: they must first be proved before they may be held. Coleridge, on the other hand, asks of received beliefs what is the truth they were formulated to express: they must first be held before they can be verified.

In varying degrees the writers of this period attempt to resolve the discontinuity between past and present. For example Coleridge expresses a view of the continuity of tradition which is very similar to Newman's. Coleridge writes: 'Great good of such revolution as alters, not by exclusion, but by an enlargement that includes the former, though it places it in a new point of view'. [4] In other words, identity perpetuates itself through change. Thus Wordsworth continued through his life to revise *The Prelude* by making explicit the religious and Christian implications of its affirmations. He was not always successful, but the interesting question arises when we compare the earlier with the later version. Is a preference for the earlier drafts merely fashionable, and the poetry better for being acceptably agnostic, or is the poetry of the later versions sometimes better for being more adequate to the poet's faith? What is the connection between poetic adequacy and adequacy of belief?

As the period develops a distinction between faith and belief becomes emphasised. For example, Tennyson in *In Memoriam* (1850) speaks of our believing 'where we cannot prove'. 'There lives more faith in honest doubt (believe me) than in half the creeds.' This is a crisis of belief, not of unbelief, as may be seen when we look more closely at the work of George Eliot. In 1841 she had translated Feuerbach's *The Essence of Christianity* – a work which was to determine her interpretation as a novelist of her characters' aspirations and beliefs. Although to her, as to Feuerbach, God is a projection in anthropomorphic images of our values and aspirations, we must live with these projections in order to live through them to the moral realities they mediate. For example, in *Adam Bede* she commends Methodism for providing a 'rudimentary culture' which connected its members' thoughts with the past, lifted their imagination above the sordid details of daily life, and suffused their souls with a sense of 'a pitying, loving, infinite presence'.[5]

As the period develops so does the sceptical tendency, but the preference for a culture which depends upon a superseded religion remains. It continues to be the source of what gives substance to imagination. Hardy, for example, speaks of himself as 'churchy', although he waits in 'unhope', 'fervourless'; but he attends God's Funeral in a spirit of devout agnosticism. He asks:

> Whence came it we were tempted to create
> One whom we can no longer keep alive?

Take away religion from his novels and you remove all source of dramatic tension. Yet because in such a culture Christianity appears to be no more than a saving lie – that is something socially desirable, but metaphysically false – it has been fruitful to turn to the Russian novelists, especially to Dostoevsky and Tolstoy. Their creative outburst in the years between 1860 and 1880 in its sheer vigour takes us back to the Elizabethans. Dostoevsky, for example, expresses a Christology which is both orthodox and yet as fully aware of the elements of Western scepticism as any of the writers I have named. It reaches its climax in the parable of the Grand Inquisitor, and in Shatov's confession of faith in *The Devils* (1871):

> 'I believe in Russia. I believe in the Greek Orthodox Church. I believe in the Body of Christ. I believe that the Second Coming will take place in Russia'.
> 'But', he is asked, 'in God? In God?' He replies, 'I shall believe in God'.[6]

Tolstoy, on the other hand, comes closer to George Eliot and Feuerbach but deals with a much wider, less provincial range of human experience. For example, at the end of *Anna Karenina*, Tolstoy shows how Levin recovers his religious beliefs; and since Tolstoy is still able to locate his characters and their questions within a tradition subserved by a strongly conservative imagination, the critical question is how far Tolstoy is being ironical. Levin decides that 'when he did not think but just lived,' he was aware of God's existence within him.[7] This ontological awareness is 'outside the chain of cause and effect' (p. 830): and Levin comes to it only as he lives 'by virtue of the beliefs in which he had been brought up' (p. 832). He concludes his soliloquy thus: 'I shall still be unable to understand with my reason why I pray, and I shall still go on praying' (p. 853).

This is not so very far from Newman's account of the convergence of probabilities into certitude in *A Grammar of Assent*. But Newman is not being ironical. Tolstoy may be so; and Matthew Arnold most certainly is when he writes that there are two things clear about the Christian religion at the present time: 'One is, that men cannot do without it; the other, that they cannot do with it as it is'.[8] The crisis of belief is common to all the writers I have cited for study. Arnold's importance consists in his ability to coin maxims and images which accurately describe its nature: we are all Scholar Gipsies standing on Dover Beach between two worlds, and waiting for the spark from heaven to fall while we listen to the melancholy, long withdrawing roar of the sea of faith. But are we? Certainly the distinctions made by poets and novelists between belief and faith, and between unbelief and honest doubt are frustrated by a static theology, whose vocabulary has not developed since its origins in the seventeenth-century conflicts of religion. On these terms Arnold and Hardy are atheists; and the suggestion made by Newman in 1845 that doctrine should and does develop was almost as uncongenial as Darwin's argument for evolution made at the same time. [9] Theology stays put. It excludes the imaginative power to 'diffuse, dissipate in order to recreate'.

Instead, as the nineteenth century ended, the dichotomy noticed by Mill as symbolised by Bentham and Coleridge became even sharper. The theologian becomes faced by two apparently irreconcilable logics – the logic of sceptical dissent and the logic of affirmation. One method of mental training seems to be hopelessly at odds with the other. Can imagination still exercise its reconciling function to secure 'the balance or reconcilement of opposite or discordant qualities'? [10]

III

To leave the nineteenth century for the twentieth is to raise the question, are the changes of religious belief between our own times and Shakespeare so profound that we must assume a radical and unique change of consciousness? With what focus are we to conclude a course in Religion and Literature? Since our method of teaching and study has been historical, we are obliged to face two events. The first is the disintegrative effect of the First World War and of the subsequent violent revolutions upon the homogeneity of European culture. The second, a consequence partly of the first, the emergence of a secular and plural society no longer founded upon a confessional affirmation of the Christian faith.

For W. B. Yeats the unity of being he saw as extending from Dante and Shakespeare to the great Venetian ladies of the eighteenth century had become fragmented by violence, civil as well as military. For him, imagination had become impaired by the growing murderousness of the world in which 'the best lack all conviction, while the worst are full of passionate intensity'. But a similar situation was also experienced by Wordsworth as a result of the French Revolutionary war. Its effect was felt as suspending the shaping or adunating power of imagination by 'abstracting the hopes of man/Out of his feelings, so that passions had the privilege to work,/And never heard the sound of their own names'.

The poets of the Great War of 1914–18 certainly experienced a comparable debasement of language, and their achievement was to forge a new language as they were faced by the clichés of conventional religion; but the poetry of Wilfred Owen draws deeply upon images from Scripture and the liturgy, as evidenced in his *Anthem for Doomed Youth* with its references to passing-bells, choirs of wailing shells, to candles and prayers. The poet even speaks of himself as becoming 'more and more Christian as I walk the unchristian ways of Christendom'. In the trenches soldiers were forced to the same conclusion as the theologians of a previous generation that men could neither do without Christianity, nor do with it as it was. Faced with the clichés of conventional religious ideology in the person of the Chaplain, with his cheery chaff and talk of scragging the Kaiser, 'the shy and uncouth muse of our savage theology unfolded her wings and flew away'.[11]

Confronted by civil violence, W. B. Yates saw himself as faced by a similar alternative: either to seek for the reconciliation of opposed beliefs, or to sharpen differences in order to gain a purer ideology. Yeats pursued the first alternative as that which nourished the imagination. He condemned the second course as leading to hatred and to the impairment of the imagination. 'The bad luck of Ireland', wrote Yeats, 'comes from hatred being the foundation of our politics':[12]

> Out of Ireland have we come;
> Great hatred, little room,
> Maimed us at the start.
>
> ('Remorse for intemperate speech')

Examples of how the imagination is impaired by revolutionary intolerance and cultural disruption have become more numerous. In *Dr. Zhivago*, for example, Pasternak shows how the spontaneity of the joyful lover, Antipov, is transformed by war into the man he has become – the ideologue Strelnikov, for whom there is no way back to a lost innocence.

Examples on a larger scale now confront us in the Third World, and especially in Africa,[13] where the general question – how may imagination be restored? – leads to further questions, such as what are the sources of religious and imaginative vitality in a nation which may have only very recently been 'invented'? What has it to inherit if it possesses no traditional religion of which its culture is the incarnation, its gods having first been discredited, and then superseded? Can it find in Christianity a source of Protean symbols which will plausibly and authentically release the African's innate capacity for joyful celebration? Or is the secular condition to which Africa has been reduced irreversible?

What seems certain is that traditional myths and symbols cannot simply be repeated, since merely 'to enumerate old themes' is to discover, with W. B. Yeats, that they are but 'circus animals', whose desertion is inevitable:

> Now that my ladder's gone
> I must lie down where all the ladders start,
> In the foul rag-and-bone shop of the heart.
> ('The Circus Animals' desertion')

IV

The enforced and violent break-up of the unity of a culture by war or revolution has effects which are not dissimilar from the deliberate determination to create a strictly secular society. But it is one thing to discuss the dissociation of religion and culture in Europe, quite another to cross the Atlantic and carry on that discussion in a society deliberately formed from the outset to be free from the claims of one over-riding confessional Christian tradition, and, as a later consequence, to be plural and permissive, its only unity being deliberately political: 'e pluribus unum'.

In his book on Hawthorne, Henry James makes the obvious point 'that the flower of art blooms only where the soil is deep, that it takes a great deal of history to produce a little literature, that it needs a complex social machinery to set a writer in motion'. James goes on to draw up a list 'of the absent things in American life'. Later, T. S. Eliot withdraws himself from North America in order to live within the European tradition – or what remains of it. Its books, paintings, cathedrals, ancient cities provide a certain residual hard currency which testifies plausibly to what *was* the case, to how religion and imagination *were* once related.

In the sense we have described it in Section II above, the United States had no nineteenth-century national religious culture to take for granted. There was nothing in common between the Boston Brahmin, the Iroquois brave and the Russian exile. What was common had, in the words of Robert Frost, to be created out of the land,

vaguely realizing westward,
But still unstoried, artless and unenhanced,
Such as she was, such as she would become.

What was this new land? It was certainly not living within the shadow of a past Christendom; whereas however much the nineteenth- and twentieth-century English writers we have cited – Hardy, Arnold, Yeats – may have consciously repudiated their inherited beliefs, it is what they assert at deeper and more unconscious levels of imagination which registers their continuing dependence upon that inheritance. Of later English writers, D. H. Lawrence anticipates the distinction in the way I have been suggesting. But, for him, perhaps because he could never cease to be a European, the dilemma remains unresolved. In *The Rainbow*, the Promethean urge which drives Ursula to leave the safety of the 'Pisgah mountain', and to go 'beyond',[14] can neither be disobeyed nor anchored in traditional pieties. And when, elsewhere in this novel, Lawrence describes the collapse of Brangwyn's faith, as it is expressed and realised in the Cathedral, he is obliged to use an analogue with all the ambivalence of an Arnold, when he speaks of a temple as 'never perfectly a temple, till it was ruined and mixed up with the winds and the sky and the herbs' (p. 206).

Although this ambivalence is never resolved (there is another view from Pisgah: it is of Pittsburgh[15]) ten years later in *St Mawr*, the rejection of 'the Augean stables of metallic filth' which has become Europe[16] is in favour of the New World, and in terms which recall Frost's poem. This new world of Mexico is free from 'the human claim'. Visually, it is 'wildly vital', but 'there was nothing behind it' (p. 140). 'Man did not exist for it. And if it had been a question of simply living through the eyes, into the *distance*, then this would have been Paradise. . . . But even a woman cannot live only in the distance, the beyond.' What characterises such a land (and Lawrence italicises his point) is '*that there was no merciful God in the Heavens*' (pp. 158–9).

Elsewhere, Lawrence writes that 'the American landscape has never been at one with the white man'.[17] To seek that it should become so is precisely what Robert Frost warns his fellow countrymen from doing. They must cease to be

colonials, possessing what we still were unpossessed by,
possessed by what we now no more possessed'.

Similarly Emily Dickinson writes that when her time had come for prayer she discovers that God has neither face nor mansion:

> Vast prairies of Air –
> Unbroken by a Settler –
> Were all that I can see –
> Infinitude, Hadst Thou no Face
> That I might look on Thee?

The conclusion we may draw is that, although the transcendent may still exist, it is no longer solely expressible in a dominant confessional tradition. The unity of culture which produced such writers as those considered in Part (1) and even (2) of our course – Dante, Shakespeare, Jane Austen, and even George Eliot, Hardy, and Matthew Arnold – is constitutionally no longer possible. Instead, conditions exist which permit, even require, a multiplicity of cultures and, therefore, a multiplicity of religious perspectives. The focus of our studies must shift. Hitherto our beliefs have been accepted and imposed 'from above', now the focus shifts from deduction to induction, from Coleridge to Bentham. We must now elucidate our beliefs 'from below' solely in the light of experience. This is how I understand Henry James when, in his preface to *The Portrait of a Lady*, he speaks of the 'moral' sense of a work of art as depending 'on the amount of felt life concerned in producing it'. Is this writer, to whom 'the entire clerical race' represented 'a new and romantic species',[18] the first secular novelist?

If, by secular, we mean no more than the absence of any privileged confessional reference, there being 'no merciful God in the Heavens', then this conception is as much applicable to the European Joseph Conrad as to the American Henry James. What then is especially characteristic of the American imagination, or is this a question which cannot be asked? Is it the theme of innocence betrayed or corrupted? How does it differ from Conrad's view that 'every age is fed on illusions, lest men should renounce life early and the human race come to a end'?[19] For Conrad the heart of darkness is reached when we can no longer 'appeal in the name of anything'. In *Victory*, the world of Shakespeare's *Tempest* and the innocence of Miranda are inevitably destroyed by Stephano, Trinculo and Caliban. There is no religious 'consolation' or, more crudely, 'compensation'; yet the paradox is stated at the end: 'Woe to the man whose heart has not learned while young to hope, to love – and to put its trust in life' (Part IV, Chapter 14). Even at his most sceptical Conrad affirms a value which transcends what we can gain solely from experience.

If the transcendent exists within a secularised imagination, then like infinitude it has no face, but its presence is to be felt in the determination to pass beyond the chain of cause and effect, and in the despair at dilemmas which cannot be resolved 'by rational innovation'. Would any reform of the marriage laws have prevented the tragic end of Jude the Obscure, or have provided the means by which Isabel Archer could have avoided the consequences of her tragic mistake in marrying Osmund? Focused as it so often is upon 'evil intelligence', corruption and savagery, the secular imagination may find its most characteristic form in tragedy. A murderous society pushes rationality to its limits and creates thereby the conditions for the rebirth of tragedy,[20] or, Nietzsche's words: 'Only after the spirit of science has been pursued to its limits, and its claim to universal validity destroyed by the evidence of these limits may we hope for the rebirth of tragedy'.[21]

V

And so one might end the course here, leaving the student with an interesting but insufficiently challenging question – is it in tragedy that the secularised imagination encounters, once again, the roots of religion? But there is more to imagination than tragedy, and to restrict religion to a merely propaedeutic role is to confine it too narrowly, since the paradox is that a plural and secular society in fact tolerates, even demands, a greater degree of religious affirmation than was sometimes permitted in earlier cultures. Is there a place for the confessional imagination which is not merely arbitrary, or even retrogressive? Or is it the case that, confronted as we are by multiple religious perspectives, the religious imagination is plausible only when it is confined to 'moments of vision' or, in other words, to its inductive mode? If so, some Christians will follow Karl Barth and reject a world which thus consummates its apostasy from the true faith. So – is the choice between the deductive assertion of beliefs, regardless of circumstances and consequences, and the inductive apprehension of isolated and fragmentary moments of vision? Either/Or? Once more we seem to be confronted by two apparently irreconcilable logics – the logic of affirmation, and the logic of sceptical dissent – but, once more, we must remember the capacity of imagination to reconcile opposite or discordant qualities. Does such a use of imagination – involving as it does a going out from religious beliefs and a coming back from the facts of experience – enable the individual to repossess that unity of being which was previously assured by unity of culture? Is the unity of being desired by Yeats and realised in Dante and Shakespeare possible in a pluriformity of faiths and cultures? It is this question which justifies us in considering writers who work from within a confessional framework. What is their effect on readers who do not share their religious beliefs?

The most obvious use of such beliefs is interrogative – to question current assumptions – but they also provide what might be called a language of 'enabling'. Take, for instance, Hopkins's poem, 'Carrion Comfort'. In its evocation of despair, and yet of its resolution of 'that time of now done darkness' it retains an authentic ambiguity which all sufferers recognise as a making real of their own condition as 'I wretch lay wrestling with (my God) my God'. Similarly, those who, in innocence and out of their vulnerability, have been the victims of violence, when confronted by the Cross, recognise in their suffering of others' sins, a reality which draws them out of themselves. Here, the language of confessional belief provides a means of recognition and realisation. For this reason it does more than extend the mental furniture by bringing a few antiques out of store, it succeeds in realising the past in the present, thereby effecting what Edwin Muir calls a transfiguration. The singer becomes the song. Such a function continues to be performed when, in its Christmas and Easter forms, belief provides a language for celebration. And how, in Yeats's words, 'but in custom and in ceremony/ Are innocence and beauty born?'

What are the roots of this language? Are they in theology? No – we must go deeper and find them in scripture and liturgy, that is in the form from which the language of theology itself derives. To refer to the liturgy is at once to make a reservation. What it effects is not gained by its beauty of music or colour. When this becomes the case, liturgy has become theatre – a sign of imminent decay. What liturgy effects demands a right ordering or sequence of acts. Thus in the descriptions of the Last Supper, for example, in scripture and liturgy 'what is remarkable is the repeated mention of the very same acts in the same order – taking, blessing, or giving thanks, and breaking'.[22]

How this use of language is first-order is evident in the ways of describing its operation. We may say that by means of scripture and liturgy we apprehend the Incarnation dogmatically, devotionally, practically 'all at once'; or we may speak of such means as ordering or unifying our response by appealing through imagination with reason to conscience. The response required is not one of mere feeling or approbation, but of performance. To quote the technical words of the Methodist theologian, Geoffrey Wainwright, 'conduct and cult are the two most immediate expressions of our doxological direction'.

To take Gerard Manley Hopkins again as an example. What he assents to is not an ideology, but a world which is literally 'charged with the grandeur of God'. In spite of man's indifference, 'The Holy Ghost over the bent/World broods with warm breast and with ah! bright wings'. But, as he remarks in the *Wreck of the Deutschland*, there is also 'the dark side of the bay of thy blessing' (II. 12); and at the heart of the terrible sonnets is the language of *De Profundis* and of the psalms. Here, where God is worshipped in fear and trembling, the language is dense and substantial: it partakes of the reality it renders intelligible.

This use of language – irreducibly symbolic and metaphorical – challenges the reader by its unqualified assertion of reality. The unity of being expressed by the poet does not depend upon a prior unity of culture (as Yeats assumed), but is for Hopkins as it is later for Eliot the consequence (or reward) of religious assent. Although this is language which is conservative of faith, it is of a faith which seeks understanding: 'the symbol gives rise to thought'. The subject of our response – one personal and ever present God as revealed in Jesus Christ – perpetuates his identity through change, that is, through the developments of our understanding; and the sign of a successful development is in its power to reconcile such opposing tendencies as the present with the past, or affirmation with scepticism.

I would suggest that one of the great achievements of the poetry of T. S. Eliot lies in his ability to resolve such opposing tendencies; and it is for this reason that I should prefer a course in Religion with Literature to conclude with an intensive study of Eliot's craftsmanship as a poet. Elsewhere[23] I have claimed that theologically Eliot provides a significant and independent exemplification of what Newman understood to be the way in which we grow to the explicit certitude of belief, and Eliot reconciles this understanding, worthy of Newman and Coleridge, with a sharply sceptical hope that 'Christianity will probably continue to modify itself, as in the past, into something that can be believed in'. 'Thus', for him, 'doubt and uncertainty are merely a variety of belief.' His method is Newman's: he says and unsays to a positive result, subjecting the language of religious affirmation to an antagonistic analysis, setting right one error of expression by another, and protesting against it while we do it. The words are Newman's, but they exactly describe Eliot's practice in *Four Quartets*, as he describes the wrestling with language in each of the movements of the poem. They also explain the method used to describe prayer, for example, in *Little Gidding*.

> And prayer is more
> Than an order of words, the conscious occupation
> Of the praying mind, or the sound of the voice praying.

But Eliot goes further. In *Four Quartets* he continues a practice begun in *The Waste Land* of using imagery from Indian religion and assimilating it to an explicitly Christian exposition in, for example, The Fire Sermon. In each case the imagery serves a double purpose by fitting the Indian religion as well as it fits the Christian. This is the case with his treatment of Time and Incarnation in *Four Quartets*: in the *Gita* the highest self is timeless, and a person always becomes whatever being he thinks of at the moment of death. By this and other means Eliot deliberately opens up his poetry to multiple perspectives, and in so doing *universalises* his imagery by freeing it from a single confessional interpretation. This subserves his intention to see the present in focus with the past; and as the two worlds become 'much like each other', so opposite or discordant states are reconciled, and the end of all our exploring

> Will be to arrive where we started
> And know the place for the first time.

I have spoken of the need to examine intensively Eliot's craftsmanship as a poet, and this returns me to the first and fundamental question. When religion and imagination are successfully related, what is guaranteed? Does adequacy of expression somehow validate the adequacy of the beliefs it embodies? Is it the truer for being well said? Or is their conjunction at least a sign that the right questions have been adequately stated, as Chekov, in commending Tolstoy, suggests? And that a proper sense of felt life has been successfully realised? Such a success is always signalised by great technical ability, as Eliot remarks of Blake. Hence we characterise such achievements as where the right words are in the right order. The attempt to discover the unknown, or reveal the transcendent, unless it is accompanied and subserved by this passion for form, can end in cliché, since, as Coleridge remarks, we stop in the sense of life just when we are not forced to go on. It is then that we need the extenders of consciousness – sorrow, sickness, poetry and religion. But although to yield thus to imagination is to be taken into worlds not realised, imagination may be impaired or at least inhibited by the violent disruption of its culture. Even so its recreative and adunating power survives, however deeply it is buried by war, by a hostile ideology, or in religion by a fanatical hard-headedness; and one of the aims of a course in Religion and Literature is to show how this happens in history.

I should like to conclude by making two statements of fact. Firstly, that however secular or plural our culture, the relation of religion and imagination persists, and that, consequently, the literary imagination has not separated itself from the transcendent. Secondly, that however complex and contested they may have become, older confessional forms (as Hopkins and Eliot testify) have not been superseded, but (as in the case of Eliot) they have been revived in new and original transfigurations. For the theologian especially, it follows that, since we live in a plural and fragmented culture, what have to be taught are habits of collaboration, particularly between theologians and literary critics. But is this justified academically, or ought it to be extra-curricular? I would reply by claiming that it is only by such habits that *both sides* can maintain an appreciation adequate to the fact that 'things truly made preserve themselves through time in the first freshness of their nature'.[24] We must trust in 'the mystery of words' and in what the 'turnings intricate of verse'[25] will continue to reveal.

NOTES

1. 'I use the term as Dante used it when he compared beauty in the *Convito* to a perfectly proportioned human body. My father, from whom I had learned the term, preferred a comparison to a musical instrument so strung that if we touch a string all the strings murmur faintly.' *The Trembling of the Veil* (London, 1922), pp. 75–6.

2. Joseph Butler, *The Analogy of Religion*, Part II, Chapter 8.

3. Joseph Butler, *Fifteen Sermons*, Sermon II.

4. S. T. Coleridge, *The Notebooks*, Volume 2, edited by Kathleen Coburn (Princeton, 1961), 2912.

5. George Eliot, *Adam Bede* (1859; London, 1967), p. 39.

6. Fëdor Dostoevsky, *The Devils*, translated by David Magarshack (Penguin Classics, 1973), p. 259.

7. Leo Tolstoy, *Anna Karenina* (1874–76) translated by Rosemary Edmonds (Penguin Classics, 1954), p. 826.

8. Matthew Arnold, Preface to *God and the Bible*, popular edition (London, 1884), p. viii.

9. Charles Darwin, *The Origin of Species* (1859). A draft was in existence from 1842.

10. S. T. Coleridge, *Biographia Literaria*, edited by J. Shawcross, 2 vols (Oxford, 1907), II, p. 12.

11. C. E. Montague, *Disenchantment* (London, 1924), p. 81.

12. W. B. Yeats, *Dramatis Personae* (New York, 1936), p. 104.

13. I refer to a seminar which the anthropologist Dr Aylward Shorter and I ran as part of the final year for the Religion with Literature course at Bristol, and to Dr Shorter's paper, 'Creative Imagination and the Language of religious traditions in Africa', published in *The African Ecclesiastical Review* (1980), pp. 175–203.

14. D. H. Lawrence, *The Rainbow* (1915; Penguin, 1970), p. 195.

15. D. H. Lawrence, 'Climbing down Pisgah' (1924) in *Phoenix: Posthumous Papers* (New York, 1936), Chapter VI.

16. D. H. Lawrence, *St Mawr* (1925; Penguin, 1950), p. 164.

17. D. . Lawrence, *Studies in Classical American Literature* (1923; Penguin, 1971), p. 61.

18. Henry James, *Notes of a Son and Brother* (New York, 1914).

19. Joseph Conrad, *Victory* (New York, 1915), Part II, Chapter 3.

20. See Wole Soyinka, *Myth, Literature and the African World* (Cambridge, 1978), pp. 46–8.

21. F. W. Nietzsche, *The Birth of Tragedy* (1872), translated by Francis Golffing (New York, 1956), pp. 93–112.

22. J. H. Newman, *Discussions and Arguments on Various Subjects* (London, 1872), p. 180.

23. John Coulson, *Religion and Imagination* (Oxford, 1982), Chapter 4.

24. Edwin Muir, *An Autobiography* (London, 1954), p. 280.

25. William Wordsworth, *The Prelude* (1850) Book V, lines 595–605.

2 Mystery and Mediation: Reflections on Flannery O'Connor and Joan Didion

D. Z. Phillips

I

At a time when professions of faith are made in a muted voice, or with a deadening insensitivity to difficulty and application in human life, the following words of Simone Weil startle us with their bold directness:

> There is a reality outside the world, that is to say, outside space and time, outside man's mental universe, outside any sphere whatsoever that is accessible to human facilities.
>
> Corresponding to this reality at the centre of the human heart, is the longing for an absolute good, a longing which is always there and is never appeased by any object in this world.[1]

Reflecting the difficulties such words have come to have for us Dr M. O'C. Drury asks,

> . . . but suppose someone was to say to me, 'what in the world do you mean, outside of space and time?' The word 'outside' only has a meaning *within* the categories of space and time. [Drury concedes] This is a perfectly logical objection, the words 'outside space and time' have no more meaning than Plato's beautiful expression 'the other side of the sky'. Again if someone were to

object, 'I don't feel any longing for an absolute good which is never appeased by any object in this world', how could you arouse such a desire? What right have you to make the psychological assertion that such a desire lies at the centre of the human heart? [Despite these difficulties, however, Drury says] Yet I believe Simone Weil is right when she goes on to say that we must never *assume* that any man, whatsoever he may be, has been deprived of the power of having the longing come to birth. But how then can this desire for the absolute good be aroused? Only, I believe, by means of an indirect communication. By so limiting the sphere of 'what can be said' that we create a feeling of spiritual claustrophobia. The dialectic must work from the inside as it were. [2]

Notice that Drury says that the dialectic *must* work from the inside. This is no optional strategy, a philosophical method which we can choose to adopt or not. On the contrary, what we have to do with here are fundamental issues concerning concept formation in religious belief; the ways in which central notions in religious belief get a hold on human life. Again, in Simone Weil, we find a striking expression of what is at stake here: 'Earthly things are the criterion of spiritual things . . . Only spiritual things are of value, but only physical things have a verifiable existence. Therefore the value of the former can only be verified as an illumination projected on to the latter'. [3] Commenting on these remarks, Peter Winch says, 'This is not to say that the expression "God" really *refers* to such facts; it is to say that the reality which it expresses is to be found in the conditions of its application'. [4]

If we infringe these grammatical requirements we shall soon find ourselves engaged in trivialities or nonsense. The most common infringements come about by trying to sever a concept from the conditions of its application. In the present context, it would amount to an attempt to characterise spiritual things independently of the illumination which the spiritual casts on the physical; to succumb to the temptation of thinking that the spiritual can be approached directly; to ignore the reminder that the presentation of concepts here has to be by indirect communication. Our fallacy is to think our task is to establish a relation between two distinct realms, the spiritual and the physical, whereas what we need to realise is that the spiritual only has sense in relation to the physical. As Drury says, 'The dialectic must work from the inside'.

The conceptual requirements I have been discussing are, of course, essential if we are to have any grasp on notions of religious mystery. Here, too, there are constant temptations to sever these notions from the conditions in which they have their sense. Mysteries must be mediated. Without the mediation of mysteries in human life, their sense as mysteries is lost or distorted. There are many forces which bring about such loss or distortion. I want to discuss some of these by reference to two American writers, the novelist, short-story writer and essayist, Flannery O'Connor, and the essayist, Joan Didion.

II

As Drury pointed out, there are plenty of people who would deny any longing or need in themselves for an absolute good. Similarly, there are plenty of people who would deny any sense to the notion of religious mystery. When such people are writers, they are not faced with the problem by which Flannery O'Connor found herself confronted. 'The writer operates at a peculiar cross-roads where time and eternity somehow meet. His problem is to find that location.'[5] Without a sense of mystery, its mediation cannot become problematic since it simply does not arise. One reason for this lack of a sense of mystery, Flannery O'Connor tells us, comes from a severance of manners from mystery.

It is possible to stay at the level of manners in such a way that no space can be found for mystery. This is a level at which we are content with relativistic judgements about the customs, practices and values we see around us. We are content with saying that according to one group, such-and-such is of value, but that according to another group, something else is of value. Within such relativities there is little room for mystery. There is no room either for the question, 'What *is* of value?' Flannery O'Connor will not allow such questions to be put aside. She says in her typically forthright manner: 'My standard is: when in Rome, do as you done in Milledgeville'.[6]

One reason why we hear little of mystery from the midst of relativities is that in such a context values often become organisational concepts. Whether something is of value depends on probabilities: the probability of that something leading to personal integration or social solidarity. Flannery O'Connor sees clearly that whether organisation at an individual or social level is worthwhile depends on its *character*, not simply on the fact of it. To say that something is valuable simply because it contributes to some form of organisation could never be, for her, a mode of vindication, let alone a final vindication. In this she is at one with those moral philosophers who have stressed the primacy of the moral; a primacy by which any form of organisation would itself be subject to an additional, moral mode of discrimination.

Whether writers are content to remain with relativistic judgements will have a great deal to do with whether they can recognise any logical space for religious mystery. As Flannery O'Connor says, 'All novelists are fundamentally seekers and describers of the real, but the realism of each novelist will depend on his view of the ultimate reaches of reality'.[7] If these ultimate reaches are no more than relativistic judgements of a social or individualistic kind, there is no room for mystery. Manners will have been divorced from mystery.

III

'On the other hand', Flannery O'Connor tells us, 'if the writer believes that our life is and will remain essentially mysterious, if he looks upon us as human beings existing in a created order to whose laws we freely respond, then what he sees on the surface will be of interest to him only as he can go through it into an experience of mystery itself' (p. 41). Everything depends, however, on how we understand what it is to have 'an experience itself'. We have seen that no such experience can be recognised if manners are divorced from mystery. It is equally important to recognise that the notion of mystery is lost or distorted if we divorce mystery from manners. When Flannery O'Connor says that the writer must work through the surface phenomena to the experience of mystery itself, she does not mean that the surface phenomena, manners, can be dispensed with, or that the 'working through' is simply a means to an end which is intelligible apart from it. On the contrary, mystery, to have any sense, must be mediated through manners, through the details of people's lives. Such mediation is a precondition of mystery being able to come in at the right place.

What if someone were to think otherwise? What if someone thought that he could dispense with the working through manners and instead go direct to the experience of mystery? Irritated or daunted by complexities, he thinks he has found a short-cut by which religious mysteries can be possessed directly, all at once. Kierkegaard described such tendencies of thought as the desire to foreshorten eternity, to take eternity by storm. He compares a person in the grip of these tendencies with the possessor of a map who delights in its beauty and construction, but without realising that that map is something to be used. When this man is set down in an actual countryside with its daunting miles and winding roads, he does not know his way about.[8] The map is of no use to him because he has divorced it from the conditions of its application and, hence, its sense. Similarly, those who try to divorce religious mysteries from the detail of life rob them of their sense. Flannery O'Connor locates, theologically, the effort to divorce the spiritual from the concrete as the heresy of Manicheanism: 'The Manicheans separated spirit and matter. To them all material things were evil. They sought pure spirit and tried to approach the infinite directly without any mediation of matter. This is pretty much the modern spirit . . .'[9] She had little doubt what effect this has on our understanding of religious belief:

> The problem of the novelist who wishes to write about a man's encounter with this God is how he shall make the experience – which is both natural and supernatural – understandable, and credible, to his reader. In any age this would be a problem, but in our own, it is a well-nigh insurmountable one. Today's audience is one in which religious feeling has become, if not atrophied, at least vaporous and sentimental. When Emerson decided, in 1832, that he could no longer celebrate the Lord's Supper unless the bread and wine were removed, an important step in the vapourization of religion in America was taken, and the spirit of that step has continued apace. When the physical fact is separated from the spiritual reality, the dissolution of belief is eventually inevitable.
>
> (pp. 161–2)

In Joan Didion's essays, written between the mid-1960s and the late 1970s, we have, it seems to me, countless examples of the inevitable dissolution of belief Flannery O'Connor speaks of. This dissolution is shown in the final conclusion she reaches. Unless I do her an injustice, Joan Didion concludes that she has little confidence in anything that has wider pretensions to be anything more than loyalty to loved ones, a shared sense of adversity, or primitive reactions to the rights and wrongs of a shared social code. Horrified by the violence, murders, rapes, atrocities committed in the name of conscience, she asks, in 1965: 'Except on that most primitive level – our loyalties to those we love – what could be more arrogant than to claim the primacy of personal conscience?'[10] She is suspicious, with good reason, of those who act in the name of 'morality', but is aware of what the reaction will be to her own scepticism.

> You are quite possibly impatient with me by now; I am talking, you want to say, about a 'morality' so primitive that it scarcely deserves the name, a code that has as its point only survival, not the attainment of the ideal good. Exactly. Particularly out here tonight, in this country so ominous and terrible that to live in it is to live with antimatter, it is difficult to believe that 'the good' is a knowable quantity.
>
> (p. 159)

She is quite insistent on the point: 'You see I want to be quite obstinate about insisting that we have no way of knowing – beyond that fundamental loyalty to the social code – what is "right" and is "wrong", what is "good" and what is "evil"' (p. 162).

Even before noting how Joan Didion reaches these conclusions, we can see that they will not do. They fall foul of the dangers involved in the relativities of manners. Survival at all costs or primitive reactions to a social code cannot be given the kind of primacy Joan Didion wants to accord to them, at least, not by one who, like herself, wishes to preserve some measure of decency. Atrocities have been committed in order to attain survival,[11] and since the social code may be contemptible, a primitive reaction to it would be no guarantee against the very evils which horrify Joan Didion.

How does Joan Didion reach her conclusions? She believes that certain stories have lost their hold on us. To use Kierkegaard's comparison, we have no shortage of maps, but the maps seem to have misled us about the territory they ought to inform us of. Some of these maps are religious, but Joan Didion's reaction to them is very different from that of Flannery O'Connor. One of these maps was the following words, which hung framed in the hallway of her mother-in-law's house in West Hartford, Connecticut.

God bless the corners of this house,
And be the lintel blest –
And bless the hearth and bless the board
And bless each place of rest –
And bless the crystal windowpane that lets the starlight in
And bless each door that opens wide, to stranger as to kin.

Joan Didion reacts:

> This verse had on me the effect of a physical chill, so insistently did it seem the kind of 'ironic' detail the reporters would seize upon, the morning the bodies were found. In my neighbourhood in California we did not bless the door that opened wide to stranger as to kin. Paul and Tommy Scott Ferguson were the strangers at Ramon Navarro's door, up on Laurel Canyon. Charles Manson was the stranger at Rosemary and Leno La Bianca's door, over in Los Feliz. Some strangers at the door knocked, and invented a reason to come inside: a call, say, to the Triple A, about a car not in evidence. Others just opened the door and walked in, and I would come across them in the entrance hall. I recall asking one such stranger what he wanted. We looked at each other for what seemed a long time, and then he saw my husband on the stair landing. 'Chicken Delight,' he said finally, but we had ordered no Chicken Delight, nor was he carrying any. I took the licence number of his panel truck. It seems to me now that during these years I was always writing down the licence numbers of panel trucks, panel trucks circling the block, panel trucks parked across the street, panel trucks idling at the intersection. I put these licence numbers in a dressing-table drawer where they could be found by the police when the time came.[12]

In such contexts as these, between 1966 and 1971, Joan Didion begins to doubt the premises of all the stories she had been told. Why do we tell such stories? She replies,

> We tell stories in order to live. The princess is caged in the consulate. The man with the candy will lead the children into the sea. The naked woman on the ledge outside the window on the sixteenth floor is a victim of accidie, or the naked woman is an exhibitionist, and it would be 'interesting' to know which. We tell

ourselves that it makes some difference whether the naked
woman is about to commit a mortal sin or is about to register a
political protest or is about to be, the Aristophonic view, snatched
back to the human condition by the fireman in priest's clothing
just visible in the window behind her, the one smiling at the
telephoto lens. We look for the sermon in the suicide, for the social
or moral lesson in the murder of five. We interpret what we see,
select the most workable of the multiple choices. We live entirely,
especially if we are writers, by the imposition of a narrative line
upon disparate images, by the 'ideas' with which we have learned
to freeze the shifting phantasmagoria which is our actual
experience.

(p. 11)

Even though the stories failed, Joan Didion argues that their
failure was itself a cultural revelation.

We were seeing the desperate attempt of a handful of
pathetically unequipped children to create a community in a
social vacuum. Once we had seen these children, we could no
longer overlook the vacuum, no longer pretend the society's
atomization could be reversed. This was not a traditional
generational rebellion. At some point between 1945 and 1967 we
had somehow neglected to tell these children the rules of the game
we happened to be playing. Maybe we had stopped believing in
the rules ourselves, maybe we were having a failure of nerve
about the game.[13]

The force of these remarks cannot be denied. Coupled with the
minimal trust she thinks we are left with, Joan Didion's standpoint,
though powerful, remains a negative one. The stories, because they
were confused, could not be lived out. But although the cures
offered cannot work, at least they reveal a prevalent sickness. Yet, if
we ask why the stories Joan Didion refers to had to fail, we find they
afford secular instances of what Flannery O'Connor identified as
the Manichean heresy, the separation of the spiritual from the
physical, the desire to foreshorten eternity and the embracing of
instant solutions. Moreover, as I shall try to show, these tendencies
appear sometimes in Joan Didion's own reflections and not simply
in the stories she criticises.

Some of the stories Joan Didion refers to were the product of

places such as Joan Baez's Institute for the Study of Nonviolence in
Carmel Valley. Speaking of Joan Baez, Joan Didion says,

> If her interest was never in the money, neither was it really in
> the music: she was interested in something that went on between
> her and the audience. 'The easiest kind of relationship for me is
> with ten thousand people,' she said. 'The hardest is with one.' She
> did not want, then or ever, to entertain; she wanted to move
> people, to establish with them some communion of emotion. By
> the end of 1963 she had found, in the protest movement,
> something upon which she could focus the emotion.[14]

The difficulty was that the dream-solution had to be complete,
given, once and for all. It consisted in people having certain
'feelings' – 'All you need is love'. The feelings were supposed to be a
kind of instant, unmediated love; a self-authenticating experience in
which utterance entailed possession. What in fact we were witnessing was an undisciplined romanticism riddled with conceptual
confusions. Sometimes, even Joan Baez is worried. After an
appearance at Berkeley she worries about the message. 'It was all
vague . . . I want it to be less vague (p. 52). But the vagueness was
no accident if what was being witnessed was a celebration of
inarticulateness, a celebration which, of necessity, is impatient with
the mundaneness of detail. The solution must be all-pervasive. A
Joan Baez song says, 'Sometimes I get lonesome for a storm. A full-
blown storm where everything changes'. Commenting on the song,
Joan Didion says, 'Although Miss Baez does not actually talk this
way when she is kept from the typewriter, she does try, perhaps
unconsciously, to hang on to the innocence and turbulence and
capacity for wonder, however ersatz or shallow, of her own or
anyone's adolescence' (p. 57). Accordingly, she says, this is why
Joan Baez is able to 'come through' 'to all the young and lonely and
inarticulate, to all those who suspect that no one else in the world
understands about beauty and hurt and love and brotherhood'.
Joan Didion has 'come through' in inverted commas. The words
could not be synonyms for 'speaks to', because all we are given in the
end is little more than a confused song appealing to an equally
confused audience. For Joan Baez and her audience to understand
what was happening would involve ceasing to take the song
seriously; seeing that such songs are themselves the product of
confusion. Joan Didion is tougher in her comments on political

movements where she finds the celebration of the inarticulate taking violent forms. In San Francisco the Black Panthers are told by their leader not to worry or even bother to work things out in words because 'a thought which needs words is just one more of those ego trips'. Joan Didion responds: 'As it happens I am still committed to the idea that the ability to think for one's self depends upon one's mastery of the language . . . They are sixteen, fifteen, fourteen years old, younger all the time, an army of children waiting to be given the words'.[15]

What we have seen is that what is described here as 'commitment to an idea' is in fact insight into a logical requirement. The attempt to divorce thought from language would leave one with no thought at all. Here, too, we find the desire to short-cut a requirement of discipline in the confused hope of instant possession of insight and understanding. Hence the result of 'an army of children waiting to be given the words'.

Yet, despite the fact that Joan Didion sees through the conceptual confusions in the stories she discusses, there are clear indications that she too is tempted by such stories. This gives her essays an added complexity and appeal. She does not moralise from a superior position. There is a kind of parallel between her essays and the way puzzles are worked through in philosophy. In philosophy too we are constantly tempted by the very confused theses we want to expose. When we look at the stories that tempt Joan Didion, we find that they too are stories which offer instant solutions, answers which are unmediated through the detail of everyday life. This much is evident in her essay, 'John Wayne: A Love Song'.

Here are the essentials of an unmediated dream:

> When John Wayne spoke, there was no mistaking his intentions; he had a sexual authority so strong that even a child could perceive it. And in a world we understood early to be characterised by venality and doubt and paralyzing ambiguities, he suggested another world, one which may or may not have existed ever but in any case existed no more; a place where a man could move free, could make his own code and live by it; a world in which, if a man did what he had to do, he could one day take the girl and go riding through the draw and find himself home free, not in a high bed with the flowers and the drugs and the forced smiles, but there at the bend in the bright river, the cottonwoods shimmering in the early morning sun. 'Hello there.' Where did he

come from, before the tall grass? Even his history seemed right, for it was no history at all, nothing to intrude upon the dream.[16]

The trouble with the story is not that the dream is of a world which has never been realised. That much could be said of allegiance to ideals. The trouble is that nothing is to intrude upon the dream. Any admission of so-called imperfections, illness, deception, destroys the dream. In that case, how can reality be informed by the dream? Is not the dream essentially romantic, an attempt to take reality by storm? In that way it is an escape from reality. There are signs of a lack of patience with the messiness and raggedness with which we are confronted in real life. For despite the fact that in such contexts Joan Didion trusts her own conscience as little as anyone else's, it is interesting to note what she would give herself to if she did heed the apocalyptic vision which informs that conscience: '. . . it would lead me out onto the desert with Marion Faye, out to where he stood in *The Deer Park* looking east to Los Alamos and praying, as if for rain, that it would happen . . . ". . . let it come and clear the rot and the stench and the stink, let it come for all of everywhere, just so it comes and the world stands clear in the white dead dawn".'[17] The price of the world's purity is indeed a high one, an all-or-nothing, instant purifying of the world. Here we are not far from the Joan Baez song which Joan Didion criticised. Here, too, the author 'gets lonesome for a storm. A full-blown storm where everything changes'. In both cases there is no mediation between vision and reality. It is the vacuum thus created that fosters the stories to which Joan Didion calls our attention. There is the constant temptation to lose patience with the realism which mediation involves, and embrace that which offers itself as an unmediated solution. We are reminded again and again of Flannery O'Connor's comments on the Manicheans: 'They sought pure spirit and tried to approach the infinite directly without any mediation of matter. This is pretty much the modern spirit.'

Joan Didion's impatience and longing for the pure place results in escapism in her essay, 'Rock of Ages', where she has the following reaction to Alcatraz, deserted apart from its caretaker and his wife: 'But the fact of it was that I liked it out there, a ruin devoid of human vanities, clean of human illusions, an empty place reclaimed by the weather where a woman plays an organ to stop the wind's whining, and an old man plays ball with a dog named Duke. I could tell you that I came back because I had promises to keep, but maybe it was because nobody asked me to stay.'[18] This does not ring true. What would it mean to stay? She wants to stay on the Rock, a Rock purged of vanities and illusions. Of course, others have sung of a Rock of Ages and have asked to hide themselves in it. What they have been seeking, however, is absorption, not escape. Thomas Merton warned those who think they have a vocation for the solitary place, 'We do not go into the desert to escape people but to learn how to find them'.[19] Such a prayer would be a form of mediation, but, as we have seen, such mediation is what is lacking in the stories Joan Didion discusses.

IV

Because she sees that certain stories have failed, Joan Didion is sceptical of *all* stories. Yet if the failure is due to attempts to offer answers abstracted from reality, why should all stories be guilty of such failure? Must all stories 'freeze the shifting phantasmagoria which is our actual experience'?

There are times when Joan Didion speaks of the kinds of voices Flannery O'Connor writes about, but she does not want to hear them. Once in Death Valley,

> Across the road at the Faith Community Church a couple of dozen old people, come here to live in trailers and die in the sun, are holding a prayer sing. I cannot hear them and do not want to. What I can hear are occasional coyotes and a constant chorus of 'Baby the Rain Must Fall' from the jukebox in the Snake Room next door, and if I were to hear those dying voices, those Midwestern voices drawn to this lunar country for some unimaginable atavistic rites, *rock of ages cleft for me.* I think I would lose my own reason.[20]

I am suggesting that if we look at some of Joan Didion's essays in the light of our discussion of the desire to take eternity by storm, the desire to achieve the ultimate experience in some unmediated purity, it may be that, by contrast, the voices she did not want to hear do not require the loss of reason to be recognised, and the rites she thought unimaginable may be seen as imaginable after all. These voices may or may not be embraced, but surely the effort to see them in their own terms is one to which an essayist, like a philosopher, ought to respond. No such response is possible, however, if we do not see how stories of eternity are mediated in the detail of human life.

One of the great visions of eternity in the Christian religion concerns the destiny of the human soul. If we say that the destiny of the human soul is a mystery, what kind of mystery do we have in mind? Is it simply a matter of eschatological ignorance which, for reasons of self-interest, we would like settled? Is it the kind of mystery about which we can be merely curious? When Flannery O'Connor shows the sense of the mystery of the soul's destiny mediated through the life of a character, these misunderstandings dissolve. We see how allowing this sense of mystery to come in at the right place is at the same time the acceptance of a spiritual truth. This can be appreciated by an examination of Flannery O'Connor's wonderful short story, *Revelation*.

To the large Mrs Turpin in the doctor's waiting-room, there is no mystery about how people are to be understood.

> Sometimes Mrs. Turpin occupied herself at night naming the classes of people. On the bottom of the heap were most coloured people, not the kind she would have been if she had been one, but most of them; then next to them – not above, just away from – were the white-trash; then above them were the home-owners, and above them the home-and-land owners to which she and Claud [her husband] belonged. Above she and Claud were people with a lot of money and much more land.[21]

There were times when she wondered what she would do if Jesus were to confront her with the following dilemma: 'There's only two places available for you. You can either be a nigger or white-trash'. Because of the changing circumstances in the community about her, operating her categories posed difficulties for her:

> But here the complexity of it would begin to bear in on her, for some of the people with a lot of money were common and ought to be below she and Claud and some of the people who had good blood had lost their money and had to rent and then there were coloured people who owned their homes and land as well. There was a coloured dentist in town who had two red Lincolns and a swimming pool and a farm with registered white-face cattle on it. Usually by the time she had fallen asleep all the classes of people

were moiling and roiling around in her head, and she would dream they were all crammed in together in a boxcar being ridden off to be put in a gas oven.

(pp. 195–6)

In the waiting-room there is another respectable white lady in whom Mrs Turpin senses a kindred soul. Unfortunately, she is accompanied by her sullen, ugly daughter. The question occurs to Mrs Turpin, 'What if Jesus had said, "All right. you can be white-trash or a nigger or ugly!"' (p. 196). Her own destiny is certainly no mystery to her. A gospel song is being played, 'When I looked up and He looked down' and she supplies the response in her mind, 'And wona these days I know I'll we-eara crown' (p. 194).

During the wait in the surgery, various conversations take place, all of which annoy the sullen daughter more and more. Her mother begins to discuss her daughter's lack of manners with Mrs Turpin, complaining that studying at Wellesley College has not improved her.

'If it's one thing I am,' Mrs. Turpin said with feeling, 'it's grateful. When I think who all I could have been besides myself and all I got, a little of everything, and a good disposition besides. I just feel like shouting, "Thank you, Jesus, for making every-thing the way it is!" It could have been different!' For one thing, somebody else could have got Claud. At the thought of this, she was flooded with gratitude and a terrible pang of joy ran through her. 'Oh thank you, Jesus, Jesus, thank you!' she cried aloud.

(pp. 205–6)

At that moment the girl's book hit her in the eye and her nails were in the flesh of her neck. The girl kicked Claud's ulcerated leg. The girl has some kind of fit, and has to be sedated, but her eyes are fixed on Mrs Turpin. Mrs Turpin leant over her:

'What you got to say to me?' she asked hoarsely and held her breath, waiting, as for a revelation. The girl raised her head. Her gaze locked with Mrs. Turpin's. 'Go back to hell where you came from, you old wart hog,' she whispered. Her voice was low but clear. Her eyes burned for a moment as if she saw with pleasure that her message had struck its target.

(pp. 207–8)

They all agree that the girl has had a fit. Some say she is destined to be a lunatic. ' "I thank Gawd," the white-trash woman said fervently, "I ain't a lunatic" ' (p. 209).

Back on the farm Mrs Turpin cannot get the image out of her mind – a wart hog from hell. She tries to greet her black workhands in the usual way. She had always said that black people should be shown love, for in that way they worked better for you. She has to tell them of the incident in the doctor's waiting-room, but, seeing through their flattery and reassurance, she finds no consolation.

In the final scene in the story, Mrs Turpin is hosing down her hogs. Suddenly, she speaks, ' "What do you send me a message like that for?" she said in a low fierce voice, barely above a whisper but with the force of a shout in the concentrated fury. "How am I a hog and me both? How am I saved and from hell too?" ' (p. 215). Her fury against God grows and in it is revealed once again the way in which she thinks of other people:

> 'Why me?' she mumbled. 'It's no trash around here, black or white, that I haven't given to. And break my back to the bone every day working. And do for the church.' . . . 'How am I a hog?' she demanded. 'Exactly how am I like them . . . There was plenty of trash there. It didn't have to be me. If you like trash better, go get yourself some trash then,' she railed. 'You could have made me trash. Or a nigger. If trash is what you wanted why didn't you make me trash?' . . . 'I could quit working and take it easy and be filthy,' she growled. 'Lounge about the sidewalks all day drinking root beer. Dip snuff and spit in every puddle and have it all over my face. I could be nasty. Or you could have made me a nigger. It's too late for me to be a nigger,' she said with deep sarcasm, 'but I could act like one. Lay down in the middle of the road and stop traffic. Roll on the ground.'
>
> (pp. 215–16)

Her railings against God come to their climax:

> 'Go on,' she yelled, 'call me a hog! Call me a hog again. From hell. Call me a wart hog from hell. Put that bottom rail on top. There'll still be a top and bottom!' . . . A final surge of fury shook her and she roared, 'Who do you think you are?' The colour of everything, field and crimson sky, burned for a moment with a transparent intensity. The question carried over the pasture and

across the highway and the cotton field and returned to her
clearly like an answer from beyond the wood.

(pp. 217–18)

Who do you think you are? – in the echo is the beginning of her
new realisation. Alone, with the hogs, the final revelation arrives:

There was only a purple streak in the sky, cutting through a
field of crimson and leading, like an extension of the highway,
into the descending dusk. She raised her hands from the side of
the pen in a gesture hieratic and profound. A visionary light
settled in her eyes. She saw the streak as a vast swinging bridge
extending upward from the earth through a field of living fire.
Upon it a vast horde of souls were rumbling toward heaven.
There were whole companies of white-trash, clean for the first
time in their lives, and bands of black niggers in white robes, and
battalions of freaks and lunatics shouting and clapping and
leaping like frogs. And bringing up the end of the procession were
a tribe of people whom she recognised at once as those who, like
herself and Claud, had always had a little of everything and the
God-given wit to use it right. She leaned forward to observe them
closer. They were marching behind the others with great dignity,
accountable as they had always been for good order and common
sense and respectable behaviour. They alone were on key. Yet she
could see by their shocked and altered faces that even their virtues
were being burned away. She lowered her hands and gripped the
rail of the hog pen, her eyes small but fixed unblinkingly on what
lay ahead. In a moment the vision faded but she remained where
she was, immobile.
   At length she got down and turned off the faucet and made her
slow way on the darkening path to the house. In the woods
around her the invisible cricket choruses had struck up, but what
she heard were the voices of the souls climbing upward into the
starry field and shouting hallelujah.

(pp. 217–18)

The necessary mystery of the soul's destiny remains. A mystery
revealed is not like a problem solved or a puzzle dissolved. One feeds
on the mystery. What the story shows is one possibility of a way in
which a mystery is mediated through the application it has in
relation to possible ways of thinking of other people. The possibility

does not mean, and neither did Flannery O'Connor mean, that all judgements of others should cease, but a great deal depends on the spirit in which the judgements are made. The story also shows how self-defeating is the attempt to penetrate a necessary mystery. To attribute, with certainty, a spiritual superiority to oneself is itself an offence against the spirit. Frantic desires and attempts to determine who is in and who is out in the sight of God, receive the reply – Who do you think you are? The eternal destiny of the individual soul is something that must be left to God. In one of her letters, Flannery O'Connor says, 'I read recently somewhere about a priest up for canonization. It was reported in the findings about him that he had said of a man on the scaffold who had been blasphemous up to the last that this man would surely go to hell; on the basis of this remark he was denied canonization.'[22] Flannery O'Connor shows us that leaving things to God is not a theoretical matter; neither is it an inevitability. It is something men find difficult to do; something which has to be worked at; something which may be revealed to us as it was to Mrs Turpin.

When such revelations take place, sudden though they may be, they are not the stormings of eternity, the instant revelations, which have been criticised in this paper. On the contrary, whether we can embrace them or not, we see such revelations as being free of such criticisms. The revelations are also free from the confusions involved in the stories to which Joan Didion directed our attention, stories she could no longer accept. The freedom from such criticisms lies in the mode of mediation by which Flannery O'Connor shows us religious mysteries. That is why the mysteries can be genuine. That is why, too, contemporary philosophy of religion has so much to learn from them.

NOTES

1. Simone Weil, 'Draft for a Statement of Human Obligations' (1943) in *Selected Essays 1934–1943*, translated by Richard Rees (Oxford, 1962).
2. M. O'C. Drury, 'Some Notes on Conversations with Wittgenstein', in *Ludwig Wittgenstein – Personal Recollections*, edited by Rush Rhees (Oxford, 1981), p. 99.
3. Simone Weil, *First and Last Notebooks* (Oxford, 1970), p. 147.
4. Peter Winch, 'Meaning and Religious Language' in *Reason and Religion* edited by Stuart Brown (Cornell, 1977), p. 210.
5. Flannery O'Connor, *Mystery and Manners*, selected and edited by Sally and Robert Fitzgerald (New York, 1969), p. 59.

6. *Letters of Flannery O'Connor: The Habit of Being*, selected and edited by Sally Fitzgerald (New York, 1980), p. 220.

7. O'Connor, *Mystery and Manners;* pp. 40–1.

8. Søren Kierkegaard, *Purity of Heart*, translated by Douglas Steere (New York, 1956), p. 14.

9. O'Connor, *Mystery and Manners*, p. 68.

10. Joan Didion, 'On Morality' in *Slouching Towards Bethlehem* (New York, 1968), p. 161.

11. For a similar criticism of the readiness to make survival a primary good see Ian Robinson and David Sims, 'Ted Hughes's Crow', *The Human World*, 9, November 1972.

12. Joan Didion, 'The White Album' in *The White Album* (Penguin, 1981), pp. 18–19.

13. Joan Didion, 'Slouching Towards Bethlehem' in *Slouching Towards Bethlehem*, pp. 122–3.

14. Joan Didion, 'Where The Kissing Never Stops' in *Slouching Towards Bethlehem*, pp. 46–7.

15. Didion, 'Slouching Towards Bethlehem', p. 123.

16. Joan Didion, 'John Wayne: A Love Song', *Slouching Towards Bethlehem*, pp. 30–1.

17. Didion, 'On Morality', ibid., p. 161.

18. Didion, 'Rock of Ages', ibid., p. 208.

19. Thomas Merton, *Seeds of Contemplation* (London, 1956), p. 49.

20. Didion, 'On Morality', p. 160.

21. Flannery O'Connor, 'Revelation' in *Everything That Rises Must Converge* (London, 1965), p. 195.

22. O'Connor, *The Habit of Being*, p. 102.

3 Job and Sophocles

Ulrich Simon

Comparisons in literature are as common as they may be either odious or boring, or both. Despite Virginia Woolf's scathing caricature in *To the Lighthouse* we are still compelled to listen to learned papers on the Influence of Someone on Someone else. Perhaps there is some justification for this procedure, for it is not a wholly sterile endeavour to find out, say, for example, where Shakespeare got his material for *Troilus and Cressida* and why he departed from the conventional treatment.

The Book of Job may claim to have a special place in comparative literature. This special place derives somewhat curiously from the negative assessment it generally earns when it is considered within the context of the Hebrew Scriptures. We cannot only not date it, but we also fail to say where this book belongs in the history and culture of Israel. The book is as much an outsider as its hero. Jewish commentators take great pains to deny this and Gordis, for example, in his magisterial *The Book of Job*[1] succeeds in regaining a Jewish provenance for the text. But this is misleading, for even he cannot disguise the fact that the language itself is, to say the least, odd and makes constant demands on extraordinary powers of perception and interpretation. After all, it was Tur Sinai who as a Jewish exponent of genius echoed the opinion that the text may have come to us as a translation from the Arabic.

But none of this can detain us in view of the greater problem: where does the Book of Job belong? Is this just Wisdom literature in the accepted sense? We find some gnomic characteristics, but the overall impression is not proverbial at all. No wonder, that most commentators have looked outside the Canon of the Old Testament to find a suitable resonance. If Job is un-Jewish, that is unrelated to Covenant, Torah, Jerusalem, Temple, Prophecy and also singularly free from a creative after-life in the Jewish-Christian tradition (except for quaint eisegesis, as in Gregory's famous *Moralia* after the *Testament of Job*) one can barely leave the book as the so-called Matterhorn, standing as a lonely peak among the majestic mountains.

The last commentary to resist this method of looking elsewhere for clues is Dhorme's masterpiece of 1926, though occasionally the Greek and Latin authors shimmer through the curtains of Patristic exegesis. But ever since the newcomer has been treated to a very wide range of possible parallels, influences, analogies. For example, F. I. Andersen in his beautiful *Job* of 1976 surveys the literary background, though he insists on the uniqueness of the Biblical scroll. Thus the Indian legend of Hariś-ćandra and the Ugaritic legend of Keret and the so-called Babylonian Job *Ludlul Bel Nemeqi* and even our old friend *Gilgamesh* only adumbrate Job without throwing direct light on its composition. Rightly Andersen mentions Egyptian sources such as The Protests of the Eloquent Peasant, Admonitions of Ipu-Wer, Dispute over Suicide, A Song of the Harper and the Gnomic texts only to stress their distance from our concern. Quite simply one concludes that once men reflect on their wretched condition and the hostility of the world they will produce some sort of articulated complaints. Goethe was not the first one who beat the torments by being enabled to say what he suffered.

However, both geographically and culturally, we move nearer a common ground when we probe into Job's relationship, if any, with the tragic theatre of Athens. If Job is given a pre-exilic date there is no more to say, except that Job may have influenced Greek authors. But this is quite improbable, and it is worth saying that, apart from a fleeting footnote referring to Job, classical scholars never even entertain the idea that Sophocles, for example, knew or owed an artistic debt to the Biblical work. Indeed, the commentators of the *Prometheus*, *Oedipus*, and *Philoctetes* proceed as if Job did not exist.

But this is not the case the other way round. European devotion to the classics wanted to establish some affinity. Robert Lowth (1710–87) as professor of poetry at Oxford devoted his research to biblical poetry. A certain Lichtenstein and soon the great Herder played with the notion that Job could be compared to something Greek and that it had the ingredients of tragedy.[2] Lesser people have followed in this train down to the present. Outstanding among these was Horace M. Kallen whose advocacy *The Book of Job as a Greek Tragedy* (New York 1918) still deserves rereading. Kallen believed that 'the original choral odes were later removed from their position in the tragedy and shifted into the dialogue to conceal the resemblance of a Greek play'. [3] There have been numerous attempts to go further than this and actually produce Job as a drama on a stage, even if the text required some severe pruning. Archibald MacLeish's play *JB*, first staged at Yale in 1958, has often been revived and acted as a kind of spur.

But Job is not a tragedy. Lowth demonstrates that it is not even a dramatic poem since the dialogue lacks plot, character and development. There is no change, no growth, no action. The speakers' attitudes, manners and sentiments exhibit a constant state. Moreover, unvarying misery is not tragic and final repentance and restoration are not dramatic but educative. Turn by way of contrast to *Oedipus Tyrannus*. If this spectacle merely contained impassioned exclamations against the gods and tender tears for the blind and disgraced hero then, says Lowth, 'the Greeks would have called such a production a monody, or elegiac dialogue, or anything but a tragedy'. Again when Oedipus reaches Colonus with his daughters and Theseus protects the dying man against brother and son for the good of the future of Athens this marvellous fable is adorned by the manners, passions, and sentiments of the characters. Yet the plot is in control of the whole.

I have no quarrel with Lowth who insists that he does not lessen the merit of Job by denying it the form of tragedy. Yet I am impressed by some informal affinities and distinctions. I would suggest that Job becomes more accessible to us by viewing it in the mirror of tragic achievement. This achievement is so rare in the history of the human theatre – less than fifty years in Athens, a little longer in Shakespeare's London, suspect in Paris, hardly at home in Weimar – that it may itself also benefit from some contact with the Hebrew-Christian world. If we engage in such an endeavour we may give an answer to George Steiner and others who maintain that tragedy has become impossible in our terrible century.

Could our reading of Job perhaps help to restore the balance? Could a tragic interpretation even give depth to the hopeless superficiality of contemporary Christian trends? If not, what are we to do with this book, where locate its centre of gravity? Since it is now generally admitted that whatever it may be, theodicy is *not* pertinent to its form and content, must we go to such extremes as to describe the work as something of a comedy, or at least as the original of all succeeding absurdities? [4] I confess that I sometimes sympathise with this extreme estimate when I read the last cycle of speeches, where weariness feeds an almost nihilistic reaction. Others lose their patience with the zoological panorama, with ostrich, horse, hippopotamus and leviathan, and therefore consign the whole work to the pile of great but meaningless literature.

So let us see what can be made of Job as tragic hero. Or rather what can be made of Job in the light of independent Greek tragedy. Clearly Job is no Prometheus: he has not rebelled and brought the fire upon earth, though he has been a benefactor to the poor and blind. Nor is he an Agamemnon for he has not led an army and sacrificed a daughter. He cannot be mentioned in the same breath as Oedipus, though some of the latter's utterances of despair have a familiar ring. But the restoration of Oedipus at Colonus differs utterly from Job's final acceptance. What about Heracles? Here is another semi-divine sufferer who labours for mankind heroically, whereas Job lacks the heroic grandeur. Only when Hyllus says to Heracles 'Ah, it is wrong to argue with a sick man, yet how can one stand to see him with such thoughts as these?', the lines remind one of Eliphaz's rebuke 'Should one dare a word, could you bear it', as Marvin Pope rightly notes. [5]

So we come to the one tragedy where the link is not contrived but organic. Sophocles' Philoctetes, like Job, has no Furies; he does not die and the final act of the play ends the disaster. But there is a plot: Odysseus brings Achilles' son Neoptolemus to Lemnos where Philoctetes has been left by his Greek allies on their way to Troy. Philoctetes, like Job, suffers from a terrible wound, which stinks and oozes filth. But his snake bite kills as little as does Job's attack of boils. Both are outcasts, but whereas Philoctetes exists in utter loneliness, Job has the doubtful pleasure of company. How Job is fed we are not told. But Philoctetes still has the bow, Heracles' bow, with which he can kill game. Moreover, without this selfsame bow the Greeks cannot capture Troy. Hence arises the deceitful embassy engineered by the crafty son of Laertes who manipulates Neoptolemus to persuade Philoctetes to join him, overtly to go home but in reality to serve the cause of Agamemnon before Troy. The bow thus becomes the centre of the plot, and this element is completely lacking in Job, who has nothing to give and whose presence is not needed anywhere. But not only the bow-question, complicated and endlessly discussed, holds our attention; even more demanding is the emergent clash of duties and the response of character, torn between what seems at first sight possible and desirable and what is moral and demanding. Thus Neoptolemus, above all, is seen to grow into a man of honour who sacrifices success, fame and advancement to integrity. No such drama exists around Job. The friends only grow in bad manners and irritability and their morality is in fact a hindrance to their own growth and to an encounter with Job. Yet, curiously, it is precisely their lack of sympathy which induces in Job his tragic self-awareness and ultimately his vision of God, not only as an enemy and spy, but also as a possible vindicator.

Neoptolemus and Philoctetes are brought to the point of decision when they cry 'What am I to do?'. Job seeks no redress by action, for action is not within his realm of possibilities. Both Job and Philoctetes prefer death to life and, if their words can be trusted, curse the prolongation of life. Their lament runs into verbal parallels, especially in their cries: 'Why gives he light to the wretched, Life to the bitter soul?', taken from Job's famous elegy in Chapter 3, beginning with 'there the wicked cease from troubling', and Philoctetes' 'Death, death, how is it that I can call on you, always, day in, day out, and you cannot come to me?' (lines 797–8). Also their plaints revolve around the same themes of endless pain and outrageous misfortune. Again they share in the paradox that despite every good reason to commit suicide they go on suffering, unable to stop the wheel of fire. Thus they are in the same plight physically and psychologically only to show that this plight allows of divergent consequences.

One of the really decisive factors is compassion. When does Neoptolemus first begin to pity and feel ashamed? 'In me a terrible pity has come to lodge, and has long been there' (lines 965ff.). The Chorus is also moved to pity at such a condition for one who had been a great man. And this pity is the pivot of the initial action which, even though mistakenly, elicits from Philoctetes a newly won confidence, the as yet false notion that a boy saviour has come. Somehow friendship and loyalty, first as a false dawn, but soon as a reality, must prevail. Philoctetes' 'Pity me' (755 ff.) does not fall on deaf ears. It could have done, for when Philoctetes is asleep – remember the famous hymn to sleep: 'Sleep, stranger to anguish . . . come, I pray, with power to heal' – Neoptolemus could, following the sailors' expectation, *use* the sleeping man and make off.

What of pity and sleep in Job? It comes to us as a great surprise that Job appeals only once to pity, namely in the famous outburst in Chapter 19: 'Have pity upon me, have pity upon me, O ye my friends, For the hand of God has touched me'. This appeal is directed to those who, he alleges, persecute him as God himself. But receiving no sign of sympathy, before or after, he then turns to the Vindicator, the Go'el, who has never been identified. The range of interpretations extends from the Go'el being the family solicitor to that of God. But why do the friends who have come to see him, be with him, and presumably intend to help him, never react with sympathy?

Their lack also accounts for the arrested development in the dialogue. They mount arguments, release diatribes, formulate accusations, but they never meet Job existentially. They show that their religious fence prevents them from entering, like Neoptolemus, into the heart of the matter. Their religion is profoundly non-tragic. Tradition, learning, duty, and ultimately vindictiveness urge a common stand against the sufferer. One is reminded also of very non-religious and great men in our age, who, like the friends, defy the stirring of pity. Goethe could not stand the sight of suffering, ordered funerals to be routed away from his house, did not visit his ailing mother nor attend her funeral. Marx regards pity, as he does religion, as a damnable opium, and Nietzsche castigates pity as the decadent aggressiveness of the have-nots and their trickery to win, not through strength and merit but through moral bribery. Job's friends pioneer the long trail towards a harsh non-involvement in suffering.

Nor does sleep come or play any part in Job. He tosses at night and hopes for the morning, and longs for the night when the sun rises (Chapter 7 v.4). [6] There is no lyrical interlude in Job to console or to test the friends' integrity. How utterly aloof is Chapter 28, the paean of Wisdom! Everything good is remote, transcendent, cosmic, beyond. The divine speeches only stress this remoteness: where were you when I made all this? Nowhere, of course. The inscrutable nature of the universe is not an intimation of immortality and the Presence of God can only be found in his absence. That is a huge and lasting paradox but, alas, it is not tragic. It does not purge us either of or by pity and terror, if the famous Aristotelian slogan still has any meaning. Hence Job is also deprived of the stirring of such an emotion as gratitude, for what should he be thankful for? Philoctetes on waking up at least sees that the boy is still there and has not deserted him. Job awake sees his friends as enemies. Philoctetes returns to life by gratitude, Job looks into an empty heaven. Blake's illustrations probably colour all our apprehensions of Jobian

despair and searching, and rightly so. For Blake the Job who suffers
is not a tragic hero but a forsaken god. Even for Blake there is a
perspective of salvation, but this perspective is not tragic in any
accepted sense. It is an inner struggle which ends in healing, a kind
of therapy, from insanity and fantasies of destruction to sanity and
integration. Blake anticipates Jung's *Answer to Job* (1952) where, if
my reading is correct, Job redeems God – an inversion taken up by
MacLeish and many moderns. God must not be prayed to but
prayed for.

If this perverse answer is unacceptable what else can be said?
Again *Philoctetes* throws light upon Job. As R. P. Winnington-
Ingram asks:[7] 'What happens to a man – a great hero – when he has
been cut off from human society for ten years?' This hero,
remember, whose festering ulcer, incessant howls, frantic wailing
may lie behind him, but who returns to Troy a spectacle worse than
the serpent's sting, is still convinced that it is a curse for a man to be
marked out of the common lot, that war always picks the best men
as its victims; in short, a hero in a rotten world, eschewing
vengeance. He is not a snarling animal, he even bids farewell to
Lemnos in the most touching verses and seems to recapture his
purity of soul. But 'the tragic consequences of a cruel act and the
tragic implications of a heroic code'[8] remain and make us question
the will of the gods. True, Heracles is sent, there will be healing and
perhaps at length a safe homeward journey. But above all, Heracles
can promise 'through suffering glory in life'. The future, too, will be
ragic, for Greeks and Trojans alike, but glory will have been
achieved. The pathos itself is redemptive.

Job does not lack pathos. When he exclaims in Chapter 13 v.15
'Though he slay me, yet will I trust in him', he testifies to an inner
conviction that the glory of God is also his despite all contradictions.
True, the forensic approach comes near to a defeat. Kafka's anti-
heroes in *The Trial* and in *The Castle* out-Job Job in the frustrating
endeavour to be acquitted on the grounds of circumstantial
evidence. In Christian theology the negation of justification sets its
seal on all attempts to regain glory or Paradise or even innocence by
winning in the Court. This way to glory is barred, just as Philoctetes
cannot win by getting his rights. Does Job, then, also regain glory
through suffering?

Jewish and Christian exegetes would answer in the affirmative. It
is enough for him to see God at the end. The history of the exegesis of
'I know that my Redeemer lives . . . ' is long and impressive. If you

take the corrupt text literally, then, after and through all the destruction of skin, the true, lasting self will see God. There is a life after death, a resurrection, a vindication. Christian exponents see in Job a prefiguration of Jesus and thus his sufferings are also a typological anticipation of the Cross. One should not dismiss these correspondences too easily in the cavalier fashion of 'we now know all this so much better', be it on linguistic or theological grounds. If Job is connected to the Christ figure with the ritual of Psalm 22 in mind, then the 'My God, my God, why has thou forsaken me . . .' becomes precisely triumphalist in the tragic sense, namely through suffering to Glory. Again if Job is also read in the light of Isaiah and specially the portrayal of the righteous servant, an even more cogent picture of kingly supremacy reaches us from one scorned, beaten and executed and yet enthroned. This Job-like figure does not only internalise his grief but deploys his wounds as a healing for the nations, making many righteous. Just as Philoctetes helps his enemies to victory, albeit a tragic one, so Job in the company of Israel's heroic saints conquers the enemy, namely the Satan, through his endurance.

It must be admitted that this traditional *via crucis* interpretation does contain a good deal of eisegesis. It lacks something of the depth of tragedy, for in vulgar hands, as in so many churches, it smacks of superficial optimism, a kind of happy ending. Moreover it ignores the fact, which Sophocles stresses, that glorification does not bring the end of the tragic existence in history. Rather, it mingles with it and opens transcendent awareness.

In this respect Sophocles and all the great writers of man's condition are united, for they circumvent total nihilism and refute the cheap success ideology which feeds nihilism. The truth is different and it is arrived at by distancing us from the terrible events. The word 'irony' recurs whenever an analysis of the text of Job or of Sophocles is attempted. It is a difficult concept and is best understood in the context of each work. For example, that Antigone should be a comfort to Oedipus cannot annul the dire future when she will oppose Creon and become the heroic, yet flawed, martyr to private conscience in a mad world of state decrees. Similarly, Job's false starts, nay Job himself, the wealthy sheikh from Uz, are portrayed with a good deal of irony. Parables and riddles are never to be taken as straightforward propositions. Gordis's painstaking notes allude forever to touches of irony in the text. For example in Chapter 8 v.19 the text oscillates between renderings of joy and/or catastrophe (Gordis prefers 'it goes on its way').[9] But minutiae apart, the prose narrative is certainly a masterpiece of ironical narrative, confounding all the literalists who want to 'explain' the Epilogue with its grotesque exaggerations.

But irony does not lessen the seriousness of this narrative. The comedy of the celestial interview between God and Satan has dimensions of terror. No-one saw this more clearly than Goethe when he appropriated the Gamble with its undeclared stakes for the Tragedy of Faustus. Through the distance of irony Goethe removes the threat of fatalism which hangs over the tragic. Sophocles also articulated a measure of freedom in personal decision, and Job never becomes a slave to fate.

Here we come up against a problem which must concern all who care for Religion and Literature, and especially Christian traditionalists. If irony pertains to the legacy of the tragic victory how can it become enshrined and made fruitful in Christian life and worship? Is not the ironic an unwelcome alien in both? True, we detect traces of irony in some Biblical books, not only in Job, but also in the Lukan narrative. The Jewish genius adds its own special brand of irony to the Greek heritage. But when all is said and done the Christian tradition does not grant ironic distance. Instead we have masters of polemic, as in Jerome and Augustine, in the Reformers and many moderns. Moreover, the frightfulness of our wars and genocides almost rules out the standing back implied in the tragic consciousness. We have learnt to metabolise the Crucifixion, perhaps too readily, but we cannot metabolise mass slaughter and nuclear holocaust. Steiner may be right, after all, in his claim that tragedy has died. No Sophocles has arisen to cleanse our generation of the horrors, though significantly the *Antigone* has been the vehicle to carry the existential dilemma of private obligation and public duty. Job, too, has provided some comfort to the despairing survivors. Perhaps the time has come when the tragic irony will liberate the stale religious positions of our time.

Confirmation for this endeavour now comes strongly from the philosophical side. Unfortunately the vocabulary of hermeneutics, such as that of Paul Ricoeur, is so far removed from daily speech that only the few trained in semiotics are likely to respond to structuralism and levels of interpretation, finding the extraordinary in the ordinary and speaking of aesthetic deliverance issuing from the tragic spectacle.[10] However, the reference back to the narrative as controlling the arguments and transforming revelation as given in the divine speech of Chapter 38 is, I think, a lasting perception. God's Rhetoric and God's Silence accordingly tell a tragic tale in which a Job concludes 'I know that thou canst do all things and that no purpose of thine can be restrained . . . wherefore I abhor myself and repent in dust and ashes', whereas a Philoctetes sings: 'Let us depart then all together when we have prayed to the nymphs of the sea to come as saviours, guardians of our return'. *Sunt lacrimae rerum* . . . The word is like that, but heroism and compassion make it bearable.

NOTES

1. Robert Gordis, *The Book of Job* (New York, 1978).
2. Theodore, Bishop of Mopsuestia (d.466) had noted similarities and been attracted to an interpretation based on such an insight.
3. See Nahum N. Glatzer, *The Dimensions of Job* (New York, 1969), p. 175.
4. See J. William Whedbee, 'The Comedy of Job'; John A Miles, 'Gagging on Job or The Comedy of Religious Exhaustion', *Semeia*, 7 (1977), *Studies in the Book of Job*, 1–39; 71–126.
5. See *The Women of Trachis*, lines 1230 ff., Marvin H. Pope, *Job. A New Translation with Introduction and Commentary* (New York, 1965), p. 35.
6. Compare *Philoctetes*, line 847: 'The sleep of a sick man has keen eyes. It is a sleep unsleeping'.
7. R. P. Winnington-Ingram, *Sophocles, An Interpretation* (Cambridge, 1980), p. 297.
8. Ibid., p. 302.
9. Gordis, *The Book of Job*, on *mesos*.
10. See 'The Book of Job and Ricoeur's Hermeneutics', *Semeia*, 19, 1–21.

4 *Horae Canonicae:*
Auden's Vision of A Rood –
a Study in Coherence

Peter Walker

I

Wystan Auden included the sixteen pages of *Horae Canonicae*, published between 1949 and 1954 but not in the order in which they stand, in the less than one hundred and forty pages of his 1968 *Selected Poems*. That is not insignificant, in a poet matter-of-fact to the point of ruthlessness (to the fury of the Beaches of this world and the suspicion of his latest biographer)[1] in discarding or amending work which had come to seem to him to lack integrity. For Auden, there was no given or autonomous 'mystic' or 'vatic' rightness about a poem to set it above the question 'Would its truthfulness stand up?'

But if the poet stood by them, these poems have proved elusive to the critics. John Fuller, whose *Reader's Guide* is seldom unillumi-native of an Auden poem, is representative:

> The whole sequence contains much striking poetry, but shows, I think, that Auden's real talent (and real interest) in this period is less for religious poetry than for poetry on the themes of nature and history, language and truth, friendship and landscape. The secular 'fifties thus contrast very much with the exploratory (and often theological) concerns of the 'forties, and 'Horae Canonicae' betrays at its centre a certain blurring of definition which the other major poems of the decade ('Bucolics', 'Memorial for the City' and so on) do not have.[2]

By contrast, I see the sequence as Auden's distilled achievement in a period when, very much because he was engaged in that religious dimension which, defined as he would define it, commanded him to the point of theological rigour of thought, he was at his best.

About a poet's proper boundaries in all this he expressed himself clearly and sometimes austerely:

> There can no more be a 'Christian' art than there can be a Christian science or a Christian diet. There can only be a Christian spirit in which an artist, a scientist, works or does not work. A painting of the Crucifixion is not necessarily more Christian in spirit than a still life, and may very well be less . . .

> Poems, like many of Donne's and Hopkins', which express a poet's personal feelings of religious devotion or penitence, make me uneasy . . . Is there not something a little odd, to say the least, about making an admirable public object of one's feelings of guilt and penitence before God?[3]

If this is what the poet is not to be about, Auden is positive on the other hand in terms of 'the sacred', the sphere of Coleridge's Primary Imagination. Here are his definitions:

(1) The subject matter of a poem is comprised of a crowd of recollected occasions of feeling, among which the most important are recollections of encounters with sacred beings or events. (*DH*, p. 67)

(2) The impression made upon the imagination by any sacred being is of an overwhelming but undefinable importance or significance . . . one is aware that a phenomenon, being wholly itself, is laden with universal meaning. The response of the imagination to such a presence or significance is a passion of awe.
    (Some sacred beings seem to be sacred to all imaginations at all times. The Moon for example, Fire, Snakes and those four important beings which can only be defined in terms of non-being: Darkness, Silence, Nothing, Death.) (*DH*, pp. 55–6)

(3) The impulse to create a work of art is felt when, in certain persons, the passive awe provoked by sacred beings or events is transformed into a desire to express that awe in a rite of worship or homage, and to be fit homage, this rite (which in poetry is verbal) must be beautiful. This rite has no magical

or idolatrous intention; nothing is expected in return. Nor is it, in a Christian sense (again at this point the reserve) 'an act of devotion'. (*DH*, p. 57)

(4) Integral to the beauty of a poem will be the way in which the poet has succeeded in reconciling contradictory feelings, transforming the 'crowd' of them with which he began into a 'community'. (*DH*, pp. 66, 71)

These are the things a poet works with and upon; and underneath his art there are these three absolute presuppositions, or dogmas:

(1) A historical world exists. The existence of such a world is a good
    i.e. the goodness of created existence.

(2) The historical world is a fallen world
    i.e. though it is good that it exists, the way in which it exists is evil, being full of unfreedom and disorder.
(It follows that a poem is a witness to man's knowledge of evil as well as good. Compare the essay on Robert Frost (*DH*, p. 338) where, after speaking of the way we want a poem to be beautiful, a 'verbal earthly paradise, a timeless world of pure play', he adds 'at the same time, we want a poem to be true, that is to say, to provide us with some kind of revelation about our life which will show us what life is really like and free us from self-enchantment and deception, and a poet cannot bring us any truth without introducing into his poetry the problematic, the painful, the ugly'.)

(3) The historical world is a redeemable world
    i.e. the possibility of regaining paradise through repentance and forgiveness.
(It follows that . . . 'Every beautiful poem presents an analogy to the forgiveness of sins; an analogy, not an imitation.') (*DH*, pp. 69–71)

I wish to suggest that the *Crucifixion*, and, more precisely, the Crucifixion as Christians have seen it, is at the heart of *Horae Canonicae*; and that, to adopt for Auden a phrase from the late Professor J. A. W. Bennett's last book, these poems stand in the great tradition of 'the early conversion of the English poetic mind to the service of the Rood'. But if so, on Auden's own account of his approach, we may expect to find, in a phrase of Professor Bennett's

about Piers Plowman, an 'abrupt alignment of the Divine with the
everyday', 'the Passion never presented as an isolated event . . . but
related directly – even forcibly – to the concerns of every day'.[4]

A second common feature in classical poetry on the Passion is
noted by Professor Bennett: 'cryptic allusiveness'. Akin to the
personal reticence to which Auden has confessed would be the use of
a 'riddling technique', 'to ensure that the emotion which the subject
calls forth was disciplined and restrained'.[5]

Yet again, I would myself suggest, there is a contemporary
theological understanding, or recovery of an understanding, associated for some of us particularly with the name of Dietrich
Bonhoeffer, of the hiddenness of God's work for us in Jesus Christ,
and indeed of the life in Christ, which could here come into its own.
Has Auden been perhaps theologically unexpectedly forward?
'Friday's Child', his own poem in memory of Bonhoeffer, might be
invoked:

> And must put up with having learned
> All proofs and disproofs that we tender
> Of His existence are returned
> Unopened to the sender . . .
> Meanwhile, a *silence* on the cross . . .

He was fond of quoting the 'Alice of a Bishop' who had said of
orthodoxy that it was reticence;[6] and in his 'Postscript: Christianity
and Art' he could write: 'The Incarnation, the coming of Christ in
the form of a servant who cannot be recognised by the eye of flesh
and blood, but *only by the eye of faith*, puts an end to all claims of the
imagination to be the faculty which decides what is *truly* sacred and
what is profane (italics mine) . . . *Christ appears looking just like any
other man* . . . the contradiction between the profane appearance
and the sacred assertion is impassible to the imagination'.[7]

But if personal reserve and sometimes riddling allusiveness and a
theological reticence should prove to be indeed features of the
poems, the subject being what it is, the more impressive then the
openness of Christian reference when it is there. And it is there in
Horae Canonicae centrally and explicitly enough for me to be grateful
for the insight, say, of Richard Johnson on the influence, 'elusive but
strong', of Heidegger,[8] and yet believe that it is not Heidegger who
will open the door for me. A knowledge of him might illuminate: but
for the poems to speak to me I must somewhere along the line be

open to reflect upon the *Christian* understanding of the crucifixion and what it might offer about life.

To move, then, towards the poetry: I am taking it, here:

(1) That the writing is closely knit, precise not only formally, or technically, but in the texture of the thought. It is an obvious maxim, but it applies particularly to Auden. The words need looking at. The maestro – who would have chosen a dictionary, and the best that money could buy, for his desert island book[9] – was a master of them.

(2) That the seven poems make a unity, possessing its own internal cohesion, or, better, movement of thought. Consistency was important to Auden. And if the harmony of a poem was vital, so, surely, the unity of a sequence which was in the making by him, to stand as a sequence, over a period of seven years.[10]

(3) That the best source of light upon the meaning, outside the poems themselves, is that collection of highly idiomatic critical writing to which I have already so often appealed.

Also, however, and as the last of my axioms:

(4) That one particular writer, the Charles Williams so often acknowledged by Wystan Auden (he was generous about such things) is to be seen as a particular formative presence throughout the poems, and this especially through one small book – one might say through twenty pages at the heart of one small book.

II

I come then to the poetry, and I observe first that if the seven poems are meant to stand as a unitary sequence, there might be point in setting the first and last of them beside each other to see whether as 'brackets' they might give a clue to what is set in between.

One thing 'Prime' and 'Lauds' have in common: they are poems of awaking. Yet how different the mood between the end of one and the start of the other. What has happened in between?

'*Prime*' moves brilliantly to evoke the moment of waking to the world

As, in complete obedience
To the light's laconic outcry, next
As a sheet, near as a wall,
Out there as a mountain's poise of stone,
The world is present, about . . .

It is indeed a world created good, and awareness of it comes through gates of the body registered at once as kind. Momentarily, then, the joy of waking. Two-thirds through the poem, however, we move into the real world from that unreal one in which we cannot stay, the world of Adam still previous to any act, of Adam sinless in our beginning. 'The earthly paradise is a beautiful place but nothing of serious importance can occur in it' – so Auden of the Ariel who has no passions: and the Serpent, we may remember, acquaintance with whom results in immediate expulsion from Eden – 'any serious need or desire'.[11]

Exactly: we are, here very explicitly, the point most precisely made, at the moment of the awakening to assertive, purposive, orectic, will-full life.

I draw breath; that is of course to wish
No matter what, to be wise,
To be different, to die and the cost,
No matter how, is Paradise
Lost of course and myself owing a death . . .

The orectic thrust, whether emerging in the desire 'to transform the self, to realise its potentialities' (see the third of the three modes of awareness in 'The Virgin and The Dynamo') – or, by ironic contrast, in the death wish, is not other than that self-assertion which is at the heart of the Fall. From that moment the world looks different and has lost, not its own physical freshness (that remains its own gift) but its uncomplicated charm for me:

The eager ridge, the steady sea,
The flat roofs of the fishing village
Still asleep in its bunny,
Though as fresh and sunny still are not friends
But things to hand, this ready flesh
No honest equal, but my accomplice now,
My assassin to be, and my name

> Stands for my historical share of care
> For a lying self-made city,
> Afraid of our living task, the dying
> which the coming day will ask.

This is the fallen world. The city so seen (and how we see our world is what the poem is about) is not quite any longer a shining, given, thing, but a part rather of the world we make ambiguously 'for ourselves'. Heidegger's evocative language of a world seen as to hand, for our manipulation, echoes here, so that George Steiner's brilliant recent exposition of Heidegger on the Fall seems almost at moments the most illuminating commentary of all on *Horae Canonicae*.[12] And extraordinarily stimulating it is. 'It was as if Heidegger's whole diagnosis of inauthenticity amounted to a quasi-secular version of the doctrine of fallen man.' But in fact there is a clear point past which we should have known from the start that Auden would accompany Heidegger no further – the point, precisely, of Auden's emphasis upon will, choice, responsibility; and, however reluctantly, we must leave Steiner's Heidegger at that point of paradox which will not do for Steiner either: 'the "positivity of fallenness" in Heidegger's analysis, with inauthenticity and fallenness the *necessary* components of existence, is', says Steiner, 'an exact counterpart to the celebrated *felix culpa* of the theologian'. Only if it is accepted, as Heidegger will not accept, on Steiner's showing, that here was *culpa*; that Verfall does, somehow, 'comport a moral value judgment'; for choice is real and responsibility, therefore, remains. We try to avoid it (see 'The Virgin and The Dynamo', *DH*, p. 62) but we may not: for 'Freedom is an immediate datum of consciousness', and integral to one's understanding of the Fall. And if responsibility, then guilt. And one thing is clear, we may not stay in Eden.

There *was* a moment of rejoicing then, and it went before 'Prime' was done: at that moment when I drew breath and that was to will.

'*Lauds*' bursts open, in precisely a transport of rejoicing, into a new day, with nothing quite laconic, this time, in the world's presentness and the very brilliance of the lines eclipsing even that of 'Prime's' opening. And there was no rejoicing in between.

> Among the leaves the small birds *sing*

(there was no music, come to think of it, in the other dawn; a passive rejoicing, unvexed for a moment, but not quite this).

The cry of the cock *commands* awaking – an awaking in solitude, yes (it can never be anything else, if aloneness, as Auden said long ago in *New Year Letter* (1.1542) is man's real condition), but for company, and

> Men of their neighbours become sensible

Awake, that is the call, to a belonging that is real. There is a realm, there is a people, to whom you belong; the green world temporal is your world, no urban desert now, and there is God's blessing on it all.

To say that this is a waking to a world renewed, redeemed, would be no more than a natural use of words. It is in fact, upon inspection, precisely what the poet is conveying. At the heart of 'Lauds' the mass bell – at the heart of the mass, it goes without saying, an act of redemption (Auden might not parade his devotion, but there are moments when, in terms of his own understanding of things, it must be remembered that he died a communicant member of his church, as I am humbled to remember recalling a Psalm Sunday morning Holy Communion (his last) in Christ Church Cathedral, Oxford at which I was the celebrant).

And to the question, what has happened between 'Prime' and 'Lauds'? the answer is, straightforwardly, a dying: a dying pointed forward to in 'Prime', 'Terce', 'Sext'; looked at, contemplated as effected, in 'Nones'; looked backward to, and forward from, in 'Vespers', 'Compline', 'Lauds'. A dying, then, which is integral in this transformation, this renewal? But of course.

And at this point I do not think that it will do to say that it was just a dying – any dying, an instance of the dying which is part of life. Dying is that, indeed, and Charles Williams once wrote on the thesis 'A kind of death attends us everywhere'.[13] But his point was that the Crucifixion, that particular dying, had a bearing on a world with which it was hardly, quite, in total discontinuity. And it is to that particular dying that the language of *Horae Canonicae* explicitly points.

It is language about a *victim*: a victim who *knows*; about the blood of a *sacrifice* upon the grass; about something that happened today between *noon and three. Immolatus vicerit*, the poet wrote under the title. And the central significance that the dying holds in the poetry, is, I am suggesting, that invested somehow in it has been precisely the poet's third presupposition as Auden has set it out – the possibility of the regaining of paradise through repentance and forgiveness, that is to say the liberation from freedom and disorder of a world created good.

III

Behind the thinking of *Horae Canonicae*, I suggested, lies essentially not Heidegger, but Charles Williams, and it is time to recall the substance of the book of his which Wystan Auden so admired.

'Did you ever see a little book by Charles Williams, *The Forgiveness of Sins*, which was published in England about two years ago? I thought it very good indeed.'[14]

Already, in fact, looking at 'Prime' we have touched phrases which are pure Williams from that source. 'But Adam may have been our name as well as our single father's, we in him and he in us in a state other than sequence. We were in him *for we were he . . .*'[15]

> . . . and I
> The Adam sinless in the beginning.

There are such echoes throughout the poems, like the body escaping in 'Compline'

> . . . to join
> Plants in their *chaster* peace,

for 'The principle of the relation of the created nature towards the Creator in that beginning is named Chastity . . .' (p. 25).

It is, however, a whole coherent, though, it must be said, pregnant, understanding of a central Christian truth in Charles Williams that I am concerned with – that which is set out, as I have suggested, at the heart of this small book, in no more than twenty pages in the third chapter of *The Forgiveness of Sins*, entitled 'The Sin of Adam' (pp. 15–34).

The theme is pardon considered 'in relation to the particular Christian pattern of the universe' (p. 15), or 'forgiveness as it appears in the theology of the Christian Church' (p. 4). The pages contain a footnote, to which I shall come much later, which seems to me quite startling in the way it will give us 'Lauds'. At this point, I need space to let us get Williams' feel.

'Victim' is Williams' particular word. Forgiveness is his subject.

All is set within a theme that informs in fact all his writing: coinherence, the coinherence, the interchanged life, the life of exchange and substitution. 'Forgiveness', he has told us at the start of his book, 'if it is at all a principle of that interchanged life, is certainly the deepest of all' (p. 2).

For Williams, the Fall – and this is the distinctive and the determinative thing of all for him – was a fall from *Joy*. The joy from which mankind fell was the joy of coinherence, that is to say of life lived together and life shared. It was a sharing between God and his creature, man, which had been intended already at the Creation in all the final fullness of an Incarnation.

> They were to be related to him and to each other by a state of joyous knowledge; they were to derive from him and from each other . . . It was to be a web of simultaneous exchange of good (p. 16).

But a response of *will* was needed from his creature and it was not forthcoming.

> He made – if we call it obedience we make the joy too dull (since we have, except at our momentary best and in our transient illuminations, lost the joy of obedience); he made – let us say the delight of a perfect response to his initiative a part of the working of the web (p. 18). Somewhere, somehow, the web loosed itself from its centre – also by its free choice. It chose; and it chose, in our phrase, wrongfully. What and how it chose we do not know. It may have been, literally, greed – some silly thing like a fruit . . . It may have been some other silly thing like pride . . . But also it may have been what it is described as being in the old myth of Genesis

– and here Williams quotes from his earlier *He Came Down From Heaven*[16] in a passage opening up a whole world, embracing for Auden criticism not only *Horae Canonicae* but also and especially 'Sonnets from China', Auden on Mr Pickwick's innocence in 'Dingley Dell and the Fleet', and much of *The Enchafèd Flood*;[17]

> It is easy for us now, after the terrible and prolonged habit of mankind; it was not, perhaps, very difficult then – as easy as picking a fruit from a tree. It was merely a wish to know an

antagonism in the good, to find out what the good would be like if a contradiction were introduced into it. Man desired to know schism in the universe. It was a knowledge reserved to God; man had been warned that he could not bear it – 'in the day that thou eatest thereof thou shalt surely die'. A serpentine subtlety overwhelmed that statement with a grander promise – Ye shall be as gods, knowing good and evil'. Unfortunately to be as gods meant, for the Adam, to die, for to know evil, for them, was to know it not by pure intelligence but by experience. It was, precisely, to experience the opposite of good, that is the deprivation of the good, the slow destruction of the good, and of themselves with the good . . . '*Nihil sumus nisi voluntates*' said Augustine . . . The coinherent will of mankind moved, and moved against its divine Original, the whole body (contrast Ephesians) disjoined and decompacted. (pp. 19–23)

But God persisted in his purpose to become man.

Mankind had had its moment, its chance of coinherent glory . . . It had devoted itself to an egotism which meant destruction, incoherence and hell. Yet God would not (though he might have) let it cease to exist.[18] But then the result was that if he was to submit to the choice of man, he was indeed to submit to that choice. He was not merely to put up with it as a Creator, he was to endure it as a Victim. (pp. 30–1)

And herein was renewal.

Creator and Victim then: the third function went with those two. He would not only endure; he would renew; that is, accepting their act he would set up new relations with them on the basis of that act . . .

They had refused the coinherence of the original creation, and had become (literally) incoherent in their suffering. He proposed to make those sufferings themselves coinherent in him, and therefore to reintroduce them (Adam, mankind) into the principle which was he. The Resurrection was the Resurrection of Forgiveness . . . he became an energy of forgiveness in the Church. (p. 65)

In Williams we are without a doubt deep in a Christian mystery. 'The Atonement is the name given to an operation; an operation beyond our comprehension, but not beyond our attention' (p. 99), and at the heart of it the identification of God with fallen man: and if man, 'in Christ', 'would know himself as the victim of his own sin – a triumphant or a defiant, but always a sacrificial – victim of sin, then it should be conceded to him to know the endured evil as good' (p. 102–3), or good, we might say, validated out of it. Forgiveness is renewal, restoration in coinherence, of man with man with God, renewal in Joy.

There, we might add, is the *felix culpa*.

'And perhaps only poetry can present the ineffable mystery', says Bennett.[19] I would like to let the poems now speak for themselves in the light (if my fourth point of method holds) of Charles Williams' writing.

IV

Part of the truth of the poetry (the Christian truth or, as Auden would probably have preferred it put, the truth Christianly taken), is its explicit acknowledgment of the fact that its subject is 'an operation beyond our comprehension but not beyond our attention'; its deep acceptance of it, so that the language has an aptness to it or, in Whitehead's words set by Auden at the head of his thoughts on 'Writing', 'embodies what it indicates', in this case, a mystery.[20] And part again of its truth is its truthfulness, in these self-same ways, to the fact that the human situation in which the operation of the Atonement was called for neither was nor is a tidy one. 'They had become (literally) incoherent in their sufferings.' And a poet 'cannot bring us any truth without introducing into his poetry the problematic, the painful, the disorderly, the ugly' – the ambiguous, one will want to say, and the near incoherent.

One key to the thought of 'Terce' and 'Sext' is that, as with 'Prime', each poem *breaks* at a two-thirds point, proceeding until then with a certain straightforward coherence, yet with hints of other things, and reaching then, as it were a breaker combing towards its fall, a moment of moving into complication, riddling ambiguity, perhaps – the fact that one is left groping for the word for it is itself an indication.

So then the actors of '*Terce*' move forward into the day, human enough, each of them; somewhat in the dark about the important role to which they go; and, in this mixture of a world, each of them with his own trivial and nervous *amour propre* or need of a modest boost.

> Now each of us
> Prays to an image of his image of himself;
>   'Let me get through this coming day
> Without a dressing down from a superior,
>   Being worsted in a repartee,
> Or behaving like an ass in front of the girls;
>   Let something exciting happen,
> Let me find a lucky coin on a sidewalk,
>   Let me hear a new funny story'.

(Civilisation is, after all, in Whitehead's words, quoted sometimes by Auden,[21] a 'precarious balance between barbaric vagueness and trivial order'.)

Not so, in the third stanza 'our victim'. For him, the outcome of the day has no uncertainty about it – what he knows is that human self-assertion will have prevailed. He who is without a wish for himself (and is thereby without self-assertion) will not assert himself to prevent it: but more, it is within the foreknown scheme of things in which he is involved that things should move in the way they will. This is indeed a redemption beyond easy comprehension, for it involves the thing that we were thinking of from Williams, the initiative of the redeemer in the events of the day, his association in the deed. *Oblatus est quia ipse voluit* – He was sacrificed because he wished it so.[22]

So, then, to the last words of 'Terce': he

> knows that by sundown
> We shall have had a good Friday.

(A single letter in a simple lower case, and in it the riddling, the allusiveness, the irony.) But what victim is this who, infuriatingly, so knows the answer to the riddle of existence?

> It is only our victim who is without a wish,
>   Who knows already (that is what
> We can never forgive. If he knows the answers,
>   Then why are we here, why is there even dust?) . . .

What, then, of '*Sext*'? The substance of the first two stanzas is straightforward enough (though for a frightening missing of the point see no less precise a critic than A. C. Partridge[23]): the brilliant evocation of the crispness of civilisation and the *ordering* of life, bringing us out of the unfreedom of feral life under Dame Kind, with its barbaric vagueness of utterance, without a consonant to our names; with the squalor of superstition; into the realms of vocation and the authority of Fortitudo, Justicia, Nous. But then comes the loaded pointer at each verse-end: crucifixion, somehow, a part of, indeed a function of, an ordered society! 'And in one of his last reviews', writes Anne Ridler of Charles Williams, 'of a "Famous Trial", he thought of the fear of the victim and wrote: "At the price of such things we live".'[24] Is that to be the message, since we cannot stay in Eden?

But from these clear edges of civility, fraught at a point but clear enough, we plunge then (is not this the irony?) into ambiguity and worse: suddenly we are with the incoherent crowd. *With*, I say: not quite *of*, for in 'Sext' and 'Nones', and the point is not unimportant, we are never quite simply exhausted in the crowd.

The crowd in *Horae Canonicae* is almost no more than a perverted way of seeing things: 'it looks on or it looks away'.[25] Anywhere, indiscriminately but ubiquitously, the negative crowd stands on the good earth (broad-chested enough to take it), perfectly still, and stillness in Auden (see 'Homage to Clio' for instance), is the context for seeing things – attentive in its perverted way: and precisely so, for how shall the crowd understand this mystery? The crowd embodies all that will not do: it is precisely the reversal of coherence; a principle, a pattern, of non-coherence; blind, not seeing the meaning, that is to say the personal which the individual will see and which civility is about; expressionless, humourless: this is the crowd. Here is the world of the Dynamo, the world of facelessness and statistics: *and* of passivity – the stillness of no direction, no commitment; the stillness of detached *irresponsibility*.

But exactly because it is the non-discriminating unit that it is, perceiving no standards of doing things properly (which is after all, again, what civility means), it is the menacing body that it is – we have it in us to be drawn into it.

> Few people accept each other and most
> will never do anything properly

> but the crowd rejects no one, joining the crowd
> is the only thing all men can do.

Deception is at the door: the deceptive sense that we have our own
belief, each of us, when uncritically we simply have one of the gods
(the lower case 'g' again) that are the crowd's; when, having lost
that separative thing, our discrimination, we are deceived into
thinking that we have found a principle of brotherhood,

> Only because of that can we say
> all men are our brothers,
>
> superior, because of that,
> to the social exoskeletons.

Lose the irony of 'Sext' here and everything is lost; and the irony
carries the poem to its ironic end.

> When
> have they ever ignored their queens,
> for one second stopped work
>
> on their provincial cities, to worship
> The Prince of this world like us . . . ?

'Occasionally', Auden wrote in 'The Poet and The City', 'the
Public embodies itself in a crowd, and so becomes visible – in the
crowd, for example, which collects to watch the wrecking gang
demolish the old family mansion, fascinated by yet another proof
that *physical force is the Prince of this world against whom no love of the heart
shall prevail*'.[26] This is the crowd of the second verse of 'Nones', and
with whom we have found ourselves in 'Sext': and this, surely, is the
Prince of this world in whose worship we are caught up before we
know it,

> 'at this noon, on this hill,
> in the occasion of this dying'
> (*this*, not *his*, the words say)

'At the price of such things we live' – and how precariously, once
violence has been invoked. (But we are still men, not ants.)

'*Nones*' comes: the moment of quintessential stillness – of dead calm.

>   It is barely three,
>   Mid-afternoon, yet the blood
>   Of our sacrifice is already
>   Dry on the grass; we are not prepared
>   For silence so sudden and so soon;
>   The day is too hot, too bright, too still,
>   Too ever, the dead remains too nothing.
>   What shall we do till nightfall?
>
>   The wind has dropped and we have lost our public.
>   The faceless many who always
>   Collect when any world is to be wrecked,
>   Blown up, burnt down, cracked open,
>   Felled, sawn in two, hacked through, torn apart,
>   (there it is in verse)
>   Have all melted away.

It is the only favour the crowd can do us: its members gone back into that chaster peace and calmly sleeping.

Nature, the kind Madonnas with the green woodpecker, of the fig tree, beside the yellow dam (they exist only here, in the poignant playfulness of the poet's imagination), the Madonnas whom civility would portray as protecting with their kind faces our cities,[27] turn their faces from us and our provincial cities which have suddenly become not more than projects under construction. For what have we done?

Yet what we have done (our *opus operatum* which can never be repeated) is the only thing to look at, even so . . .

>   The Madonna with the green woodpecker,
>   The Madonna of the fig tree,
>   The Madonna beside the yellow dam,
>   Turn their kind faces from us
>   And our projects under construction,
>   Look only in one direction,
>   Fix their gaze on our completed work . . .

and we ourselves? We find ourselves looked away from: ironically,

we, the agents, stand among our unfinished projects, identified with
them, the equipment of a spent and bankrupt city.

> Pile-driver, concrete-mixer,
> Crane and pick-axe wait to be used again,
> But how can we repeat this?
> Outliving our act, we stand where we are,
> As disregarded as some
> Discarded artifact of our own,
> Like torn gloves, rusted kettles.
> Abandoned branch-lines, worn lop-sided
> Grindstones buried in nettles.

Some things come home to us at such a moment: particularly the
violence that is there under some of life's playfulnesses . . . but
there it is, and always with us now is this thing we shall not ever get
away from –

> wherever
> The sun shines, brooks run, books are written
> There will also be this death.

And this moment of stillness which was to have been the moment
of *meaning*? But, indeed, there will be time.

> We have time
> To misrepresent, excuse, deny,
> Mythify, use this event
> While, under a hotel bed, in prison,
> Down wrong turnings, its meaning
> Waits for *our lives*.

Such will be the moments of truth (and I remember that Wystan
Auden died, alone, in a hotel bed nine years ago next week).

But what shall we do till nightfall? Rest – and look forward to
sleep – a hint, perhaps, of meaning: for the body is not so fallen that
it has lost the Creator's gift of renewal. (We are in Charles Williams'
country again, on a theme I have not had time more than just to
touch, the flesh in Williams, 'which was dragged down with the will
but which was not itself the origin of the Fall, since initiative could
only act by the assent of the will', and which 'exiled from its unity,
yearns – and more innocently than the soul – for its original joy'. [28]

That, while we are thus away, our own wronged flesh
    May work undisturbed, restoring
The order we try to destroy, the rhythm
    We spoil out of spite: valves close
And open exactly, glands secrete
    Vessels contract and expand
At the right moment, essential fluids
    Flow to renew exhausted cells,
Not knowing quite what has happened, but awed
    By death like all the creatures
Now watching this spot . . .

That was a hint, perhaps: of renewal perhaps as a hope – but could the meaning not be spelt out a little? For we have something of a mystery, having heard these things:

(1) It was a crucifixion, and it was our act; an act that the coming day had asked for from us, frighteningly, at the moment when our wills claimed our bodies as their own.

(2) It could be seen as a part of our worship of the Prince of this world, literally; but it was on the other hand a function of civilised society.

(3) Yet at another level, it was within the foreknowledge and initiative of the one who was our victim and who 'knows it all'.

'*Vespers*' is the prosaic interlude, the poet's gloss. That the meaning will be yielded as you reflect upon the City (Williams' great word) and its meaning (the life, that is, of men *together*) the opening lines make clear, the landscape no doubt contrived a little (in the setting of the scandalous pair) but precisely to focus the attention on *the citizen and his citizenship in the context of the Fall*. And that the Crucifixion is central for the City's meaning, because central to the City's life, necessary indeed for its very survival, is the concluding statement of the piece.

For without a cement of blood (it must be human, it must be innocent) no secular wall can safely stand.

It is a truth, we have just been told, we must be reminded of by being reminded of our victim. But what is the meaning of this mystery, this secret somehow shared?

You will not see it (so I read 'Vespers') if you will insist on living in your Eden or Arcadia (where confessedly the poet's own fantasies lie) – those unreal worlds where there is no thrust in things. Nor will you see it if (at poles apart) you seek your dwelling in a New Jerusalem (though they do not all turn out that way) of clinical and ruthless progress where there are no agonies about suffering inflicted on the way. But if the real world of the present is where you know that you must be and life there is seriously your concern, you may find the meaning. And perhaps indeed the uncomfortable neighbour, the stark incompatible, may disturb you by his very presence and has been sent for that. How will you live with the unlivable with?

If there was truth in Williams, that the Fall was a fall indeed into the way of incoherence, and that on the Cross we see the Creator's identification with his humanity, so caught in the toils of its own sin, but see him there with exactly the intention that from the inside of man's condition he should then energise and redirect the disabled drives; *this* would, in a word, be the renewal, the forgiveness, the taking of the guilt.

Edward Mendelson closes his *Early Auden* with an illuminating phrase – 'The only answer to the isolating will is the absolute gift of pardon'.[29] With him, I believe that *Horae Canonicae* embodies this insight. And I believe (it has been the main thrust of this paper) that the reference to the victim on whose immolation as Sin Offering all our civic life depends is explicitly a reference to the *Immolatus* of the Christian faith, the Crucified.

'But come', I hear the critic say, 'how can you be so particular? Did you not observe the parenthesis – on whose immolation (*call him Abel, Remus, whom you will, it is one Sin Offering*) arcadias, utopias, our dear old bag of a democracy are alike founded?'

'Yes', I reply, and the point is vital. Implicit in the pages of Charles Williams on which we have spent so long, it is put by him most clearly in *The Cross*, that paper for the volume *What the Cross Means to Me* so often used by Auden:[30]

'By that central substitution (his placing of himself, that is to say, in our place), which was the thing added by the Cross to the Incarnation, He became *everywhere* the centre of and *everywhere* energised and re-affirmed *all* our substitutions and exchanges.' Among them, then, those of the Abels and Remuses of our world.

We have seen the individual poems, if I am right, combining, as it were, towards a fall. So of the sequence itself – it builds towards what? a dying fall? a climax? or a resolution? The critical moment, he peak, comes towards the end of *'Compline'*.

That there is a meaning, after all, and that joy was the intended meaning, this was Charles Williams' account of things – a joy of life lived in the order and the beauty of the coinherence, the exchange.

That such joy, such order, is somewhere in the scheme of things the stars in their courses have always said to some, and so too the body's faithful rhythm (spoil it though we may through spite) – and though the day may be ending at 'Compline' in confessed defeat, with recollections of our small destructivenesses and refusals of each other from the cradle to the grave – a child's wild look of envy and an old man's greed – and though what happened today between noon and three (where surely the meaning must lie) is a total emptiness, yet still they seem to give the message, tied up it may be with a sorrow of the heart for sin: they

> Sing of some hilarity beyond
> All liking and happening

(we are back to the old vocabulary of 'Prime', of desire and event).

But these are hints and guesses, and who would wish to be deceived? 'To be happy means to be free, not from pain or fear, but from care or anxiety. A man is so free when (i) he knows what he desires and (ii) what he desires is real and not fantastic.'[31] If we must not hold on to the vain fornications of fancy, there is nothing for it now but the unreal world of dreams, not of daydreams but of dreams, one step past which, with all their untruth, is . . . what? – the final unreality of non-being itself.

But there could be an equity in that –

> . . . what comes to be
> Must go back into non-being
> For the sake of the equity, the rhythm
> Past measure or comprehending.

And at that point, the moment of potential final non-comprehension, incoherence, non-being itself, on the crest of the wave-top breaking into that, like

> Lion, fish and swan [who]
> Act, and are gone
> Upon Time's toppling wave –[32]

at the point of an acceptance, the give and take of it seen as a
rhythm, *the* rhythm perhaps, after all – at that point (counterpoint
to the critical moment in 'Prime'): *the question* – Is there after all a
possible kindness, indeed a justice, in the universe, beyond our
comprehension though it be?

> It is not easy
> To believe in unknowable justice
>   Or pray in the name of a love
> Whose name one's forgotten . . .

but still *is* salvation, a poet's salvation even (is it the nearest Auden
will ever get to a personal parade of penitence? – I like to think so), a
possibility?

> Can poets (can men in television)
>   Be saved? It is not easy
> To believe in unknowable justice
>   Or pray in the name of a love
> Whose name one's forgotten: *libera*
>   *Me, libera* C (dear C)
> And all poor s-o-b's who never
>   Do anything properly . . .

What has happened, Fuller has seen – the sequence has been
'shifted into its role as prayer'.[33] Incoherently (which does not
matter and indeed is largely the point, for we are at the end of our
resources, and have faced the truth of things, the possible abyss) we
topple over into prayer. And Fuller has seen, too, that it is a prayer
from the Mass. It is also, I think, to be noted that it is a prayer from
the *Requiem Mass*, the *Responsorium* –

> Libera me, Domine, de morte aeterna in
> die illa tremenda, quando coeli movendi
> sunt et terra; dum veneris judicare
> saeculum per ignem . . .
>
> Spare us in the youngest day (novissima illa dies) . . .

Meaning *will* be given, but only in response to that cry which is a
cry for pardon and therefore for life, and the life given will not be

short of resurrection (or its full meaning known before the day of judgement): it will be a liberation out of unfreedom, disorder and meaninglessness, into joy: yet not a private rejoicing but rather the joy that had originally been intended, the joy of coinherence, perichoresis (it is, of course, one and the same word). This is the dance. And at the centre of the dance, the tree . . .

> *libera*
> *Me, libera* C (dear C)
> And all poor s-o-b's who never
> Do anything properly

(and under the principle of forgiveness they are acceptable, and we call them brothers)

> . . . spare
> Us in the youngest day when all are
> Shaken awake, facts are facts,
> (And I shall know exactly what happened
> Today between noon and three)
> That we, too, may come to the picnic
> With nothing to hide, join the dance
> As it moves in perichoresis,
> Turns about the abiding tree.

The Charles Williams footnote that I mentioned – here, at last, it is, a reference to Milton and his *Comus* (and of comedy Williams has said 'But forgiveness is the resolution of all into a kind of comedy, the happiness of reconciliation, the peace of love'):

> It has been pointed out to me that the masque usually involved a dance, and that Milton for the actual dance substituted a philosophical. The suggestion is so much in accord with the high gaiety of *Comus* that I wish I had thought of it myself. The physical nature of the dance passes into the intellectual measure and there maintains itself in the sound of the verse.[34]

'Lauds' is the dance: the dance of resurrection, the prayed-for pardon, the restored coinherence of man and God, and man and man. It is just this: 'Lauds' *is* the dance: the dance here and now, the language embodying what it indicates.

Yet the critics, even Fuller, who saw 'Compline' as ending in prayer, and Johnson, too, who has seen the pure perfection of the form, can make nothing of it, nothing of it in the end in terms of any substance. For the one it is merely a decorative postscript; for the other, it is there to demonstrate the chasm between its formal, artistic harmony and the cacophony of existence, but with no direct reference to the events of the other poems. And we are near indeed to the aesthetic heresy 'that a poem has no subject' (*DH*, 37).

V

'We read Dante for his poetry not for his theology because we have already met the theology elsewhere.'[35] How many of us in fact met the rather special stream of Christian theology which is Charles Williams, and to which Auden acknowledges his indebtedness, I do not know. I do believe that it is a stream which comes into its own today; and *Horae Canonicae*, caught by it thirty years ago, leaves my own mind, in John Coulson's words from Hopkins, 'swinging, poised but on the quiver . . . the ecstasy of interest'.[36]

That the Passion and its poetry could 'come into its own' today for us to 'repossess the mystery of the Cross'[37] as something not discontinuous with our own suffering world, is indeed a thought. Yet there are different degrees of disciplined understanding and, as Professor Bennett said perceptively in that last book of his,

> To see the Cross as the epitome of the world's woe requires no special grace. It is on the efficacy of its redemptive and vicarious sacrifice that Christian hope must rest, and though some modern Hindu and Buddhist teachers come close to an understanding of the Crucifixion only the Christian creed accepts the figure of the Cross as a fountain of life-giving blood. (pp. 196–7)

On this, three observations may be offered, in terms of men's need today. First, it is a corporate, a social, redemption that would be to the point for us, and not less than that.

> Christian insight . . . differs from a secular humanist estimate of man . . . First, it knows that good aims are not enough. St. Paul had strong aims before he became a Christian and he knew the agony of finding 'another law in his members warning against the

law of his mind' – an inner division only healed by his becoming open to an influence outside himself. *The same problem afflicts societies.* The aims of men in a particular period are often thwarted by the equipment of a civilisation which has acquired a momentum of its own and pulls against what men want to achieve.[38]

The point had been long ago taken by Auden. 'But, first, money and then machinery have created a world in which . . . we are all mutually dependent.' Then, significantly, there follows a long quotation from Williams' 'Taliessin through Logres', ending:

For the wealth of the self is the health of the self exchanged.
What saith Heraclitus? – and what is the City's breath? –
dying each other's life, living each other's death.[39]

And so Fr Cornelius Ernst O. P. was writing, in that same year as Demant, the year of Wystan Auden's death, of 'a *newly-discovered* sense of the solidarity of human kind, a solidarity of alienation and despair and a solidarity of liberation and life. It is such a solidarity that Paul tries to represent when he talks about the "body" of redeemed humanity.'[40]

There is another human solidarity: the solidarity of human kind with this green world temporal. And this brings me to my second observation.

We yearn (it is a Charles Williams' word) with a new sensitivity towards the environment – a care which Auden shared in fact with Heidegger. Certain phrases leap out from the pages of Steiner's little book: 'today's penitential ecology and attempts at reparation, probably futile'.[41] We need an affirmation of the material world that can give us a confidence to meet such a despair. 'The Cross', wrote Professor Bennett of the Anglo-Saxon 'Vision of a Rood', 'is not only king of all the forest trees, it is the source of a cleansing flood that pours over terra, pontus, astra, mundus (earth, sea, stars, world) – eall þeos moere gesceaft, "all this wondrous creation" '.[42]

I think, yet here again, of Auden's criticism.

The images of the Just City, of the civilised landscape protected by the Madonna, the 'Fior, frondi, ombre, antri, onde, aure soavi' which look at us from so many Italian paintings, and of the rose garden or island of the blessed, are lacking in Romantic literature because the Romantic writers no longer believe in their existence. What exists is the Trivial Unhappy Unjust City . . .[43]

The redemption with which Auden is most distinctly concerned is, indeed, of the City: but the creaturely world is there in the picture: not only our own wronged flesh but, awed too by this death and watching,

> the hawk looking down
> Without blinking, the smug hens
> Passing close by in their pecking order,
> The bug whose view is balked by grass,
> Or the deer who shyly from afar
> Peer through chinks in the forest,

and the eager ridge, the steady sea of 'Prime', were there to be seen as friends.

If my first observation pleaded for the affirmation of *society* as part of the Christian understanding of redemption, and my second for the affirmation of *the material world* as likewise important, my third would be to do with the affirmation of *responsibility*.

We touched at an early moment in this chapter on the concept of *felix culpa*, to make the point that responsibility is too deeply serious a notion for Auden to allow us to trade in any final sense in Heideggerian terms ('positivity of fallenness', the sheer givenness of the fall in the 'facticity of inauthenticity') in expounding Auden on the Fall: choice is integral, for him, and a moral value judgement is somehow comported.

I believe it to be part of the greatness of the sequence that it 'embodies' throughout the poetry one deep tension – elusive, at moments, to define, but inescapable in any serious treatment of the Fall and the Atonement. It is a tension nowhere put more concisely than in a page or two of that almost exact contemporary of Wystan Auden (whom he met in the United States at a fateful moment of his life, in summer 1939) the Dietrich Bonhoeffer to whom I have already referred. I refer to the *Ethics*, put together afterwards from those papers of his which came so exactly out of an 'abrupt and forcible alignment' of theology with the everyday.

'Yet the crucifixion of Jesus does not simply mean the annihilation of the created world, but under this sign of death, the cross, men are now to continue to live, to their own condemnation if they despise it, but to their own salvation if they give it its due.'[44] And then, under the title 'The Acceptance of Guilt', these words: 'From His selfless love, from His freedom from sin, Jesus enters into the guilt of men and takes this guilt upon Himself . . . If any man tries to escape guilt in responsibility, he detaches himself from the ultimate reality of human existence, and what is more he cuts himself off from the redeeming mystery of Christ . . . He sets his own personal innocence above his responsibility for men'[45] – poignant words, the fullness of whose meaning, we remember, waited for Bonhoeffer at the moment remembered in Auden's dedication of 'Friday's Child' (or 'He told us we were free to choose')

In memory of Dietrich Bonhoeffer,
martyred at Flossenburg, April 9th, 1945

We cannot stay in Eden: we must carry responsibilities, sometimes dreadful, which will open with a new dawn.

That the dawn opens on a world redeemed – with pardon a real possibility when, as we shall do indeed, we have gone down a wrong turning – is its brightness. Already the mass bell goes dong-ding – *and* the dripping mill-wheel is again turning, the world's business to be done. That we are to see ourselves redeemed from fear and unreality into the courage of such realism is a word that is needed in any real proclamation of the Atonement today. It is a frightening world, and we can easily find ourselves standing passive with the Crowd.

VI

So we must leave the poetry. Auden has been true to his own word. A world created good, but fallen; the possibility of regaining paradise through repentance and forgiveness – things, in Dr Coulson's words describing the function of the Imagination, seen in a new light and with recreative power . . . 'Its use in literary criticism (as in theology) is to denote a particular kind of cognitive perception. It marks the arousal of a state of deep but highly ordered feeling, which is never mere feeling but has as its object a new sense of reality.'[46]

Wystan Auden would surely have liked that. And it takes me

back to his own thoughts on Imagination and the encounter with sacred things, sacred events.

Quickness to be touched by them, to see them so, is, I come to see more clearly, the credential of the poet. And he was quick.

I ask myself (with gratitude to him for the sharing) what were the things he saw and as he saw them found them invested with an importance overwhelming and undefinable, evocative, irreducibly, of *awe*: the moments, the events, such as

> the world seen in the immediacy
> of its freshness at awaking
> and that glimpse overtaken by a cloud

or

> the moment before losing consciousness,
> going into non-being,
> after a day that has made no sense;
>
> the look in a man's eye, the set
> of a man's mouth, as though all
> civilisation were explained in it

or

> the blankness of the crowd's look
> the incoherence of its roar,
> a child's wild look of envy.

And among the events, most deeply, surely, the reading of that small book and its pondering over a time, a solid time. If the argument of this paper holds it had helped him to make public his own crowd of recollected occasions of feeling in all its problematic contradictoriness.

At the centre, this understanding of a Fall – the vexation and unease ('Prime's' words) that are involved for men when life demands, as demand it must if it is to be life, a choice in things and so finds a will-fullness built in from the start. Could we indeed have stayed in Eden? At the price of certain things, including innocence, we live. To that mystery of fallen humanity, which we must not forget, the poems pay their homage.

But inescapably part of this illumination, and giving us indeed the courage to face the reality of things so, is the explicitly Christian account of a world redeemed, and by an act which is both acceptance of the human situation and its transformation. Here is human responsibility redeemed, said 'Yes' to – which is what the possibility of pardon means: and here is the possibility of joy.

To that, 'Lauds' pays homage: but the sequence as a whole, the *Horae Canonicae* which is a movement and a unity, embodying as it does this tension (with which we must still live), is homage to it too.

NOTES

1. Joseph Warren Beach, *The Making of the Auden Canon*, (New York, 1957), passim; and Humphrey Carpenter, *W. H. Auden: A Biography* (London, 1981), pp. 415f.
2. John Fuller, *A Reader's Guide to W. H. Auden* (London and New York, 1970), p. 238.
3. W. H. Auden, 'Postscript: Christianity and Art' in *The Dyer's Hand and other essays* (in future references, *DH*) (London, 1963), pp. 456–61, p. 458.
4. J. A. W. Bennett, *Poetry of the Passion, Studies in Twelve Centuries of English Verse* (Oxford, 1982), pp. 3, 89, 86.
5. Ibid., p. 6.
6. Auden, *DH*, p. 21.
7. Auden, *DH*, p. 457.
8. Richard Johnson, *Man's Place, An Essay on Auden* (Cornell, 1973), pp. x, 186ff.
9. Auden, *DH*, p. 4.
10. Thinking began on *Horae Canonicae* in 1947. See *W. H. Auden: A Tribute*, edited by Stephen Spender (London, 1974, 1975), p. 116 (Ursula Niebuhr).
11. In 'Robert Frost', *DH*, p. 340 and 'Dingley Dell and The Fleet', *DH*, p. 411.
12. George Steiner, *Heidegger* (London, 1978), pp. 94f.
13. Charles Williams, 'The Cross' in *The Image of the City and other essays*, edited with an Introduction by Anne Ridler (Oxford, 1958), p. 134.
14. Auden, in a note to Ursula Niebuhr sent while he was at Swarthmore, 1942–5. See Spender (ed.), *A Tribute*, p. 112.
15. Charles Williams, *The Forgiveness of Sins* (London, 1942), p. 22.
16. Charles Williams, *He Came Down From Heaven* (London, 1938).
17. W. H. Auden, *The Enchafèd Flood* (London, 1951).
18. Compare Dietrich Bonhoeffer in *Ethics* (London, 1955), passim (the concept of the 'penultimate').
19. Bennett, *Poetry of the Passion*, p. 3.
20. Auden, *DH*, p. 13.
21. W. H. Auden, 'The Greeks and Us', in *Forwards and Afterwards* (London, 1973), p. 8.
22. Isaiah 53.7, quoted by Bennett, *Poetry of the Passion*, p. 6.
23. A. C. Partridge, *The Language of Modern Poetry, Yeats, Eliot, Auden* (Andre Deutsch, 1976) p. 295. 'The dedicated craftsman will even neglect religious duties, such as prayers to saints . . . the names of the saints have no bearing on Auden's line of thinking!'

24. A. Ridler, *The Image of the City* (London, 1958), Introduction, p. xxxi.
25. Auden, 'The Poet and The City', *DH*, p. 82.
26. Auden, *DH*, p. 83.
27. See *The Enchafèd Flood*, p. 32 'Memorial for the City' (In Memoriam Charles Williams d. April 1945) section 2: 'nursed on the smile of a merciful Madonna'.
28. Williams, *The Forgiveness of Sins*, pp. 26, 33.
29. Edward Mendelson, *Early Auden* (London, 1981), p. 364.
30. Williams, *The Image of the City*, p. 137.
31. Auden, 'Red Ribbon on a White Horse', *DH*, p. 327.
32. Auden, 'Fish in the unruffled lakes', *Collected Poems* (London, 1976), p. 118.
33. Fuller, *A Reader's Guide*, p. 238.
34. Williams, *The Forgiveness of Sins*, pp. 14, 25 n.2.
35. Auden in 'D. H. Lawrence', *DH*, p. 277.
36. John Coulson, *Religion and Imagination 'in aid of a grammar of assent'* (Oxford, 1981), p. 73.
37. Amos Wilder, *Theopoetic, Theology and the Religious Imagination* (Philadelphia, 1976), p. 12.
38. V. A. Demant, 'Humanism, Christian and Secularist', *Theology* (June 1973), 30.
39. Auden, 'Brothers and Others', *DH*, p. 235.
40. Cornelius Ernst O. P., *he Theology of Grace* (Wisconsin, 1974), p. 24.
41. Steiner, *Heidegger*, p. 130.
42. Bennett, Poetry of the Passion, p. 14.
43. Auden, *The Enchafèd Flood*, p. 32.
44. Bonhoeffer, *Ethics*, p. 109.
45. Ibid., p. 210.
46. Coulson, *Religion and Imagination*, p. 6 (on Coleridge).

5 Poetry and Prophecy: Bishop Lowth and The Hebrew Scriptures in Eighteenth-century England

Stephen Prickett

To the modern reader one of the most puzzling features of Wordsworth's *Prelude* is a kind of disconcertingly inappropriate religiosity that suddenly obtrudes into the narrative without any very obvious 'objective correlative'. In Book XIII of the 1805 text, for example, after describing his vision of the 'sea of clouds' by moonlight from the top of Snowdon, Wordsworth goes on to use it as the culminating symbol of the poet's mind – a magnificent pre-Freudian intuition of the power of the unconscious mind in artistic creativity.[1] But, having made his disclosure with admirable economy, he then proceeds to labour the point with what seems like abstract pieties:

> Such minds are truly from the Deity,
> For they are Powers; and hence the highest bliss
> That can be known is theirs – the consciousness
> Of whom they are, habitually infused
> Through every image and through every thought,
> And all impressions; hence religion, faith,
> And endless occupation for the Soul,
> Whether discursive or intuitive;
> Hence sovereignty within and peace at will,

Emotion which best foresight need not fear,
Most worthy then of trust when most intense.
Hence cheerfulness in every act of life,
Hence truth in moral judgements and delight
That fails not in the external universe.

(lines 108–19)

Most critics omit the passage when discussing the Snowdon scene. Its grandiose and pious abstractions do not seem to belong to the unconscious as we have come to think of it. Wordsworth's egotistical sublime seems to have gone over the top a bit. We perhaps feel about it as we do about Shelley's claim in the *Defence of Poetry* that the poet ought to be, and is 'the happiest, the best, the wisest, and the most illustrious of men'. [2] Yet, for Wordsworth, the passage was clearly of some importance since in the 1850 text the tone is even more overtly religious, and a number of extra lines are added to reinforce the point, concluding:

Hence, amid ills that vex and wrongs that crush
Our hearts – if here the words of Holy Writ
May with fit reverence be applied – that peace
Which passeth understanding, that repose
In moral judgements which from this pure source
Must come, or will by man be sought in vain.

(lines 124–9)

The religious dimension of the poet's task is clearly central to Wordsworth. We may get some clue to the origins of this spontaneous overflow of pious feelings if we look back to the previous book of *The Prelude* where he addresses his friend Coleridge on the 'genius of the Poet':

Dearest Friend!
Forgive me if I say that I, who long
Had harboured reverentially a thought
That Poets, even as Prophets, each with each
Connected in a mighty scheme of truth,
Have each for his peculiar dower, a sense
By which he is enabled to perceive
Something unseen before . . .

(1805: Book XII, lines 299–305)

This claim, that the poet is a prophet, who, like those of the Old Testament, proclaims the great hidden truths of human existence, is one of the central tenets of Romanticism.

William Blake, in an early work polemically entitled *There is No Natural Religion* (1788), argues (incidentally, on sound Kantian lines) that not merely religion, but *all* knowledge, of whatever kind, is ultimately dependent upon the poetic or 'prophetic' leap of the imagination.

> If it were not for the Poetic or Prophetic character the Philosophic and Experimental would soon be at the ratio of all things, and stand still, unable to do other than repeat the same dull round over again. [3]

The same year, 1788, in another piece with the equally aggressive title *All Religions are One*, Blake's 'Voice of one crying in the Wilderness' announced that 'The Religions of all Nations are derived from each Nation's different reception of the Poetic Genius, which is everywhere call'd the Spirit of Prophecy'. [4]

Shelley goes even further than the first generation Romantics. In his *Four Ages of Poetry* (1820) his friend Thomas Love Peacock had ironically described the poets of ancient times as being

> not only historians but theologians, moralists, and legislators: delivering their oracles *ex cathedra*, and being indeed often themselves regarded as portions and emanations of divinity: building cities with a song, and leading brutes with a symphony: which are only metaphors for the faculty of leading multitudes by the nose. [5]

Shelley's reply, in his *Defence of Poetry*, was to out-top all previous claims for the status of the poet, supporting his assertion that 'poets are the unacknowledged legislators of mankind' with reference to their traditional prophetic role:

> Poets, according to the circumstances of the age and nation in which they appeared, were called, in the earlier epochs of the world, legislators or prophets: a poet essentially comprises and unites both these characters. [6]

Moreover, as rapidly becomes clear, Shelley, the atheist, is not using the word 'prophet' in any merely metaphorical sense. The main thrust of the rhetoric of the *Defence* is towards a scarcely secularised language of divine inspiration. The phrases tumble over each other. 'Poetry lifts the veil from the hidden beauty of the world . . . A man to be greatly good, must imagine intensely and comprehensively . . . The great instrument of moral good is the imagination . . . Poetry strengthens the faculty which is the organ of the moral nature of man, in the same manner as exercise strengthens a limb . . . Poetry is the sword of lightning, ever unsheathed, which consumes the scabbard that would contain it . . . Poetry is indeed something divine.'

Though it is argued just a little too vehemently to be a critical commonplace, the identification of the poet with the prophet of old so permeates Romantic thought that it is easy to lose sight of just how dramatic a critical revolution lies behind it. As with most 'new' ideas, its roots can be traced back a long way. Sidney, in his *Apology for Poetry* (1595), remarked that 'Among the Romans a Poet was called Vates, which is as much as Diviner, Fore-seer, or Prophet. . .'[7] and noted that the Delphic oracles were delivered in verse. Thomas Percy, the antiquarian collector of poems, and, if truth be told, part-composer of the anthology published under the title *Reliques of Ancient Poetry*, added to it an 'Essay on the Ancient Minstrels in England' in which he dilates upon the 'northern SCALDS, in whom the characters of historian, genealogist, poet, and musician, were all united'. These Norse 'Scalds' 'professed to inform and instruct, and were at once the moralists and theologues of their Pagan countrymen'.

Alongside this pagan tradition was another, specifically Christian and Augustinian concept of the prophet as poet and orator which finds expression in, for instance, Milton's prose works and even in Blake's *Jerusalem*.[8] It was given a more precisely-argued form within English literature with the publication of John Dennis's *The Grounds of Criticism in Poetry* in 1704. According to him 'Poetry is the natural Language of Religion . . . the Prophets were Poets by the Institution of their Order, and Poetry was one of the Prophetick Functions'.[9] Though the strands of thought between pagan and Christian, Homer and the Old Testament, cross and recross throughout the eighteenth century, their essential difference is, once again, beautifully illustrated by Wordsworth in *The Prelude*.

From his meditation on the poet as prophet in Book XII he goes on at once to what he calls a 'reverie', first of ancient Britons, 'with

shield and stone-axe' striding 'across the wold', and then of Druid
sacrifices

> . . . fed
> With living men – how deep the groans! the voice
> Of those in the gigantic wicker thrills
> Throughout the region far and near, pervades
> The monumental hillocks, and the pomp
> Is for both worlds, the living and the dead.
>
> (lines 331–6)

At other times, he tells us, he saw before him

> on the downy Plain
> Lines, circles, mounts, a mystery of shapes
> Such as in many quarters yet survive,
> With intricate profusion figuring o'er
> The untilled ground, the work as some divine,
> Of infant science, imitative forms
> By which the Druids covertly expressed
> Their knowledge of the heavens . . .
>
> (lines 339–46)

But though Wordsworth hopes to catch 'a tone/An image, and a
character' from these 'bearded teachers', he distances it all as an
'antiquarian's dream'. They may well be in a historical sense his
spiritual ancestors, but, though he recognises the connections, he
does not cast himself as a new 'Druid' – the reference to the
screaming victims being burnt alive in the wicker cages is sufficient
reminder of the gulf between the ancient Celtic bards and the
modern poet. If we want to find in Wordsworth echoes of the same
tone of high seriousness and sense of divine meaning to the high
calling of the poet that so obtruded themselves in the lines with
which we began, we must look, for instance, to the passage in Book
IV of *The Prelude* where the young Wordsworth is coming home
after an all-night dance. As he walks across the fields in the first light
of dawn he is caught up in a sudden mood of exaltation:

> Ah! need I say, dear Friend! that to the brim
> My heart was full; I made no vows, but vows

Were then made for me; bond unknown to me
Was given, that I should be, else sinning greatly,
A dedicated Spirit.

(lines 340–4)

The contrast in language with the previous passage about the pagan bards is total. He is not now concerned with the poet as guardian of esoteric mysteries, or with the sense of tradition that inspired an 'antiquarian's dream', but with personal commitment, 'vows' and 'dedication'. Nor, in spite of the title of a recent book centring on Wordsworth's 'natural methodism',[10] is this the language of contemporary Methodist or Evangelical conversion. Though to break those vows would be 'sinning greatly', they are not ones that he himself has made; he has, rather, become aware of them as an existing condition that affects his entire life. This is not the language of the northern bards and druids, nor that of the classical world: it is that of a specific minority tradition running from the Old Testament through certain kinds of individual experience into the later tradition of the Church. It is that of St Augustine in the *Confessions*, and behind him the stories of Samuel, of David, and of Hosea. The vows made for the infant Samuel by his mother, Hannah, are echoed by Monica's prayers for her son, Augustine, and now, metaphorically, by Wordsworth's 'foster-mother', Nature, for her dedicated son. Though Wordsworth was well aware of the pagan and classical antecedents for the divine status of the poet, his stress is not on the powers bestowed by the gift of prophecy on the poet, but on the process of *election*.

Wordswoth stands at a peculiar and, in some ways, a unique moment in the history of biblical criticism. To understand something of the complexity of his aesthetic vision we need to turn to the middle of the eighteenth century: to the publication of a book that was to transform biblical studies in England and Germany alike, and was to do more than any other single work to make the biblical tradition, rather than the classical one, the central poetic tradition of the Romantics: Robert Lowth's *The Sacred Poetry of the Hebrews*. Delivered first as the Oxford Poetry Lectures in 1741, this was first published in Latin in 1753, and achieved much wider circulation with its English translation in 1787.

Lowth was not merely one of the most distinguished theologians of his day, he was also an outstanding Orientalist – in the eighteenth-century sense of the word – an expert on the manners, customs, and thought of the ancient Hebrews. His translation of *Isaiah* (1778) rapidly became a standard work, and his *Short Introduction to English Grammar* (1762) showed a linguistic sophistication that kept it still in use at Harvard University in the mid-nineteenth century. After a highly successful Oxford career (he was only 31 when he became Professor of Poetry), he became successively, Bishop of St David's (1776), Oxford, in the same year, and finally of London (1777).

To Lowth we owe the rediscovery of the Bible as a work of literature within the context of ancient Hebrew life. Hitherto, it had been understood almost exclusively in terms of allegorical and typological meanings: a timeless compendium of divinely inspired revelation. Old Testament events were read in relation to those they might pre-figure in the New, especially in the life of Christ. Thus one popular mid-eighteenth-century commentary explains that the story of Elijah on Horeb, confronted by the earthquake, the wind, and the fire, followed by the 'still small voice' (I Kings 19. 8–12), is a 'type' of the way in which 'the soft and gentle persuasions' of Jesus in the New Testament were to follow 'the storms, thunders, lightnings and earthquakes which attended the promulgation of the law' in the Old.[11] Even as late as 1806, we find Mrs Trimmer, that formidable engine of the SPCK Tract Society, in her *Help to the Unlearned in the Study of the Holy Scriptures*, telling her readers that 'The LORD's *speaking in a small still voice*, was a sign that He was graciously disposed to show lenity and forebearance towards the idolatrous people of Israel, and to preserve the land of Israel for those who had not yet bowed the knee to Baal . . .' Though the later example is significantly less 'typological', in the traditional sense, than the former, for neither is the event itself of primary interest. What is important is its *meaning* within the whole of the divine plan. As Mrs Trimmer had succinctly put it in her Introduction:

> The Histories they [the Scriptures] contain differ from all other histories that were ever written, for they give an account of the *ways of GOD*; and explain *why GOD protected and rewarded* some persons and nations, and *why* he *punished* others; also, *what led* particular persons mentioned in Scripture to *do* certain things for which they were approved or condemned; whereas writers who compose histories in a common way, without being *inspired of God*, can only form guesses and conjectures concerning God's dealings with mankind, neither can they know what passed in the hearts of

those they write about; such knowledge as this, belongs to GOD alone, whose ways are *unsearchable and past finding out, and to whom all hearts are open, all desires known*!

There can be no argument about divinely inspired history. The Bible was not a historical document so much as the yardstick by which the authenticity of historical documents might be judged. But behind this attitude to inspiration lay a quite different attitude to history itself. It was not a matter of particularities but of generalities: the grand generalities that illustrated Natural Law. History, in essence, was a useful collection of examples for pedagogical purposes.[12] The purpose of sacred history was to provide the types by which God revealed his grand design from the Fall to the eventual redemption of man.

In contrast, Lowth argued that

> He who would perceive the particular and interior elegancies of the Hebrew poetry, must imagine himself exactly situated as the persons for whom it was written, or even as the writers themselves; he is to feel them as a Hebrew . . . nor is it enough to be acquainted with the language of this people, their manners, discipline, rites and ceremonies; we must even investigate their inmost sentiments, the manner and connexion of their thoughts; in one word, we must see all things with their eyes, estimate all things by their opinions: we must endeavour as much as possible to read Hebrew as the Hebrews would have read it.[13]

Commonsense as this kind of approach might seem to us today, as we have seen, Lowth's aesthetics involved a new and even revolutionary kind of scholarship. In the words of Friedrich Meinecke:

> Lowth's book was perhaps the most intellectually important product of the whole pre-Romantic movement in England. It was free of all dilettantism and superficiality of taste, and had the indirect result of contributing to the liberation of historical research from the bonds of theology by displaying the purely human and historical content and value of the Bible. It set forth a genuine science of the humanities, and gave it new organs.

(p. 206)

In Germany the pioneer biblical scholar Johann David Michaelis brought out an annotated Latin edition in 1758 (Volume 2, 1761) and various continental translations quickly followed. His notes were reprinted in subsequent English editions. Lowth's *Lectures* were to be a major influence on the new generation of biblical critics and historians in Germany, such as Eichhorn, Gesenius, and above all, Herder, whose own *Spirit of Hebrew Poetry* owes much to them. As a historian of ideas working specifically on Herder and the rise of the modern notion of 'history', Meinecke has his own perspective on Lowth, but his assessment of the influence of the *Lectures* on the subsequent development of German thought is the more significant in consequence.

In England Lowth's emphasis on the historical context of Hebrew poetry was closely paralleled by a similar development in classical scholarship. In 1735 Thomas Blackwell had published his *Life and Writings of Homer* which had linked together the destinies, customs, and language of a people in a mutually interacting chain. To understand Homer, he argued, it was essential to imagine oneself in his audience, as part of a warrior people wishing to hear something of the heroic deeds of their ancestors.[14] Lowth, like Blackwell, insisted that there could be no break between historical and aesthetic scholarship. The clue to the relationship between the prophecy and poetry of the Bible, already noted by, for instance, Dennis, must lie in detailed study of the social setting from which they arose.

> It is evident from many parts of the Sacred History, that even from the earliest times of the Hebrew Republic, there existed certain colleges of prophets, in which the candidates for the prophetic office, removed altogether from an intercourse with the world, devoted themselves entirely to the exercises and study of religion.[15]

The Hebrew word Nabi', explains Lowth, was used in an ambiguous sense denoting equally 'a Prophet, a Poet, or a Musician, under the influence of divine inspiration'. He cites the case of Solomon, who 'twice makes use of the word, which, in its ordinary sense, means prophecy, strictly so called, to denote the language of poetry' (II, p. 12).

From all these testimonies it is sufficiently evident, that the prophetic office had a most strict connexion with the poetic art. They had one common name, one common origin, one common author, the Holy Spirit. Those in particular were called to the exercise of the prophetic office, who were previously conversant with the sacred poetry. It was equally part of their duty to compose verses for the service of the church, and to declare the oracles of God.

(II, p. 18)

The difference between Dennis's speculative and theoretical argument and Lowth's sense of historical context is illustrated over the relationship between Jesus and the Old Testament prophetic tradition. Dennis saw as a prophet: 'the method of his Instruction was entirely Poetical: that is, by Fables or Parables, contriv'd, and plac'd, and adapted to work very strongly upon human passions'. [16] Lowth anchors this assertion by pointing out that 'Mashal', one of the words commonly used for a poem in the Old Testament (especially in terms of *content*) is also the word translated in the New Testament as 'parable'. In other words, he concludes, Jesus's parables are not an innovation, but merely an extension, by the greatest of the biblical 'poets', of the basic mode of Hebrew thought as it had been handed down through the prophetic tradition. [17]

In spite of coming frequently from humble backgrounds – like David, the shepherd boy – the prophets of Israel were not to be seen as rustics, but as men whose religious training had included an elaborate grounding in aesthetics – in particular, in the arts of music and verse. The prophets were, in short, the inheritors of a highly sophisticated aesthetic and intellectual tradition. Though Lowth's *Lectures* were to feed directly into the revival of primitivism in English poetry during the latter part of the eighteenth century, he refutes any suggestion that the poet Isaiah or the authors of the Psalms were themselves 'primitives', any more than those they inspired, like Smart, Cowper, Blake or Wordsworth were. What Lowth implicitly rejects are the stilted conventions of Augustan poetic diction. He praises, instead, the 'simple and unadorned' language of Hebrew verse, that gains its 'almost eneffable sublimity' not by elevated diction, but from the depth and universality of its subject matter. In his humble origins, and in the simplicity and directness of his language, Jesus is thus also a continuation of the Old Testament poetic tradition. Unlike the modern European poets, the Hebrew ones had never been part of a courtly circle at the centre of power, but had remained, often in opposition to the political establishment of the day, in close touch with the rural and pastoral life of the ordinary people, using in their verse (or 'parables') the homely metaphors of agriculture and everyday life (I. pp. 123, 311).

Lowth's capacity to bring out, anticipate, and even originate critical principles that were only to come to fruition with Romanticism is everywhere extraordinary. Though previous critics had made play with terms like 'enthusiasm' and 'sublimity' in the context of the Bible, they had remained, as ideas, relatively unfocused. Dennis, for instance, cites the authority of Longinus to show 'that the greatest sublimity is to be deriv'd from Religious Ideas. . . '[18] (something which, incidentally, Longinus never said), but the question of whether this is by definition *all* 'religious ideas', or some more than others is of less interest to him. In contrast, as we have seen, Lowth's idea of the 'sublime' stresses naturalness as against artificiality, the irregular as against the regular, the mysterious as against the comprehensible, in a way that closely anticipates Burke's own *Enquiry into the Sublime and the Beautiful* (1757) by several years. For him, as for Burke, it is the ultimate criterion of greatness in art. Foreshadowing Blair and Wordsworth, Lowth goes on to describe the language of poetry as the product of 'enthusiasm', 'springing from mental emotion'.[19] It is hardly surprising that through Lowth's influence the Bible was to become for the Romantics not merely the model of sublimity, but also a source of style and a touchstone of true feeling.

But Lowth's most original scholarly contribution was the rediscovery of Hebrew prosody: the technique of its construction. It had always been clear, of course, that a great deal of the Bible was 'poetic', and earlier critics as far removed from each other as Dennis and Addison had laid great stress on the poetic qualities of the scriptures, but even the Psalms (which were known to be songs) showed perplexingly little evidence of either rhyme or regular metre in the original Hebrew. Even among contemporary Jews the traditional art of Hebrew verse-construction seemed to have been completely lost. Earlier scholars, such as Bishop Hare (1671–1740), had made valiant efforts to discover in the Psalms a system of scansion and a rhyme-scheme, but their results looked distinctly unconvincing. Lowth now demonstrated, with impressively detailed evidence, that Hebrew poetry had never depended upon the normal conventions of European verse at all, but was constructed instead upon a quite different principle which he called 'parallelism';

> The Correspondence of one verse, or line, with another, I call *parallelism*. When a proposition is delivered, and a second subjoined to it, or drawn under it, equivalent, or contrasted with it in sense; or similar to it in the form of grammatical construction; these I call parallel lines; and the words or phrases, answering one to another in the corresponding lines, parallel terms.
>
> (II. p. 32n)

This 'correspondence of one verse, or line, with another', Lowth argued, was the basic principle on which Hebrew metre was constructed. Its origins lay in the antiphonal chants and choruses we find mentioned in various places in the Old Testament. Lowth cites, for example, I Samuel 18.7, when David returned victorious from battle with the Philistines the Hebrew women greeted him with the chant of 'Saul hath smote his thousands', and were answered by a second chorus with the parallel: 'And David his ten thousands' (II. p. 53). This simple, rhythmic, antiphonal structure of statement and counter-statement, though it may have originated spon-taneously in song, gave the Hebrew psalmists and prophets a basic pattern of extraordinary flexibility. Its commonest form is what Lowth calls 'synonymous parallelism, when the same sentiment is repeated in different, but equivalent terms', as in Psalm 114:

> When Israel went out from Egypt;
> The house of Jacob from a strange people:
> Judah was as his sacred heritage;
> Israel his dominion.
> The sea saw and fled;
> Jordan turned back:
> The mountains leaped like rams;
> The hills like the sons of the flock.

Lowth himself distinguishes no less than eight different kinds of parallelism. From the simplest forms of repetition or echo that we find in synonymous parallelism, it could provide endless variation, comparison, contrast – as between David and Saul, for instance, in the example noted above, where their respective ratings in the charts was not lost on Saul – through to antithesis and even dialectic. Indeed, parallelism could be said to have shaped the whole structure of Jewish thought. Moreover, form helped to shape content in a way that was almost unknown in European poetry, and this extraordinary coincidence of style and content had another, apparently providential, consequence for European readers of the Bible.

Dennis had seemed to have a certain *a priori* logic on his side when he had argued 'that all those parts of the Old Testament which were writ in Verse, ought to be translated in Verse, by Reasons which may have force enough to convince us, that Verse translated into Prose is but half translated'.[20] Now, in the wake of Lowth's rediscovery of parallelism, it could be appreciated how *little* of the Hebrew poetry was in fact lost through the normal processes of translation. Whereas contemporary European poetry, which relied heavily on essentially untranslatable effects of alliteration, assonance, rhyme, and metre, was extremely difficult to render in another language with any real equivalence of tone and feeling, Hebrew poetry was almost all translatable. As Lowth put it:

> . . . a poem translated literally from the Hebrew into the prose of any other language, whilst the same form of the sentences remain, will still retain, even as far as relates to versification, much of its native dignity, and a fair appearance of versification.[21]

Translated into Greek or Latin, however, with a different word-order 'and having the conformation of the sentences accommodated to the idiom of a foreign language' it 'will appear confused and mutilated'. We may hear in this the convictions of the man who was later to publish one of the most highly acclaimed translations of *Isaiah*.

The point was eagerly taken up by succeeding critics, who noticed also the corollary: that, contra Dennis, Hebrew poetry was actually *better* translated into prose than verse. As Hugh Blair, one of Lowth's most influential admirers put it in his *Lectures on Rhetoric and Belles Lettres* (1783):

> It is owing, in a great measure, to this form of composition, that our version, though in prose, retains so much of a poetical cast. For the version being strictly word after the original, the form and order of the original sentence are preserved; which by this

artificial structure, this regular alternation and correspondence of parts, makes the ear sensible of departure from the common style and tone of prose.[22]

Though Lowth could hardly have foreseen the consequences of his work, its effect was nothing less than a critical revolution. Not merely did the Bible now give authority for the prophetic status of the poet as the transformer of society and the mediator of divine truth, but it was also stylistically taken as a model both of naturalness and of sublimity – with the added assurance that its precious content was almost providentially preserved in the rich prose of the English Authorised Version. As Freidrich Meinecke, Isaiah Berlin, and Elinor Shaffer have detailed,[23] Lowth's 'historical' approach was to prove seminal to the German historians and biblical scholars of the second half of the eighteenth century, and to play a key part in the development of the Higher Criticism. Yet, for all the interpretative brilliance of his scholarship, Lowth was never a 'historian' in the modern sense of the word. He accepts the biblical narrative at its face value, and never questions the textual history of the material he is dealing with, any more than he questions the miracles or the chronology of Genesis. For him, as for his forebears, the Bible was still the inspired Word of God. For all the emphasis on its context in the religious and cultural life of its day, Hebrew poetry is still regarded by Lowth as having 'one common author' – in the person of the Holy Spirit. Lowth has, similarly, no doubts that the books of Jonah and Daniel are 'the bare recital of fact', and the nearest he gets to speculation about authorship is when he discusses whether Moses or Elihu (the late entrant, you will recall, among Job's comforters) actually wrote the book of Job. We are still a long way from the world of Eichhorn, Lessing and Herder.

In England, however, as we have seen, Lowth's influence was to take a somewhat different course. Though Gregory's English translation was not published until 1787, the *Lectures* had already been published for a wider audience in monthly instalments in the anti-Wesleyan *Christian's Magazine* twenty years before, in 1767,[24] and were extensively summarised again by Blair in 1783. Though detailed evidence of his influence on individuals is sometimes hard to come by, his effect on Smart, for instance, is well-documented, and it is significant that the Blake references to the 'poetic genius' as 'the Spirit of Prophecy' which were quoted earlier date from 1788, the year after Gregory's translation of Lowth. What is clear is that alongside the rediscovery of the Bible within a historical context runs a no less important rediscovery of the Bible as *poetry*. The debate over the Bible opened up by Lowth is as much aesthetic as historical.

Perhaps the most important area of argument concerned the question of poetic form in the books of prophecy. This was a question on which Lowth himself had been somewhat ambiguous.

> In respect to the order, disposition, and symmetry of a perfect poem of the prophetic kind, I do not know of any certain definition which will admit of general application. Naturally free, and of too ardent a spirit to be confined by rule, it is usually guided by the nature of the subject only, and the impulse of divine inspiration.
>
> (II, p. 69)

Though it is perfectly possible to read this in a sense quite compatible with a later Romantic sense of organic form, it is clear from the actual examples that Lowth chooses that his ideas of 'regularity' and 'perfection' of form remain by and large neo-classical. Nor had he had reason to revise the caution of his defence of biblical structure by the time he came to publish his translation of the prophet who, by general accord, was given first place (after David) among the poets of Israel: Isaiah.

> Isaiah greatly excels, too, in all the graces of method, order, connexion, and arrangement; though in asserting this we must not forget the nature of the prophetic impulse, which bears away the mind with irresistible violence, and frequently in rapid transitions from near to remote objects, from human to divine: we must also be careful in remarking the limits of particular predictions, since, as they are now extant, they are often improperly connected, without any marks of discrimination; which injudicious arrangement, on some occasions, creates almost insuperable difficulties.
>
> (II, pp. 85–6)

This pusillanimity in defence of the artistic form of divine inspiration was too much for one of Lowth's sincerest admirers, Thomas Howes, Rector of Thorndon, who, in 1783, published his

Doubts Concerning the Translation and Notes of the Bishop of London to Isaiah, Vindicating Ezekiel, Isaiah, and other Jewish Prophets from Disorder in Arrangement. Howes out-Lowths Lowth. He has no doubt that the basic principles enunciated by the bishop are correct, but in adopting, however tentatively, the theory that there may be breaks in the text, or mistakes in the ordering, Lowth is being untrue to his own critical canons. Howes brings to biblical criticism contemporary theories of inspiration, natural genius, and poetic grace, thus, in the words of a recent commentator, 'making the Bible the *locus classicus* of the issue of inspiration vs. mechanical composition, artlessness vs. art'.[25] His argument is the more powerful in that it enlists, by implication at any rate, the full authority of the Holy Spirit for the new ideas of organic form. He challenges Lowth's assumption that the natural order for prophecies should be chronological, suggesting two other possible principles of arrangement: that of 'historic order', that in which the prophecies were actually accomplished, and that of 'oratorical order', that which is 'best suited to the purpose of *persuasion and argumentation*'. This last, which Howes describes as the 'still better order', he also calls 'poetic arrangement':

> For it has been long conceived, that these prophecies are replete with bold poetic ideas and expressions; the translator [Lowth] with his usual learning and accuracy, has convinced the public, that they are even composed in a similar metre to the other antient poetic works of the Jews: I have only ventured, in pursuance of his example, to advance one step farther in novelty, by shewing, that there are equally good reasons to conceive these prophecies to be put together in a connected method and order, agreeably to such modes of poetic and oratorical arrangment, as were customary in the most antient ages, and this apparently by the respective authors of each prophetic work.[26]

It has been well said by A. O. Lovejoy that 'the history of ideas is the history of the confusion of ideas'. Howes' idea of an 'oratorical order' for the prophets is, in many ways, closer to the notions of rhetoric that we find in Milton or Dennis, than it is to the Preface to the *Lyrical Ballads* or *Biographia Literaria*. Conversely, of course, Lowth's suspicion that there are problems to the text of Isaiah not wholly to be attributed to the agency of the Holy Spirit, and his hypotheses of confusion due either to the frenzy of inspiration or carelessness of an editor, place him closer to the spirit of the Higher Criticism than it does to contemporary aesthetics of the 1740s. Yet Howes' argument, that the confused, tortuous, and even apparently rambling structure to some of the prophetic books of the Bible, represented a 'poetic' structure of divinely inspired profundity, analogous to the seemingly confused yet secretly ordered structure of the natural world, may be taken as the final tread of the new Jacob's ladder by which the poet, the Grub-Street hack of Swift and Pope, has ascended to divine authority and prophetic status. The historical argument that poetry is an older mode than prose, resisted fiercely by such critics as Dennis, who believed that as the superior and more sophisticated form it was logically later than prose, could be, and was, restated as an argument that the Holy Spirit used it.

The question of the influence of these ideas on the first generation of Romantics, Coleridge, Wordsworth or Blake, is not always easy to demonstrate in detail, but the overall picture is fairly clear. By the 1790s the two traditions stemming from Lowth were beginning to come together again. The ideas of Eichhorn, Lessing, and even Herder were beginning to filter into intellectual circles in Britain, chiefly through Unitarian channels, and though there were even home-grown critics and scholars of international standing, such as Alexander Geddes, a Scottish Roman Catholic priest, it had proved a false start for the new wave of biblical scholarship. The popular reaction against the French Revolution by 1793 meant that Unitarianism, with its dangerous intellectual and radical associations, was itself suspect. As part of a witch-hunt against suspected Unitarians and radicals, William Frend was expelled from his Fellowship at Cambridge, and Thomas Beddoes from Oxford. The Higher Criticism was not merely felt to be un-Christian, it was un-English, unpatriotic and politically dangerous. For a whole generation it was virtually ignored in Britain, isolated as ever by the appalling quality of the modern language teaching in her schools and universities, and engaged in the long wars with Napoleon. It was not until the 1820s that the intellectual climate was again favourable towards the German Historical critics, but when, in 1823, Edward Bouverie Pusey, shortly to become a leading figure in the Oxford Movement, became interested in the new ideas he could only find two men in the University of Oxford capable of reading German. Yet there *were* a few, mostly outside the universities, who could and had studied the Germans. Coleridge was one. Frend had been a Fellow of his own college, Jesus, while he was an

undergraduate there, and had been a big influence on his
intellectual and religious development. It was Beddoes who had
persuaded Coleridge to go to the University of Göttingen when he
was in Germany in 1798 to read Eichhorn and attend his lectures.
The influence of Eichhorn on Coleridge's biblical criticism has been
well documented.[27] Though we have little evidence of
Wordsworth's direct contacts with the German Higher Criticism,
there seems little doubt that, at this period of their closest co-
operation, he must have learned something of it from his friend.
Similarly, there is reason to believe that Blake, though he was not
frequenting the same Unitarian circles as Coleridge, was also in
touch with the new ideas. Internal evidence from *The Marriage of
Heaven and Hell, There is no Natural Religion*, and *All Religions are One*
seem to suggest an acquaintance with the Higher Criticism.
Certainly he was in touch with people during the 1790s where the
ideas of the German critics were known and discussed. He too knew
William Frend. He also belonged to a circle that used to meet
regularly at the house of Joseph Johnson, the radical London
publisher and bookseller, in St Paul's Churchyard. Other members
of this group included William Godwin, Mary Wollstonecraft, Tom
Paine, Joseph Priestley, Richard Price and Thomas Holcroft.

What we may call the 'second' Lowthian tradition is both easier
and more difficult to trace. It is easier in the sense that, as we have
seen, the aesthetic principles enunciated by Lowth were part of a
long tradition of debate about the nature and properties of sacred
verse. It is more difficult in that the very diffuseness and widespread
nature of the debate make it more difficult to isolate specific authors
and their direct influence. To take, once again, the example of
Blake. There is no certain evidence that he had read Howes, but
Joseph Johnson was the publisher of William Newcome's translation of Ezekiel. This outlined Howes' thesis in the preface, and
reprinted some of his notes. Priestly was also likely to have known
Howes' *Critical Observations* since they included an attack on him.[28]
Coleridge, we know, had used Lowth's translation of Isaiah for some
of his 1795 Lectures, and was almost certainly also familiar with the
Lectures on the Sacred Poetry of the Hebrews. Wordsworth, apart from his
connections with Coleridge, would have known Blair's account of
Lowth even if he did not know the original work. But an
acquaintance with current debates is only a part of the story. As we
have seen, the idea of the poet as prophet is not an isolated belief
that can be separated from its matrix, but was part of a total way of

looking at human experience and perception of the world: a way that remains essentially *typological* rather than historical.

This is a point easily forgotten by literary critics. Typology did not simply disappear overnight with the advent of the Higher Criticism. Indeed, the new historicism took almost a hundred years to gain complete hold. As late as 1860 Kingsley's lectures on *The Roman and the Teuton* as Regius Professor of History in Cambridge still show markedly typological elements – as disgruntled colleagues were quick to observe. Moreover, as the notion of a divinely engineered scheme of history slowly retreats during the nineteenth century, it tends to be replaced by an internalised version of the same belief in literature: a theory of symbolism. Just as one might say that a 'type', in the sense of the old-style biblical criticism, is a symbol written, as it were, into history by its Author, so one can say that a symbol is an internalised and secularised type within a work of art.[29]

Wordsworth is in contact with both worlds, and even uses the two terms in tandem. When he had crossed the Alps in Book VI of *The Prelude*, for instance, he describes the natural grandeur in terms of deliberate ambiguity.

> The immeasurable height
> Of woods decaying, never to be decayed,
> The stationary blasts of waterfalls,
> And everywhere along the hollow rent
> Winds thwarting winds, bewildered and forlorn,
> The torrents shooting from the clear blue sky,
> The rocks that muttered close upon our ears,
> Black drizzling crags that spake by the wayside
> As if a voice were in them, the sick sight
> And giddy prospect of the raving stream,
> The unfettered clouds and region of the Heavens,
> Tumult and peace, the darkness and the light –
> Were all like workings of one mind, the features
> Of the same face, blossoms upon one tree;
> Characters of the great Apocalypse,
> The types and symbols of Eternity,
> Of first, and last, and midst, and without end.
> (1805. lines 556–72)

The tone of gratuitous piety that we noted at the beginning is here

present once again, though less obtrusively. The contradictions of
Nature, apparently jarring and discordant, are mysteriously reconciled into a harmony and unity that is both a type and symbol of
eternity. The two terms, the one religious, the other literary, give us
some clue as to the kind of elipsis or compression that underlies this
extraordinary passage. It is as if every term is given dual reference.
The overpowering sense of sublimity in Nature is charged, by a
typical Wordsworthian ambiguity, with a corresponding sense that
it has been 'arranged' or planted there by God for man to read. If we
see in this the role of the poet as prophet, receiving, Moses-like, the
inspiration from Sinai the apocalyptic reference becomes more
comprehensible. The task of the poet, in Coleridge's terms 'reconciling opposite or discordant qualities' is simultaneously that of the
prophet, reading God's signature in his creation, and imaginatively
recreating it for the reader.

This bring us back, at last, to the Snowdon scene in Book XIII
with which I began. I myself some years ago was guilty of the error
of describing it as 'symbolic', but, of course, it is not – or only in a
secular reading; it is one of the most striking pieces of *typology* in
Romantic literature. Only unfamiliarity with the terminology
prevents us from seeing at once what Wordsworth is saying, for here
he is quite explicit:

> . . . above all
> One function of such mind had Nature there
> Exhibited by putting forth, and that
> With circumstance most awful and sublime,
> That domination which she often times
> Exerts upon the outward face of things,
> So moulds them, and endues, abstracts, combines,
> Or by abrupt and unhabitual influence
> Doth make one object so impress itself
> Upon all others, and pervade them so
> That even the grossest minds must see and hear
> And cannot choose but feel. The power, which these
> Acknowledge when thus moved, which Nature thus
> Thrusts forth upon the senses, is the express
> Resemblance, in the fullness of its strength
> Made visible, a genuine counterpart
> And brother of the glorious faculty
> Which higher minds bear with them as their own.

(lines 74–89)

Now it is possible, of course, to interpret what Wordsworth is here describing simply as a psychological experience, for that, at one level, is certainly what it is. Wordsworth is meditating on that shock of discovery by which we can suddenly find mirrored for us in the external world a symbol for an internal or abstract state: here, of the creative unconscious, the mind of the poet. It is an experience perhaps parallel to, and not unlike that of Kekule's 'discovery' of the benzine ring. But that is only half the story. What he is also describing is the 'typology' of Nature. Just as the Old Testament prophet-poets exercised their dual office by discerning and proclaiming God's judgements in contemporary events, so Wordsworth, the poet-prophet of his own age, is perceiving the language of God in Nature: 'catching', 'creating', 'transforming' it into a symbol within the work of art which is the poem we have before us. The compulsive religiosity that we started by puzzling over is thus not a gratuitous piece of piety, but a direct reminder of the divine election of the poet for whom 'vows' had been made. The creative imagination is also the prophetic vision.

Yet, of course, there *is* a fundamental difference – and it is a very revealing one. By an interesting irony the Hebrew poets had no word in their vocabulary for anything corresponding to our idea of 'Nature'.[30] For them there was no essential difference between the regular rhythm of the seasons, the fall of Babylon, or the bodily assumption of Elijah in a chariot of fire. All were equally the direct actions of a God who habitually manifested himself through purposeful change. Wordsworth is no less conscious than the Hebrew poets of living in a world of profound, even cataclysmic changes, such as the French Revolution, but for that very reason, perhaps, he tends to find the evidence of divine meaning and order less in the processes of history than in the great unchanging permanencies of Nature against which they must be set. The fall of Robespierre or the career of Napoleon may indeed exemplify the inexorability of God's judgements, but in so doing, they merely reflect flickeringly and by contrast the truths permanently exemplified in the ordered harmony of man and his natural environment. Though *The Prelude* purports to be a 'history', its whole movement is curiously anti-historical. In other words, while Hebrew typology is essentially diachronic, working through history, Wordsworthian typology is in effect, if not in intention, synchronic.

If before we were justified in detecting the influence of Lowth on Wordsworth's idea of the poet as prophet, now we encounter something that looks suspiciously like that of Howes. The unity in diversity, the mysterious harmony that is revealed through the apparent randomness and arbitrariness of natural phenomena in the Simplon Pass is a dramatic reassertion of the way in which the poet, under the guidance of the Spirit, brings order out of disorder. The list of abstract pieties, read in this context, takes on a precise and poetically important meaning: they are no less than the powers of the prophet to link his own inner harmony with a 'delight/That fails not in the external universe'. They are also a clue towards the structure of *The Prelude* itself. If its outward structure, with the thirteen books (I refer to the 1805 text) and the crisis over the French Revolution bears a strong resemblance to that earlier spiritual autobiography, Augustine's *Confessions*; its inner structure, lacking in any immediately chronological thread, anecdotal and digressive, bears a strong similarity to the 'poetic order' detected by Howes in the Old Testament prophets. The Higher Critics may well insist that this is a mistake; the poets, by a fine irony standing within the same Lowthian tradition, may not be all that wrong in replying that it is the basic language of the Spirit.

NOTES

1. For a discussion of this see my *Coleridge & Wordsworth: The Poetry of Growth* (Cambridge, 1970), pp. 37–42.
2. Percy Reprints No 3, edited by H. F. B. Brett-Smith (Oxford, 1921), p. 56.
3. *Complete Writings*, edited by Geoffrey Keynes (Oxford, 1966) p. 97.
4. Ibid., p. 98.
5. Percy Reprints No 3, Brett-Smith, p. 6.
6. Ibid., p. 27.
7. Ibid., p. 88.
8. See Leslie Tannenbaum, *Biblical Tradition in Blake's Early Prophecies: The Great Code of Art* (Princeton, 1982), p. 37.
9. *The Critical Works of John Dennis*, edited by F. N. Hooker (Baltimore, 1939), pp. 364, 370.
10. Richard E. Brantley, *Wordsworth's 'Natural Methodism'* (Yale, 1975).
11. *The Royal Bible*, with a commentary by Leonard Howard (London, 1761).
12. Freidrich Meinecke, *Historism: The Rise of a New Historical Outlook*, translated by J. E. Anderson (London, 1972), p. lviii.
13. *Lectures on the Sacred Poetry of the Hebrews*, translated by G. Gregory, 2 vols (London, 1787), I, pp. 114, 113.
14. Meinecke, *Historism*, pp. 203–4.
15. *Lectures*, II, p. 12.
16. Hooker, *John Dennis*, p. 371.

17. *Lectures*, I, pp. 76–8, 224.
18. Hooker, *John Dennis*, p. 358.
19. *Lectures*, I, p. 336.
20. Hooker, *John Dennis*, p. 331.
21. *Lectures*, I, pp. 71–2.
22. Hugh Blair, (Edinburgh, 1820), II, pp. 270–1.
23. Meinecke, *Historism*; Isaiah Berlin, *Vico and Herder: Two Studies in the History of Ideas* (London, 1976); Elinor Shaffer, '*Kubla Khan*' *and* '*The Fall of Jerusalem*': *The Mythological School in Biblical Criticism and Secular Literature 1770–1880* (Cambridge, 1975).
24. Tannenbaum, *Biblical Tradition*, p. 10.
25. Ibid., p. 29.
26. Howes, *Critical Observations on Books, Antient and Modern*, 4 vols (1776–1813), reprinted (New York, 1972), II, pp. 442–3.
27. Shaffer, *Mythological School*, Chapters 1 and 2.
28. Tannenbaum, *Biblical Tradition*, p. 36.
29. See, for instance, George P. Landow, *Victorian Types, Victorian Shadows: Biblical Typology in Victorian Literature, Art and Thought* (Boston, London and Henley, 1980).
30. H. Wheeler Robinson, *Inspiration and Revelation in the Old Testament* (Oxford, 1962), p. 34.

6 Literature and Commitment: 'Choosing Sides'

Martin Jarrett-Kerr

In January 1982 a new poem by the veteran American poet Richard Eberhart appeared entitled 'Old Dichotomy – Choosing Sides'. Here are a few lines from it:

> Why don't you like the wild cry of the madman
> Who does not know what makes him cry as he does?
>
> Because Aristotle said the world was measurable,
> Took leaves off every tree, and measured them.
>
> He began the scientific method. But the wild man
> Was perhaps older, subjective, would scoff at the objective.
>
> We have to choose between the wild in us, and the sober,
> The intensity of genius may be best.[1]

It is, to be frank, not a very good poem; indeed it is almost a parody of one kind of Dichotomy, one way of taking sides. but it provides a good way into our subject.

There is a story that Reinhold Niebuhr and William Temple were together at a small theological meeting.[2] Niebuhr had been talking about 'paradox' – the paradoxical nature of this and that. Finally Temple intervened with 'Well, no doubt paradoxical to all of us, but not paradoxical to Dr Niebuhr, for he appears to understand it?' 'No, no,' said Niebuhr vigorously, 'the ultimate paradox of existence.' 'Surely,' said Temple blandly, 'Surely Dr Niebuhr does not expect us to imagine that the Blessed Trinity suffer from eternal perplexity in their contemplation One of Another?' We hear of no further discussion; perhaps the company dissolved into laughter. But in fact Dr Niebuhr *could* have had the last word: he could surely have said in reply, 'Ah, William: but you see only a Hegelian like you could find the doctrine of the Blessed Trinity non-paradoxical'.

I

The debate between the Hegelian and the Paradoxical, which could also be called that between the Essentialist and the Kierkegaardian, or perhaps in more immediately contemporary terms between the Structuralist and the Deconstructionist (unless I have gravely misunderstood this last altercation) – these debates are very old, very confused, and perhaps by now very tedious. But the relation of Literature to Commitment is on any view of it going to be affected by what sort of philosophical, or post-philosophical, or even anti-philosophical assumptions may lie behind the commitment.

Let us start with yet another version of the debate: that between 'Content' and 'Form'; or 'Life' and 'Art'. This, too, is a tired affair; yet in various forms it keeps turning up. And since it can be put in concrete terms we will start here and return to 'Niebuhr versus Temple' later.

In 1874, Tom Hughes added a Preface to the Sixth Edition of his extremely popular novel, *Tom Brown's Schooldays* (1857). He commented on the correspondence he had received since the first publication.

> Several persons, for whose judgment I have the highest respect, while saying very kind things about the book, have added, that the great fault of it is 'too much preaching;' but they hope I shall amend in this matter should I ever write again. Now this I must distinctly decline to do. Why, my whole object in writing at all was to get the chance of preaching! When a man comes to my time of life [he was fifty when he wrote this] and has his bread to make, and very little time to spare, is it likely that he will spend almost the whole of his yearly vacation in writing a story just to amuse people! I think not. My sole object in writing was to preach to boys: if ever I write again, it will be to preach to some other age.
>
> (pp. xii–xiv)

There could hardly be a less equivocal statement of didactic purpose. *Tom Brown's Schooldays* is barely 'literature', but it represents in extreme form a position which has been taken, consciously or unconsciously, by great writers in works of abiding value – Philip Sydney's *Apology*, Ben Jonson's 'Epistle Dedicatory' to *Volpone*; John Keble's 'medicinal' view of poetry in his *Praelectiones Academicae* as Professor of Poetry in Oxford; most strikingly Tolstoy in his later novels; Brecht, of course; and many others. Ezra Pound wrote unashamedly 'I am perhaps didactic; so in a different sense, or in different senses are Homer, Dante, Villon and Omar . . . A revelation is always didactic. Only the aesthetes since 1880 have pretended to the contrary, and they aren't a very sturdy lot.'[3] And finally we may cite, for its wider context, Bernard Shaw's Preface to *Back to Methuselah*:[4]

> Art has never been great when it was not providing an iconography for a live religion – compare Flaxman and . . . [other minor 19th century painters] with Phidias and Praxiteles . . . Michael Angelo and Cimabue . . . and you must feel that until we have a great religious movement we cannot hope for a great artistic one.
>
> (pp. Lxxix–Lxxx)

But what is the logical conclusion of this position? Wordsworth warned us – and remember that he wrote this at a time when he was moving in a conservative position, politically and religiously – in 1815:

> No poetry has been more subject to distortion, than that species, the argument and scope of which is religious; and no lovers of art have gone further astray than the pious and the devout.[5]

But this warning should apply not only to 'religious' poetry or literature; almost any type of 'commitment' can have this distorting effect. We might recall the 'Albert Hall Festival of Poetry' on 11 June 1965. The poems recited there were published in the collection *Children of Albion*.[6] The editor, Michael Horowitz, in his Afterword writes: 'This sort of poetry is good as it does good'. He criticised traditional criticism and teaching of English: Oxford English, for instance, provides 'a conformist programme which [proves] a two-dimensional concept-cage'. By contrast he praises the revival of oral tradition as represented in local and national festivals of spoken verse. 'Most people ignore most poetry because most poetry ignores most people.'

It is interesting that two of the poets represented in this anthology, *Children of Albion*, turn up also in the *Oxford Book of Twentieth Century English Verse* (1973) edited by Philip Larkin. It may be remembered that this book was reviewed in *The Listener* by Donald Davie, and that he concentrated his fiercest criticism upon the last section (recent verse), and especially upon a poem by Brian Patten, 'Portrait of a Young Girl Raped at a Suburban Party'. Davie's comment is blunt.

> At no point, by not one of the many ways available, has imagination entered, penetrated, opened up, transformed. By the end of the fourth dishevelled stanza we are precisely where we were after we had read the title. [7]

Davie went on to damn the anthology for other like inclusions.

The Battle of the Books was now fully engaged. Fierce correspondence followed, some of it along 'class' lines. Davie, said one correspondent, had got 'excited over the riff-raff getting into his Royal Enclosure of Poetry'. Another compared 'the more readily communicative verse of this century' (represented by such as Brian Patten and the 'Liberpudlians') with the 'esoteric rambling' of Davie's own poetry; and another simply stated that the sort of poetry Larkin had included in his anthology 'has been part of the scene for some years . . . [and therefore] it would be dishonest of any anthology not to recognise this'. (This last argument has a hospitable openness which is no doubt admirable in itself; but it could also be contended that squatters' 'rights of occupation' are not so easily established.)

It is interesting, however, that both Davie and, earlier, Horowitz, used the notion of poetry 'doing something', although with rather different meanings. Horowitz's formula was 'this poetry is good as it does good' (meaning, perhaps, stimulates us, affects the adrenalin, brings the revolution nearer?); Davie's use is also active, but in a subtler sense – of enlarging the understanding, focusing the emotions, expounding a deeper meaning. Curiously enough an earlier critic had used the same phrase when assessing Matthew Arnold's *Poems* of 1849. 'What does it do' he asked, 'all this pure and brilliant imagination?' [8] This is a strange reversal of charges. The pragmatic Victorian critic (who turns out to have been Charles Kingsley) reproaches the would-be classical poetry of Arnold; while the classical critic, Davie, objects to the down-to-earth, 'with-it' pop poetry – both on the same grounds that it 'doesn't *do* anything'.

II

A reaction against any form of 'committed' poetry in favour of a purer conception of the function of literature is not surprising. The extreme type seems to be epitomised in a famous remark attributed to James Joyce. His elder brother, Stanislas, had to leave Italy in 1936 because of his opposition to Mussolini. The two brothers met in Paris some time afterwards, and Stanislas tried to tell Jim of the horrors of fascism. James stopped him: 'Don't talk to me about politics; I'm only interested in style'.[9] No wonder Joyce was attacked in the 1934 Soviet Writers' Congress by Karl Radek, who described the method of *Ulysses* as naturalism 'reduced to clinical observation' and 'a heap of dung, crawling with worms, photographed by a cinema apparatus through a microscope – such is Joyce's work'.[10] For Joyce was puzzled: 'I don't know why they [the Marxists] attack me, nobody in any of my books is worth more than £1,000'; and, 'I've never written about anything but common people'.[11] Today Marxist critics are more sensitive; they appreciate Joyce's powerful and penetrating social understanding. Nevertheless the whole thrust of Joyce's work up to and including *Finnegans Wake* is surely towards the exaltation of 'form' over subject-matter. Kingsley's review of Matthew Arnold, quoted above, asks 'To what purpose [is] all the self-culture through which the author must have passed?' One wonders what Kingsley could have made of Stephen Daedalus.

The importance of the debate – of which that between Joyce and his Marxist contemporaries is but one example – was revealed in a curious outburst some three years ago in the *Times Literary Supplement*. Professor John Carey came out with a brash, swashbuckling announcement that 'the displacement of "evaluation" has been effected with remarkably little fuss'.[12] (He is, of course, parodying the late Dr Leavis's 'dislodgment' of Milton.) Carey supported his contention with three arguments: (a) that all literary evaluations are merely subjective, since no demonstration of their universality or objectivity has ever been or could be produced; (b) that in any case only scientific statements of fact are objective, therefore all 'values' are subjective, that is, man-made; and (c) that both (a) and (b) can be supported by the obvious position which man holds in the universe. Carey asks:

> How can such values retain their credibility in the godless universe which most people now inhabit? [13] Modern man is more used to the idea that we are temporary occupants of a cooling solar system; that human life is an accident of chemistry; that all the ages, from the first dawn on earth to its extinction, will amount to no more than a brief parenthesis in the endless night of space, that good and evil and other such ephemers were created by the human mind in its attempt to impose some significance on the amoral flux which constitutes reality. From this perspective, literary evaluation of any kind might seem almost comically irrelevant.

As I read that extraordinary outburst I had a sharp sense of the *déjà-écouté*. Compare Bertrand Russell:

> Brief and powerless is man's life; on him and all his race the slow, sure doom falls pitiless and dark. Blind to good and evil, reckless of destruction, omnipotent matter rolls on its relentless way; for Man, condemned to-day to lose his dearest, to-morrow himself to pass through the gate of darkness, it remains only to cherish, ere yet the blow falls, the lofty thoughts that ennoble his little day . . . Proudly defiant of the irresistible forces that tolerate, for a moment, his knowledge and his condemnation, to sustain alone, a weary but unyielding Atlas, the world that his own ideals have fashioned despite the trampling march of unconscious power. [14]

The language is a trifle more lush and the thought a deal more stoical than that of Professor Carey, but the general meaning is the same. T. S. Eliot had fun with the passage – both its style and its content. [15] But let us look at Carey's argument. Of his three propositions only two have any connection with each other. It is certainly true that (a) 'literary evaluations are subjective', is strictly entailed by (b) all values are subjective because only scientific statements are objective. For (b), however, he gives no reasons whatever. Indeed it is almost incredible that such confident display of words like 'fact', 'reality', 'science' and the rest could be

made in 1980 after all the discussion in the philosophy of science
from, for example, the mathematician Henri Poincaré at the turn of
the century down to Michael Polanyi, Karl Popper and the post-
Popperians (Kuhn, Lakatos and others). Carey's cosmic *wel-
tanschauung*, of course, leaves us with a darkness which blots out not
only his own distinctions between 'fact' (whatever that is) and
'value', but all distinctions – full stop. Certainly his view would
make a 'Conference on Religion and Literature' worthless; but it
would render equally worthless the writing of a commissioned
article in the *Times Literary Supplement.*

As to commitment: if any logic could be detected in Carey's
argument its logical conclusion could only be close to that of Simone
de Beauvoir. (Would Professor Carey be flattered by the association?) When she joined the students in the famous incidents at the
Sorbonne (1968) she was far more starry-eyed than they were about
the significance of the occupation of the university premises at
Nanterre, which she saw as 'the crisis of society as a whole . . . [the
creation of] a vanguard capable of carrying a revolution in the
capitalist countries through to a successful conclusion'.[16] By
contrast Cohn-Bendit and his supporters were perfectly well aware
of the limited nature of their enterprise. But when Simone de
Beauvoir was later asked why she did not, in that case, join the
students on the barricades she replied that it was not her place; she
was not a student; and anyway 'she *did not want to,* [and] one must
always follow one's own inclinations and desires . . . Although I
was totally involved I was not very active myself, because after all I
am an intellectual'.[17]

III

So far we have been operating at a fairly superficial level. For is
there not a third possible commitment – to a 'middle way' between
the two contenders? The first work by F. R. Leavis which I ever read
was 'Under Which King, Bezonian?', in *For Continuity*,[18] and I
underwent instant conversion. It rejected the dichotomies of Right
and Left, and this extremely persuasively at the time. Later Leavis
was to state this middle way more positively.

[D. H.] Lawrence's account of why and how a creative work
matters is one that I would ascribe to. A creative work, when it is

such as to challenge and engage us to the full, conveys the artist's basic allegiances, his sense of ultimates, his real beliefs, his completest sincerity, his profoundest feeling and thought about man in relation to the universe. When I say that a great work will inevitably have a profound moral significance I am thinking of such a significance as will need to be described as religious too.[19]

A graphic example of this 'middle way' can be found in Lionel Trilling's novel, *The Middle of the Journey*. (I read this first when it appeared in 1948 without the Introduction which was added to the second edition of 1978, giving the politico-historical background to the work and the extent to which it reflects the cases of Alger Hiss and Whittaker-Chambers.) One passage has remained with me. Gifford Maxim, the Marxist, is predicting that Marxists and Catholics will have to make common cause to 'establish ourselves against the anarchy of the world'. He points to Nancy Croom, the Catholic, and says to John Laskell, the 'Liberal':

'I'm sorry – but we [Gifford and Nancy] must go hand in hand. Let it be our open secret. You will preach the law for the masses. I will preach the law for the leaders. For the masses, rights and the freedom from blame. For the leaders, duties and nothing but blame, from without and from within. We will hate each other and we will make the new world. And when we've made it and it has done its work, then maybe we will resurrect John Laskell. But resurrection implies –' And he shrugged.

'Giff, I swear I think you're crazy,' Kermit said earnestly. 'I swear I do.'

'He is crazy. He's insane,' Nancy said.

'No,' said Laskell. 'He's not.'

Maxim pointed his finger at Laskell. 'Remember it!' he said to the others. 'It is the last time that you will see it.' He spoke gaily, as if the conversation had been the brightest, most successful nonsense among friends. 'The supreme act of the humanistic critical intelligence – it perceives the cogency of the argument and acquiesces in the fact of its own extinction.'

'You have been very clever, Maxim,' said Laskell. 'Cleverer than I thought a man could ever be. But you are wrong on one point – I do not acquiesce.'

'Yes,' said Maxim, still in his gay, bright excitement. 'Of course I was wrong. You cannot possibly acquiesce. But it does not matter, John,' he said kindly, 'whether you do or not.'

'It matters,' Laskell said. 'Oh, it matters very much. It is the only thing that matters.'[20]

The case for the 'middle of the journey', for choosing the centre between the two extremes, between Left and Right, between scepticism and dogmatism, any form of 'old dichotomy', is a powerful one. But is there not a necessary *caveat* even here? May not the very fact of commitment, even to the 'middle way', be dangerously anti-rational? Is not the very posing of commitment as a pivotal concept a precarious first step towards the arbitrary and the mindless?

In a valuable little book entitled *Reason and Commitment*,[21] which has not had the attention it merits, Roger Trigg discusses the dangers of all types of fideism. He concedes that the difference between the entertaining of a scientific hypothesis and the holding of a religious belief is important and undeniable. But, he says, the wrong interpretation of that difference can lead to intellectual confusion. Wittgenstein, for instance, held that science and religion simply involve different systems of thought and that what counts as 'truth' in each case is radically different. We do not, he says, talk about hypothesis or high probability in religious contexts: there are not those who say about the Resurrection, 'Well, possibly'. One is either committed or not.[22] But, replies Trigg, what results from this is that the Resurrection is only important in the influence it has on one's life. And this pragmatic approach has its extreme logical conclusion in the following, quoted by Trigg, from a writer on aesthetics:

> Why, to put the point incisively, if painfully, should we demand a birth certificate of Jesus of Nazareth, any more than of Odysseus or Buddha or Hamlet? Why can we not live and grow in these beings imaginatively, without feeling any nagging guilt because we cannot recite their social security numbers? Are they not in human terms more important than they would be if they were merely literal and historical?[23]

But, says Trigg, there is a confusion here which arises from

> a failure to differentiate between propositional belief and the commitment which is the normal response to it . . . If all our

attention is diverted to the fact of commitment and none to the importance of certain beliefs, it becomes unimportant why someone rejects Christianity. He is uncommitted, and that is all that matters.

But there are surely different reasons for the rejection: you can understand the claims of Christianity and reject them because you find them false, nonsensical or unintelligible, or irrelevant. In the last case you understand the claims but do not see the need to commit yourself.[24]

And of course it is not only religious commitment which can be anti-rational. The sociologist, David Hay, gives an example from the political 'Left' of what commitment can do to a man's outlook. In his Questionnaire on religious attitudes taken from Nottingham he elicited one response from a member of a Marxist revolutionary group. Hay quotes it to illustrate

the effects of commitment to a belief system which rejects religion as false consciousness. His [the young man's] refusal of even the possibility of religious experience is based on a moral revulsion. 'At times of selfishness' (the young man said) 'I stumble into other worldliness, when I feel the need to lean on some emotional peg. I suppose some people would call it prayer.) But when I catch myself, I stop it by saying: "There is no power that can help me . . ." The aspect of subservience disgusts me.'[25]

One is inclined to applaud his sense of independence and demand for autonomy, perhaps in the words G. K. Chesterton once used to a young sceptic in the audience. Chesterton had been lecturing in reply to George Bernard Shaw. At question-time the young man accused him of making statements without proof. 'Young man,' said Chesterton 'do you believe that *you* exist?' The questioner, being something of a pyrrhonist, replied cautiously, 'Well, I prefer to say that I have an intuition that I exist'. 'Cherish it – cherish it', said Chesterton.

There can be equally non-rational commitments to something so inchoate as to be almost meaningless. The late President Eisenhower once solemnly stated: 'Our Government makes no sense unless it is founded in deeply felt religious faith – and I don't care what it is'.[26] He might have cared if it had been pointed out to him that his definition could include the Theology of Revolutionary Liberation.

If we look carefully at what has been happening I think that we shall see that the word 'commitment' has become almost mystically identified with decisions to act, with the 'leap of faith', with conversion and the twice-born as contrasted with the once-born personality. This assumes that there can be no commitment to rationality, to the stable or the conservationist. The notion of 'inspiration' in Literature and Religion suggests a similar narrowing. We need not undervalue this notion of 'inspiration', but it is only one mechanism among others; indeed, it plays much the same part in literature as 'locutions' or 'visions' play in the mystical life – welcome if vouchsafed but secondary and often perilous. The tasks to which commitment in literature is vital are as various, that is, as exalted and as humdrum, as life itself. But the most basic commitment must always be to language/speech. Professor L. C. Knights in his Clark Lectures referred to sociological research in America which seemed to show that 10 per cent of American Freshmen had a *usable* vocabulary of only about 800 words; that in the four years in College there was a 20 per cent *decrease* in these figures; and that ten years after graduation there had been an even greater decline. Knights concluded:

> If we regard with suspicion the language of the mass media it is not because it offends against our canons of taste, but because, in Chomsky's phrase, it leads to 'the narrowing of the range of the thinkable'.[27]

IV

If the only 'safe' kind of commitment (that is, safe from the charge of irrationality or arbitrariness) is commitment to language, will not that mean that we shall simply have come down on the side of 'form' as against 'content', 'medium' as against message? But when we force ourselves to take a wider view, and look at literature in its historical and in its geographical (indeed, global) context, the problem of 'old dichotomy' becomes more complex. I can illustrate this best by quoting (with his permission) from a paper by a former colleague, Mr Arthur Ravenscroft, written in the context of 'Third World Literature'.[28] Writers in India, Africa and the Caribbean would of course be insulted if any but the highest literary standards were to be applied to their work. But we cannot escape the fact that the critical criteria evolved in 'Eur-America' have been deeply marked by cultural forces derived from colonial political history. Mr Ravenscroft quotes Arnold's famous dictum from 'The Function of Criticism at the Present Time', concerning 'the best that is known and thought in the world', concluding that the business of criticism is to concern itself with this and no more, 'to leave alone all questions of practical consequences and applications'.[29] Faced, however, with the formation of post-colonial élites, with vast gaps between educated minorities and the non-literate 'masses', it would be unrealistic to 'leave alone all questions of practical consequences'. Ravenscroft points out that the best East African novelist of today, Ngugi Wa Thiong'o, was imprisoned for his part in a play produced by a communal enterprise among largely illiterate villagers; and that, in India, Professor Narasimhaya plans to use his retirement from Mysore University to involve a neighbouring village in his new Centre for Postgraduate Literary Studies. Ravenscroft is right. Of course if there is a common humanity we cannot make out Third World Man as a special case. Unless we accept Professor Carey's arbitrary subjectivism, or Wittgenstein's nominalist pluralism, there must be some universal critical standards. But since man is always *in via* he cannot have every consideration of time, place and situation simultaneously in mind. The 'Developing Nations' are a sharp, often painful reminder of one vitally important situation.

V

'Since man is always *in via*.' This brings us back at last to Niebuhr and William Temple and to Kierkegaard versus Hegel. Since, as we have seen, commitment can be either to 'form' or to 'content', or to both, can we say that it might be to both Temple and Niebuhr – not just to the 'middle way' but to both ends? It is clear that because man is *in via* there is bound to be a certain asymmetry in his tasks. Karl Popper long ago asserted that

> the greatest mistake of utilitarianism . . . [is] that it does not recognize that from the moral point of view suffering and happiness must not be treated as symmetrical; that is to say, the promotion of happiness is in any case much less urgent than the rendering of help to those who suffer . . . Human suffering makes

a direct moral appeal . . . for help, while there is no similar cal
to increase the happiness of a man who is doing well anyway.[3

In other words we are committed to a journey, or development, ir
which there are already pressures which we did not choose. This i
the real significance of Pascal (sometimes called 'the first existential
ist'): his 'Wager' may seem an unworthy metaphor for Christiar
living, but the point of it is that we can not refuse to make a choice
'vous êtes embarqué'.[31] And it is interesting that the very 'ur
existentialist' Joseph Addison seems to have picked this up. Th
difference between Milton and Aristotle, said Addison, is that ir
Paradise Lost we have a situation utterly foreign to Greek tragedy
the principal Actors (Adam and Eve) are 'not only our Progenitor
but our Representatives . . . It is not considered what may possibl
be, but what actually is our own Case; since we are *embark'd* witl
them on the same Bottom'.[32]

And this brings me to my conclusion. There is a type c
commitment which has not yet been mentioned, although it relate
to Addison, Pascal, Milton and a whole mountain-range behinc
them. So far we have considered only man's commitmen
to . . . (beliefs, principles, systems, forms, styles, aspirations . . .)
But what of a commitment believed to have been made (o
continually being made) not *by* man, but *to* man? Commitment b
whom or what? Let us call it by some 'outside' power or powers

To be able to talk about such a commitment we need the prio
ability to talk about the 'outside' or the 'power(s)'. This is ar
enormous task for the end of a long chapter. I will take but tw
aspects of it.

The first is negative. I constantly come across writers who by
dismissing the possibility of talking about an 'outside', limit thei
understanding of what they are studying. I can give two examples o
this. In 1951 the distinguished anthropologist, Raymond Firth
stated categorically that

> a funeral rite is a social rite *par excellence*, its ostensible object is the
> dead person, but it benefits not the dead but the living.[33]

(Firth's example is from Tikopia ritual, but he generalised from tha
to other funerary rites.) I was at a conference of Anthropologists anc
Theologians in 1976 at which Professor Firth was also present. I hac
been describing the post-funerary rites of the Malagasy people

called *famadihana*, which quite clearly (like many other *rites de passage* of this sort) cannot be described exhaustively in terms of the living but imply benefit believed to be conferred upon the departed. I suggested that Professor Firth's account did not do justice to this fact. Unfortunately he did not reply.

Second, an example from literary criticism. M. H. Abrams in his fine and learned study of the English Romantics, *Natural Supernaturalism* misstates (I believe) the position at two crucial points. Commenting on the passage in *The Prelude* about the blind beggar with the paper on his chest explaining his identity, Abrams quotes:

> And on the shape of this unmoving man
> His fixed face, and sightless eyes, I looked,
> As if admonished from another world.
>
> (1805 VII ll.621–3)

Abrams comments: 'The typical Wordsworthian "as if" quietly absorbs the world beyond time and space into the world of the apprehended here-and-now'.[34] With respect, No. Hamlet's cloud is 'almost the shape of a camel' (III. i. 400). But if the camel is 'absorbed' into the cloud it ceases to be a metaphorical object. And the importance of observing the analogical principle is even more central when, *à propos* Wordsworth's discussion of his vocation in *The Prelude* Book III, Abrams says: 'God has not quite dropped out, but He is only mentioned after the fact, and given nothing to do in the poem . . . What does God do in the poem? . . . Nothing of consequence'.[35] But even in the 1850 version, where the analogy with divine activity is made more explicit, Wordsworth still does not give God any more to 'do' in the poem. And he is right not to. The important feature of an analogy is that the two sides – the analogous and the analogate – must not cross. As well say 'Chess is like a military engagement', and then proceed to bomb the bishop.

Of course this negative argument does not prove the existence of 'power(s)'; it only suggests the limitations of those who deny them. For a positive argument I will commend what I consider one of the keenest recent pieces of thinking in philosophical theology: Mr Roger White's essay, 'Notes on Analogical predication and Speaking about God' in the recent *Festchrift* for Donald Mackinnon.[36] It is an unusual essay which moves from Barth and Aquinas to Wittgenstein, especially to Wittgenstein on colour, and so to our ability to form an 'ideal' or 'standard' without appeal to Platonic 'Forms'; and so, *via* the life and death of Jesus, to a reinstatement of the notion of 'divine revelation'. I hope it may prove a seminal work.

But the same argument can be filled out by referring to a longer and more detailed study which I shall leave you with: the brilliant book by Robert Alter, *The Art of Biblical Narrative*.[37] With that I shall couple an earlier study, which Professor Alter himself commends, Herbert Schneidau's *Sacred Discontent*.[38] Schneidau is not a Hebrew scholar, he is an English Literary critic, but he has read widely in Near Eastern anthropology and archaeology. His theme is that the Biblical revolution was a challenge to the polytheistic culture in which it grew up and against which it rebelled. There is no word in Hebrew for 'goddesses', and spells and divinations, which proliferate in Near Eastern remains, are largely absent from the Bible. Robert Alter, who is a Professor of Hebrew as well as of Comparative Literature, considers that Schneidau exaggerates the distinctness and stark difference of the Hebrew-Biblical complex from its surroundings; but he fully accepts one of Schneidau's main contentions, that the narrative techniques of the Old Testament (which is for Alter, as a Jew, 'the Bible') are uniquely able to express 'the ambiguities of history', and in so doing witness to the escape of Hebrew thought from the 'stable closure' of the old mythological world. Alter is able to use his own expertise in Hebrew language and literature – and he draws also on the most recent Israeli scholarship – to introduce us to the paradoxes of Biblical achievement. (Here Niebuhr's, and also Schneidau's, Lutheran backgrounds perhaps assist in appreciating this paradoxical complex.) The paradox, above all, is that the Bible 'is a very secular book. . . far less religious than Dante'.[39] Alter expounds the dialectical tensions between, first, 'The divine plan and the disorderly character of actual historical events'; and, second, between 'God's will, His providential guidance, and human freedom, the refractory nature of man'. These tensions are the result of

> the monotheistic revolution which . . . profoundly altered the ways in which man as well as God was imagined, and the effects of this revolution probably still determine aspects of our conceptual world more than we suspect.
>
> (pp. 129–30)

And so Alter's unique combination of Hebrew scholarship and literary-critical expertise is employed to demonstrate how a 'spiritual urgency' lies behind even the most racy and enjoyable tales: so that, again paradoxically,

> by learning to enjoy the biblical stories more fully as stories, we shall also come to see more clearly what they mean to tell us about God, man, and the perilously momentous realm of history.

(pp. 188–89)

CODA

We face today an improbable alliance between two, perhaps three, very different teams. The first is that which is opposed to 'The Personal Heresy': C. S. Lewis, T. S. Eliot of the early essays, especially 'Tradition and the Individual Talent', D. H. Lawrence in his famous instruction, 'Don't trust the teller, trust the Tale'. The second team (if it needs to be distinguished from the first) is that which campaigns against the 'Intentionalist Fallacy': especially W. K. Wimsatt and M. C. Beardsley. The third is of a later generation, and stems from French Structuralism: especially the late Roland Barthes, with his battle-cry 'Death to the Author'. Since the sorts of commitment we have been considering may suggest a reversion to the priority of the Author, it is worth pointing out that the first types of commitment in this paper could be considered as commitment not merely by individuals but by groups, families, tribes; and that the second type, commitment *to* man from outside 'power(s)' is certainly in its religious sense commitment both to individual man and to the whole body. It is therefore appropriate that we should have taken our last example from the Bible. It is a book which should come through unscathed while these literary battles rage round it: for not many of its contents have ascribable authors, and even of those that have, no biographies have survived.

NOTES

1. *Times Literary Supplement*, 1 January 1982, p. 3.
2. The meeting was probably in 1943.
3. *Letters, 1907–1941*, edited by D. D. Paige (London, 1951), p. 248.
4. Bernard Shaw, *Back to Methuselah* (London, 1921).

5. *Essay, supplementary to the Preface* (1815), in *Poetical Works*, edited by Thomas Hutchinson. New edition, revised by Ernest de Selincourt (Oxford, 1969), p. 744.

6. *Children of Albion. Poetry of the Underground in Britain* (Harmondsworth, 1969).

7. The Listener, 29 March 1973, 420–1, and subsequent numbers for correspondence.

8. *Fraser's Magazine*, 39 (May, 1849), pp. 570–86.

9. Stanislas Joyce, *My Brother's Keeper* (London, 1954), p. 23.

10. 'Contemporary World Literature & the Tasks of Proletarian Art', in *Problems of Soviet Literature*, edited by H. G. Scott (London, 1955), pp. 155–4.

11. *James Joyce and Modern Literature*, edited by W. J. McCormack and Alistair Stead (London, 1982), pp. 111, 134.

12. John Carey, 'Viewpoint', *Times Literary Supplement*, 22 February 1982, p. 203.

13. This sentence suggests that some people inhabit a god-ful universe. Carey presumably meant 'the universe which most people consider to be godless'. It makes a difference.

14. Bertrand Russell, 'A Free Man's Worship' (1902), collected in *Mysticism and Logic and Other Essays* (London, 1918), pp. 56–7.

15. T. S. Eliot in *Revelation*, edited by John Baillie and H. Martin (London, 1937), pp. 1–39, 7.

16. Simone de Beauvoir, *Tout compte fait* (Paris, 1972), translated as *All's Said and Done* (London, 1974).

17. Anne Whitmarsh, *Simone de Beauvoir: the Limits of Commitment* (Cambridge, 1981), p. 131, quoting Dyan and Ribowska, *Simone de Beauvoir* (Paris, 1979), pp. 72–3.

18. F. R. Leavis, *For Continuity* (London, 1933).

19. F. R. Leavis, *Times Literary Supplement*, 19 September 1958. Reprinted in *Letters in Criticism*, edited by J. Tasker (London, 1974), p. 67.

20. Lionel Trilling, *The Middle of the Journey* (London, 1948), p. 323.

21. Roger Trigg, *Reason and Commitment* (Cambridge, 1973).

22. L. Wittgenstein, *Aesthetics, Psychology & Religious Belief* (Oxford, 1966), pp. 56–7.

23. D. N. Morgan, 'Must Art Tell the Truth?' in *Journal of Aesthetics and Art Criticism*, 26 (1967), p. 26.

24. Trigg, *Reason and Commitment*, pp. 37, 82–3.

25. David Hay, *Exploring Inner Space* (Harmondsworth, 1982), p. 154.

26. Ibid., p. 66.

27. L. C. Knights, *Public Voices* (London, 1971), pp. 114–15; N. Chomsky *American Power and the New Mandarins* (New York, 1969).

28. Arthur Ravenscroft, 'Third-World Literature: Purpose or Indulgence'. A paper for a forthcoming book to mark the retirement of Professor Narasimhaya, doyen of English Studies in India, from the Chair of English at the University of Mysore.

29. Matthew Arnold, *Essays in Criticism*, First Series 1865 (London, 1898), pp. 18–19.

30. K. R. Popper, *The Open Society & Its Enemies*, 2 vols (London, 1945), I, p. 205, n. 6; p. 241, n. 21.

31. B. Pascal, *Pensées*, no. 418/343.

32. Joseph Addison, *Spectator*, no. 273 (1712). (Reprinted in *Milton: The Critical*

Heritage, edited by J. T. Shawcross (London, 1970), p. 154. (Italics mine.)
33. Raymond Firth, *Elements of Social Organization* (London, 1951), p. 63.
34. M. H. Abrams, *Natural Supernaturalism* (Oxford, 1971), p. 389.
35. Ibid., p. 90.
36. *The Philosophical Frontiers of Christian Theology*, edited by Hebblethwaite and Sutherland (Cambridge, 1982), pp. 197–226.
37. Robert Alter, *The Art of Biblical Narrative* (London, 1982).
38. Herbert Schneidau, *Sacred Discontent* (Berkeley, 1977).
39. Alter, *Biblical Narrative*, p. 19.

7 Simone Weil – Sacrifice: a Problem for Theology

Ann Loades

We read in a recent essay that 'The love of God in Christ that . . . embraced sacrifical suffering is the pattern for the Christian. By incorporation "in Christ" he must continually seek more and more completely to reproduce it in his own life, and St. Paul believes that this can bring benefit to the Body of Christ which is the Church.'[1] Flemington suggests that there are in our own time 'some whose life and conduct force us to ask whether St. Paul's conviction about the Cross of Christ may not give us the clue to the secret of this strange and baffling universe'. Lash approves of Flemington's point by arguing that 'Christian practice consists (by analogy with the practical interpretation of dramatic, legal and musical texts) in the performance or enactment of the biblical text: in its '"active reinterpretation"'.[2] He is at pains to remind us that such a 'faithful "rendering"' of those matters to which the texts bear witness is frequently problematic. Flemington instances Maximilian Kolbe, whose story is well known even to those who have no concern with the categorisation of him as 'blessed' or 'saint'. Elements in his story include the information that as a child he believed he was destined for martyrdom; that as a Franciscan, suffering from tuberculosis, he founded religious houses in Poland and Japan; that by the time he left Japan for the last time in 1936 he was tormented by headaches and abscesses brought on by eating food to which his body could not adapt itself; that in Auschwitz he took the place of another man picked out to die in the starvation cells in order to help the others destined to end their lives there to die; that as the last man of the group still alive after a fortnight he offered his arm, still praying, to the man who came to finish him off with a shot of carbolic acid.[3]

Few examples seem so unambiguously impressive, though it seems foolish to suppose that one *understands* the kind of choice Kolbe made, or choices in situations of comparable horror though it is to these situations that the language of sacrifice seems appropriate. Nothing else will do, even if the situation is too terrible to comprehend, so that the language of sacrifice itself marks the bounds of intelligibility. As an example, one might take *Sophie's Choice*,[4] a novel which in its own particular way provides a 'faithful "rendering"' of the kind of *context* in which Kolbe made his choice, and which in any case may draw upon the recollection of someone who survived witnessing events of the kind Styron narrates. Confronted on arrival at Auschwitz with a doctor involved in the prisoners' 'golgotha . . . of selection', in her terror of being identified with the Jews, Sophie helplessly blurted out that she was Polish, born in Cracow, that she and her children were racially pure, German speakers, and 'I'm a Christian. I'm a devout Catholic'. The response from the doctor she confronted was, 'So you believe in Christ the Redeemer? . . . Did He not say, "Suffer the little children to come unto Me"? . . . You may keep one of your children . . . The other one will have to go. Which one will you keep?' Styron says that his 'subtle magnanimity' forced Sophie to choose her boy, though she screams that she cannot choose, and one might say, on reading the novel, to 'sacrifice' her little girl. Although Sophie somehow survived the camp (her boy did not) in the end the knowledge and the memory of her choice contributed to her eventual suicide in the safety of post-war America. She too was a 'sacrifice' in the sense of being a 'victim' of her times.

'Sophie' may be a fiction; Simone Weil (1909–43) was not. Her own writings, and the memories of those who knew her, present us with the case of someone who came to interpret her own life and death in terms of the sacrifice of Christ, as one may presume Kolbe did, but the manner of whose death required a coroner's inquest. This took place on 27 August 1943, three days after she had died. The verdict was that the cause of death was 'cardial failure due to myocardial degeneration of the heart muscles due to starvation and pulmonary tuberculosis', with the assessment that: 'The deceased did kill and slay herself by refusing to eat whilst the balance of her mind was disturbed'.[5] Simone Weil could never become a candidate for official ecclesiastical approbation, since she adamantly refused to become part of the official church, originally having the idea that she was 'born inside' it[6] and some Roman Catholics have given perceptive and sympathetic treatments of her writings. One of her most devoted friends made an apt response to the charge of her heterodoxy with his remark commenting on the pious book where everything is second or *n*th hand, where strict orthodoxy is no more than hearsay and repetition, 'expressing the mechanical docility of a mind incapable of rising to the level of religious preoccupation and intellectual curiosity where heresy germinates . . .'[7] Her heterodoxy had much to do with her obsession with the universality of salvation, and the correlation of Christ's passion with the suffering of the guilty as well as of the innocent. 'We no longer imagine the dying Christ as a common criminal . . . the death on the Cross is something more divine than the Resurrection, it is the point where Christ's divinity is concentrated. Today the glorious Christ veils from us the Christ who was made a malediction; and thus we are in danger of adoring in his name the appearance, and not the reality, of justice.'[8]

She had at any rate one important strand in her spirituality in common with Kolbe, which was her devotion to the figure of St Francis of Assisi. There is a particular feature of Franciscan spirituality of which Mary Douglas reminds one when writing of the death of the Dinka spearmaster. He makes 'a stiffly ritual act' in giving the sign for his own slaying. 'It has none of the exuberance of St. Francis of Assisi rolling naked in the filth and welcoming his Sister Death. But his act touches the same mystery. If anyone held the idea that death and suffering are not an integral part of nature, the delusion is corrected.' Ritual shows another side to anyone tempted to treat it as 'a magic lamp to be rubbed for gaining unlimited riches and power', and 'If the hierarchy of values was crudely material, it is dramatically undermined by paradox and contradiction'.[9] Sympathetic appreciation of this tradition will hardly be developed by those who tend to examine human conduct within narrow boundaries, or who employ the kinds of ethical theories which dominate contemporary moral philosophy, characterised by optimism, order and progress. These theories will not help us even to begin to understand Simone Weil, any more than the letter of Sister Teresia Benedicta (Dr Edith Stein) writing to her Mother Superior on Passion Sunday 1939, 'I beg your Reverence to permit me to offer myself to the heart of Jesus as a vicarious sacrifice for true peace . . .'[10]

The sort of examples one seems to need are those of St Gemma Galgani or St Elizabeth of the Trinity, possible illustrations of those who skip other levels of contemplative religious development and start with 'Passionist' manifestations. As Margaret Masterman remarked[11] these usually die before missed levels can be gone through and what she referred to as 'plasticity' reattained. Thibon wrote of Simone Weil that 'the tension and rigidity of her obedience to her vocation were a sign, not indeed of inauthenticity, but of the green immaturity of her spiritual life. The best fruit remains hard as long as it is green . . . '[12] It seems that someone operating at the 'passionist' level presents him/herself as a total physical sacrifice to the destructive elements of the world rather than 'hitting back', regarding his or her self-sacrifice as the only way 'safely' to meet persecution, since either the persecutors will repent, or at any rate death will keep the victim from revenge. It is also worth noticing that the next level is what Margaret Masterman identified as the 'Hostic' level, 'only sacramentally portrayed', at which 'The saint desires not only to be killed but eaten'. Simone Weil noted: 'To live the death of a being is to eat him. The reverse is to be eaten by him. Man eats God and is eaten by God – and that in two senses, one in which he is lost, and another in which he is saved Communion.'[13] In an extended analogy she wrote:

> The beauty of the world is the mouth of a labyrinth. The unwary individual who on entering takes a few steps, is soon unable to find the opening. Worn out, with nothing to eat or drink, in the dark, separated from his dear ones, and from everything he loves and is accustomed to, he walks on without knowing anything or hoping anything, incapable even of discovering whether he is really going forward or merely turning round on the same spot. But this affliction is as nothing compared with the danger that threatens him. For if he does not lose courage, if he goes on walking, it is absolutely certain that he will finally arrive at the centre of the labyrinth. And there God is waiting to eat him. Later he will go out again, but he will be changed, he will have become different, after being eaten and digested by God. Afterwards he will stay near the entrance so that he can gently push all those who come near into the opening.[14]

It is obvious that the language of sacrifice and the language of a certain kind of eucharistic theology run into one another, but this only in part prepares one to read the appalling prayer Simone Weil wrote towards the end of her life,[15] though she did insist to herself that one could not voluntarily demand what the petitions were for, that it was despite oneself, though with consent, entire and without reservation, a movement of the whole being. The prayer included petition to the Father to grant her in the name of Christ, 'That I may be unable to will any bodily movement, or even any attempt at movement, like a total paralytic. That I may be incapable of receiving any sensation, like someone who is completely blind, deaf, and deprived of all the senses. That I may be unable to make the slightest connection between two thoughts . . .' She asked for will, sensibility, intelligence, love to be stripped away, 'devoured by God, transformed into Christ's substance, and given for food to afflicted men whose body and soul lack every kind of nourishment. And let me be a paralytic – blind, deaf, witless, and utterly decrepit.'

This is just one example of what are from the ordinarily moral point of view monstrous images by which to conceive of God's dealings with his creatures, images which for their violence are perhaps among the most perplexing features of her writings, and which were in their employment disastrous for her personally. For one might regard her as someone who inflicted on herself, by accident, the kind of death she might have come to in a concentration camp, to whom the 'ghastly verbal witticism *être suicidé*' would have been appropriate,[16] except that she died in fact as the consequence of 'the employment of false metaphors'.[17] To suggest this is to criticise a tradition, unless one can find some way to justify it. If such a justification is unavailable she might well, with others who have employed this language, be another instance of someone in whom the creative imagination had atrophied and finally failed: 'the "artist" of suicide is a grasping, blundering, failed artist' whose artwork remains only as 'a mockery of feminine achievement'. The prayer she wrote would then be analogous to Sylvia Plath's poem 'Lady Lazarus', in which the author, writing only a few months before her suicide in February 1963, wrote to relate her own sufferings with those of the tortured Jews of an earlier generation. This was a matter of particular horror for her, since her own father was of Prussian origin, and her mother an Austrian, who could conceivably have been related to one another as Nazi and Jew. Some of the lines from 'Lady Lazarus' run as follows:

> A sort of walking miracle, my skin
> Bright as a Nazi lampshade,
> My right foot

A paper weight,
My face a featureless, fine
Jew linen . . . . .
These are my hands
My knees.
I may be skin and bone,

Nevertheless, I am the same, identical woman . . . . .
Dying
Is an art, like everything else.
I do it exceptionally well.
I do it so it feels like hell.
I do it so it feels real.
I guess you could say I've a call . . . . .
For the eyeing of my scars, there is a charge
For the hearing of my heart
It really goes.

And there is a charge, a very large charge
For a word or a touch
Or a bit of blood

Or a piece of my hair or my clothes.[18]

Sylvia Plath's poem is illuminating in regard to Simone Weil in certain important respects. To begin with, Simone Weil was deeply at odds with her own Jewishness, though she had little sense of it during her childhood, living as she·did as part of a family group which was assimilating itself into French urban culture. For Simone Weil herself complete assimilation to French culture and total rejection of her inheritance were all too conventional alternatives, though at least she had learned a conception of Judaism which would provoke anti-Semitism[19] and it would be almost miraculous for some one person to be able to tackle this on their own. In learning this conception she had learned something about self-hate which in itself was bound to precipitate a problem about becoming a Christian in the ecclesiastical sense: for 'new-born Christianity did not know how to detach itself from a tradition which, after all, had ended up with the murder of Christ'.[20] If Martin Buber's views are any guide[21] she made the same sorts of criticism of Judaism and of the Roman Catholic church as he did of that church, though her Left-wing political philosophy and activism might have made membership of the church at that time a major problem also. The only parts of the Old Testament to survive a scrutiny worthy of Pierre Bayle were those which matched up to criteria derived from her knowledge of Greek classical literature and philosophy.

Chaim Potok's novel *My Name is Asher Lev*[22] helps to illuminate the predicament of a Jew who came as she did to feel constrained to use Christian imagery. The novel is about a Jewish boy with artistic gifts comparable to those of Chagall, gifts which in themselves were a source of deep distress and conflict within his family and religious community. Eventually, largely due to the influence of his Rebbe, no less, he is apprenticed to a great artist, himself a Jew by race, who teaches him to draw and paint nudes, and to study paintings of the crucifixion in New York's galleries and museums. 'It was only later, on my way home, that it occurred to me how strange it must have been to see a red-haired boy in a black skullcap and dangling earlocks standing in a museum and copying paintings about Jesus' (p. 151). On seeing his drawings his mother was horrified. 'Do you know how much Jewish blood has been spilled because of him, Asher? How could you spend your precious time doing this?' His father's father had been murdered by a Russian peasant celebrating a holiday to do with 'that man'. When in Italy Asher was deeply distressed by Michelangelo's *Pietà* in the Florence Duomo.

> I was an observant Jew, yet that block of stone moved through me like a cry, like the call of seagulls over morning surf, like – like the echoing blasts of the shofar sounded by the Rebbe. I do not mean to blaspheme. My frames of reference have been formed by the life I have lived. I do not know how a devout Christian reacts to that *Pietà*. I was only able to relate it to elements in my own lived past. I stared at it. I walked slowly round it. I do not remember how long I was there the first time. When I came back out into the brightness of the crowded square, I was astonished to discover that my eyes were wet.
>
> (p. 270)

Travelling to Rome, and drawing the *Pietà* from memory, he discovered with horror that the woman supporting the twisted arm of the crucified Jesus bore a faint resemblance to his mother (p. 274). Thinking intently of his mother, he began to sense something of her anguish, keeping alive her son's gift, her dead brother's work, her husband's work, always with the fear that someone she loved would be brought to her dead. Asher was ultimately driven to paint her anguish and torment, and drew her as the central figure in a crucifixion scene, framed by the living-room window of his Brooklyn home.

> The torment, the tearing anguish I felt in her, I put into her mouth, into the twisting curve of her head, the arching of her slight body, the clenching of her small fists, the taut downward pointing of her thin legs . . . I painted swiftly in a strange nerveless frenzy of energy. For all the pain you suffered, my mama. For all the anguish this picture of pain will cause you. For the unspeakable mystery that brings good fathers and sons into the world and lets a mother watch them tear at each other's throats. For the Master of the Universe, whose suffering world I do not comprehend.
>
> (p. 285)

Asher works with this image 'because there was no aesthetic mould in his own religious tradition into which he could pour a painting of ultimate anguish and torment'. The painting was a sensation at the New York showing of his work because it was a brilliant piece of work. 'The colours, look at how he worked the colours. But isn't he an Orthodox Jew? one of those – what do you call them – Hasids? How could he paint that? Who's the woman? Christ, look at the agony on her face. Christ, he's good' (p. 311). Asher found it impossible to explain what he had done, not least because it was beyond his own comprehension. The showing of the painting leads not surprisingly to a radical break with family and community. How might even an 'assimilated' Jewish family react to what in Simone Weil's case is virtually a self-portrait in these terms and what inner conflict did it bring her once she had done it?

Attention to Buber's representation of Jewish faith[23] alerts one to an inevitable criticism of Simone Weil from another angle, given her deep suspicion of anything that could be construed as 'consolation' for suffering, which seemed to include what others would deem to be 'blessings'. Any exponent of the Jewish or Christian tradition which celebrates flourishing and fruition was likely to be critical of her, and set her at odds with herself again, since the criticism would be that in taking 'the Man of Sorrows' as her paradigm, she was substituting 'the falsity of a near-masochism for the falsity of complacency'.[24] She commented on the words addressed to Thomas[25] and argued that these could not refer to those who, without having seen it, believed in the fact of the resurrection. 'Surely those who are blessed are they who have no need of the resurrection in order to believe, and for whom Christ's perfection and the Cross are in themselves proof.' So she affirmed that 'Christ curing the sick, raising up from the dead; this is the humble, human, almost menial part of his mission. The supernatural part is the bloody sweat, the unsatisfied desire to find consolation among his friends, the supplication to be spared, the feeling of being forsaken by God'.[26] And further: 'There is only one proof of the goodness of God – it is that we love him. The love that we have for him is the sole benefit worthy of our gratitude, and consequently this love contains within itself the proof of its legitimacy. When it has no other incentive than itself, nothing can shake it; for even at the point of "Why hast thou forsaken me" love does not falter, but takes on the form of absence instead of that of contact. It thus attains the extreme limit of purity' (p. 267). So in her meditations on the 'Our Father' she wrote that as well as actual literal food, all incentives are sources of energy. 'Money, ambition, consideration, decorations, celebrity, power, our loved ones, everything which puts into us the capacity for action is like bread.' All these (and it is important to notice 'our loved ones' in this list) made up 'the daily bread of the world', depending on circumstances. 'We should ask nothing with regard to circumstances unless it be that they may conform to the will of God. We should not ask for earthly bread.'[27] Again and again she insisted that her haven was the Cross: 'If it cannot be given me to deserve one day to share the Cross of Christ, at least may I share that of the good thief. Of all the beings other than Christ of whom the Gospel tells us, the good thief is by far the one I most envy. To have been at the side of Christ and in the same state during the crucifixion seems to me a far more enviable privilege than to be at the right hand of his glory' (p. 26).

There is another way in which Simone Weil's anguish may be illuminated by 'Lady Lazarus', in that by ordinary standards one would have to say that she was deeply at odds with herself about her femininity, which may not have been helped by her mother's preference for values associated with little boys rather than little girls, such as forthrightness, though one could hardly criticise her for that in particular.[28] She seems to have been like Lûmir in Claudel's play *Le Pain dur* who says 'I am not very beautiful. If I were very beautiful, perhaps it would be worth the trouble of living. /I do not know how to dress. I have none of the arts of woman. /I have always lived like a boy. Nothing but men around me. /Look how everything hangs on me. It's flung on anyhow.'[29] It was recalled that 'Her usual costume was a loose, tailored dress of masculine cut, with large side-pockets that were always full of tobacco, worn with the low-heeled shoes of a little girl'.[30] She could and did find a 'religious' justification for what might originally have been no more than the self-image of a member of the revolutionary intelligentsia of her day. 'To accept poverty in the literal sense of the word, as St. Francis did, is to accept being nothing in the appearance which one presents to oneself and to others, just as one *is* nothing in reality.'[31]

One can readily see how both this language and the language of 'sacrifice' could be deeply damaging to her, rather as in another of Claudel's plays, *L'Annonce faite à Marie*, Violaine says, 'The male is the priest but it is not forbidden to the woman to be a victim'.[32] Simone Weil wrote of 'the infinitely tender love which has made me the gift of affliction' (*Waiting on God*, p. 63), and, 'To use the flesh to hide ourselves from the light – is not that a mortal sin? Terrible thought. Better to be a leper' (*Notebooks*, II, 623). Claudel as it happens expressed what she may have meant in a poem to the lepers of the Hôpital St Louis:

> So much the worse for this poor house
> If I have destroyed it a bit!
> This God with you, this Brother,
> You haven't paid too dearly for Him.
> I am fire! He who touches me
> Must consent to be burnt.
> A victim, a living sacrifice,
> Do you cease to be My child?
> My child, My only child!
> And if I took your tunic from you
> Of what use was that vesture?[33]

Moreover, enthusiasts for asceticism, and for sexual virginity as one of its manifestations are not always aware of its importance in the early church or in modern society, of its significance as a symbol of revolution against coercion, though women may still define themselves in relation to the male divinity, the male apostle, even those extraordinary creatures, male but allegedly sexless angels.[34] To use a paradoxical adjective, Simone Weil was notoriously 'touchy' about any physical contact or expression of affection, and her asceticism may well have been one way of trying to get control of her formidable talents and personality in a society which would have been more comfortable for her had she continued to work as a teacher, or at any rate fulfilled some other socially acceptable rôle. Trotsky correctly identified her need 'to defend her personality against society'[35] but her determination to push herself to the limits of her endurance was another disastrous trait in a person who apparently took to asceticism so easily, eating all too little, and smoking incessantly – a necessary stimulant despite its being the Achilles heel of that asceticism. At least one medical practitioner, Dr Bercher, whom she met in Marseilles seems to have realised that she was in some way ill. 'I also told Simone a story that I had heard from my sister, the story of a nun who had gone for a very long time without eating. "She nourished herself on the holy eucharist," my sister said. Simone found this story quite reasonable. When I told these stories to Simone, I wasn't very happy with myself. I had the sensation that I was both giving her pleasure and doing her *harm*. That was how it was with this creature who was at war with her own life. If you did one side of her good, you wounded the other side.'[36]

It is very likely that she was in fact a sufferer from anorexia nervosa, possibly triggered off by her fear of failure. She herself recounted how at the age of fourteen she fell into a pit of bottomless despair, and seriously thought of dying because of her mediocre abilities – which were to take her to the Ecole Normale Supérieure in 1928 in the same year as Simone de Beauvoir, two women together at the top of their year. She believed herself to be inferior in comparison with her brother, 'who had a childhood and youth comparable to those of Pascal'. She claimed not to mind visible success, but grieved until she convinced herself that no matter what her natural abilities she could 'penetrate to the kingdom of truth reserved for genius' if only she longed for it and perpetually concentrated for attention upon its attainment (*Waiting on God*, p. 30). She was to refer to this goal of her life in an all too revealing way when she wrote of 'those beings who have, in spite of flesh and blood, spiritually crossed a boundary equivalent to death, receive on the farther side another life, which is not primarily life, which is primarily truth, truth which has become living, as true as death and as living as life. A life, as Grimm's fairy tales put it, as white as snow and as red as blood. It is that which is the breath of truth, the divine Spirit' (*The Need for Roots*, p. 238). In *La deuxième sexe* Simone de Beauvoir hit by chance on an apt commentary on the fairy-tale imagery all too suitable for the sufferer from anorexia nervosa when she said: 'St. Blandine, her white body blood-streaked under the lion's claws, Snow White laid out as if dead in a glass coffin, the Beauty asleep, the fainting Atala, a whole flock of delicate heroines bruised, passive, wounded, kneeling, humiliated, demonstrate to their young sister the fascinating prestige of martyred, deserted, resigned beauty' (p. 319). Simone Weil might have flourished had she been able to acknowledge that 'all sanity depends on this: that it should be a delight to feel the roughness of a carpet under smooth soles, a delight to feel heat strike the skin, a delight to stand upright, knowing the bones are moving easily under the flesh. If this goes, then the conviction of life goes too.'[37]

It is already clear how Simone Weil would have responded to an argument that concludes that resurrection 'is the fulfilment in which the pattern of each person shall again become presence, our own real presence of which we may each say (perhaps in surprised delight) "This is my body"'.[38] Rather, the crucified man-God is a sort of 'reversed image of the white, blood-stained martyr' with whom a little girl may have come to identify herself, here a man has assumed her rôle.[39] Whereas one *might* read the imagery as carrying with it the promise of resurrection, Simone Weil could read it only as a symbol of much longed-for total peace, so it was not to be wondered at if she longed for oblivion: 'my greatest desire is to lose not only all will but all personal being' (*Waiting on God*, p. 26). Her fear of failure came to be couched in terms of a fear of failing 'at her death', a fear which 'never ceased to grow more and more intense'.[40] She argued that wherever there is what she called 'complete, authentic and unconditional consent to necessity, there is fullness of love for God; and nowhere else. This consent constitutes participation in the Cross of Christ' (*Intimations*, p. 184). That is to say, participation in the redemptive suffering of Christ by consenting to death, the precise moment at which God seems to be absent. Death then represented 'the centre and object of life . . . the instant when, for an infinitesimal fraction of time, pure truth, naked, certain and eternal enters the soul' (*Waiting on God*, pp. 29–30). So she persuaded herself that

> Those who place their life outside their own
>   bodies are really stronger than the rest, who
> appear to be invulnerable . . . But fate discovers
>   where their life is laid up and deflates them.

The man who places his life in faith in God
    can lose his faith. But the man who places
his life in God himself – he will never lose
    it. One must place one's life in something
one cannot touch on any account. It is impossible.
    It is a death. It means no longer being alive.
And that is exactly what is wanted.'

                        (Notebooks, II, ll 94–95)

She realised her own danger, at any rate sometimes, but preferred it
to relying on her parents, and when it came near to the time of her
death, she could not bring herself to warn them of the imminence,
except possibly by indirect suggestion. 'Antigone has gone through
a few bad patches, it's true. But they didn't last. It's all far away
now' (*Seventy Letters*, p. 191). She only half-knew what she was doing
to herself and wrote that 'No one ever inflicts disaster on himself,
neither out of love nor perversity. At the most one can, under one or
the other inspiration, take distractedly and as if unconsciously two
or three steps leading to the slippery point where one becomes a
prey to gravity and from which one falls on stones that break one's
back' (*Intimations*, p. 183). Even more obviously: 'There is a certain
similarity between the extreme penalty of the cross and that of
immuring inflicted on Antigone. This is no doubt due to the same
motive – the search for an alibi. One doesn't actually kill; one places
the condemned person in a situation in which he or she must
necessarily die' (*Notebooks*, II, 517–18). Her most recent 'reason' for
refusing to eat had been that she would not take more food than she
believed the French were getting, but this was as it were built on to
her existing asceticism. 'Thirst, hunger, chastity – carnal privations
of all kinds – in the search for God. Sensible forms of the void. The
body has no other way of accepting the void' (*Notebooks*, I, 137). In a
situation of terrible privation such asceticism could have manifested
itself as a love dominating the whole personality, as Dorothy Emmet
relates by means of a story told to her by Leonard Wilson when
Bishop of Singapore, imprisoned by the Japanese. When it came to
handing out plates of food, he could bring himself to offer them to his
companion that the latter might take the smaller helping, though he
could not bring himself deliberately to hand him the larger one. But
he knew a man in the prison who could do just that.[41]
    Deprived of such an object of love in the needs of those sharing
privation, she became conscious only of desperate fatigue, and

eventually a total lack of patience with herself. 'Catholic communion. God has not only made himself flesh once; every day he makes himself matter in order to give himself to man and be consumed by him. Conversely, through fatigue, affliction, death, man is made matter and consumed by God. How refuse this reciprocity?' Exhaustion she understood as 'the mechanism of resignation' to affliction, killing the desire for deliverance from it (*Notebooks*, I, 99, 139–40). She expressed her attitude to herself as 'contempt and hatred and repulsion' (*Seventy Letters*, p. 139), and reminded herself of 'My two enemies: *fatigue* and *disgust* (physical disgust for all kinds of things). Both of them wellnigh invincible; and under certain circumstances can, in a flash, make me fall very low' (*Notebooks*, I, 153). For someone who could be extraordinarily perceptive about herself and others, it was disastrous for her not to recognise her illness for what it was and to judge herself as harshly as she did. 'The refuge of laziness and inertia, a temptation to which I succumb very often, almost every day, or I might say every hour, is a particularly despicable form of consolation. It compels me to despise myself' (*Seventy Letters*, p. 142). So she made use of a particularly puzzling bit of biblical material when she confessed that 'I never read the story of the barren fig tree without trembling. I think that it is a portrait of me. In it also, nature was powerless, and yet it was not excused. Christ cursed it . . . the sense of being like a barren fig tree for Christ tears my heart' (*Waiting on God*, p. 64). She could not allow 'Qaerens me sedisti lassus', the very words from the Franciscan 'Dies Irae' on the cover of her 1941 notebook[42] to be used of herself in her approximation to the sufferings of Christ, as she became increasingly self-critical at the limits of her natural strength. 'There are some words in Isaiah which are terrible for me: They that love God "shall run and not be weary; and they shall walk and not faint." This makes it physically impossible for me to forget, even for a moment, that I am not of their number' (*Seventy Letters*, p. 170).

It is not only the sufferer from anorexia nervosa who arouses deep feelings of anxiety, guilt and resentment among relatives, friends and among 'the medical staff, particularly female, concerned with her treatment'.[43] For instance: 'Porridge time came around one morning and in bustled one of those guardian angels, a nurse. "Come on dear," said the 20-year-old to the 70-year-old, "Eat up your nice porridge." The woman sat unspeaking while the nurse tried to push the spoon into the unwilling mouth. The ward was quiet, the helpless looked away while the helper forced in the porridge. The woman turned her head, wordlessly, tears streaming down her face. The nurse, momentarily defeated, angrily turned to the helpless for support, "She's got to eat it, it's good for her."'[44] Simone Weil didn't, and the result was inevitable, whatever she intended. Sylvia Plath wrote another poem about death, entitled 'Contusion'.

> Colour floods to the spot, dull purple.
> The rest of the body is all washed out,
> The colour of pearl.
>
> In a pit of rock
> The sea sucks obsessively,
> One hollow the whole sea's pivot.
>
> The size of a fly,
> The doom mark
> Crawls down the wall.
>
> The heart shuts,
> The sea slides back,
> The mirrors are sheeted.

(*Ariel* p. 84)

NOTES

1. W. F. Flemington, 'On the interpretation of Colossians 1.24', in *Suffering and Martyrdom in the New Testament*, edited by W. Horbury and B. NcNeil (London, 1981), pp. 84–90 (p. 89).
2. N. Lash, 'What might martyrdom mean?' in *Suffering and Martyrdom*, pp. 183–98. (pp. 196–7).
3. M. Craig, *Blessed Maximilian Kolbe: Priest Hero of a Death Camp* (London, 1973).
4. W. Styron, *Sophie's Choice* (London, 1979), pp. 480–7.
5. S. Pétrement, *Simone Weil: A Life*, translated by R. Rosenthal (London, 1976), p. 537.
6. S. Weil, *Waiting on God*, translated by E. Crauford (London, 1974), p. 32.
7. J. M. Perrin and G. Thibon, *Simone Weil as We Knew Her*, translated by E. Crauford (London, 1953), p. 168.
8. S. Weil, *Intimations of Christianity among The Greeks*, translated by E. C. Geissbuhler (London, 1976), pp. 142–3.
9. Mary Douglas, *Purity and Danger* (London, 1966), p. 178.
10. H. Gollwitzer, *Dying We Live*, translated by R. C. Kuhn (London, 1958), pp. 205–6.

11. M. Masterman, 'The Psychology of Levels of Will or, the Possibility of constructing a Psychology of Growth as well as of Sex', *Proceedings of the Aristotelian Society*, New Series 48 (1948), 75–100.
12. Perrin and Thibon, *Simone Weil as We Knew Her*, p. 118.
13. S. Weil, *The Notebooks*, translated by A. Willis, 2 vols (London, 1976), I, 329.
14. Weil, *Waiting on God*, p. 119.
15. S. Weil, *First and Last Notebooks*, translated by R. Rees (London, 1970), pp. 243–4.
16. D. Daube, 'The Linguistics of Suicide', *Philosophy and Public Affairs* (1972), 387–437.
17. J. C. Oates, 'The Art of Suicide' in *Suicide: The Philosophical Issues*, edited by M. Pabst Battin and D. Mayo (New York, 1980), pp. 161–8 (p. 162).
18. S. Plath, *Ariel* (London, 1965), pp. 16–19.
19. D. M. Mackinnon, *Borderlands of Theology* (London, 1968), p. 103.
20. Weil, *Waiting on God*, p. 187.
21. *The Philosophy of Martin Buber*, edited by P. A. Schlipp and M. Friedman, (La Salle, Illinois, 1967), p. 558.
22. C. Potok, *My Name is Asher Lev* (Harmondsworth, 1977).
23. P. Vermes, *Buber on God and the Perfect Man* (Chico, CA, 1982), pp. 141–4, 157–8.
24. H. Oppenheimer, 'Christian Flourishing', *Religious Studies*, 5 (1969), 163–171 (p. 170).
25. S. Weil, *The Need for Roots*, translated by A. F. Wills (London, 1978), p. 257.
26. Weil, *Notebooks*, I, 263.
27. Weil, *Waiting on God*, pp. 171–2.
28. Pétrement, *Simone Weil: A Life*, p. 278.
29. E. Beaumont, *The Theme of Beatrice in the Plays of Claudel* (London, 1954), p. 86.
30. J. Cabaud, *Simone Weil: A Fellowship in Love* (London, 1964), p. 32.
31. Weil, *Intimations*, p. 175.
32. P. Claudel, *L'Annonce faite à Marie* (Paris, 1940), p. 124.
33. K. O'Flaherty, *Paul Claudel and 'the Tidings brought to Mary'* (Oxford, 1948), p. 75.
34. See S. de Beauvoir, *The Second Sex* (1949) translated by H. M. Paishley (Harmondsworth, 1972), pp. 317–18.
35. Pétrement, *Simone Weil: A Life*, p. 178.
36. Ibid., p. 420.
37. D. Lessing, *The Golden Notebook* (St Albans, 1981), p. 591.
38. H. Oppenheimer, 'Life after Death', *Theology*, 82 (1979), 328–35 (p. 335).
39. de Beauvoir, *The Second Sex*, p. 686.
40. S. Weil, *Seventy Letters*, translated by R. Rees (London, 1965), p. 178.
41. D. Emmet, *The Moral Prism* (London, 1979), pp. 156–7.
42. L. Allen, 'Simone Weil', *Stand*, 19 (1978), 4–9 (p. 9).
43. P. Dally, *Anorexia Nervosa* (Bath, 1969), p. 1.
44. *Images of Ourselves: Women with Disabilities Talking*, edited by J. Campling (London, 1981), p. 46.

8 *Middlemarch* as a Religious Novel, or Life without God

T. R. Wright

How George Eliot lost her belief in God and lived unhappily ever after is a well-worn tale but one which never ceases to comfort the faithful. How the pious provincial girl refused one day to go to church, made herself Strauss-sick by translating over two agonised years his dissection of the beautiful Gospel stories into their compound of myth and legend, how she made matters worse by turning next to the rabidly anti-theological Feuerbach, and how she spent the rest of her life seeking for a replacement for the God she had come to find inconceivable: this has been the subject of much scholarship and reflection. Christians in her own time, such as the liberal Catholic Richard Simpson, marvelled that 'the godless humanitarianism of Strauss and Feuerbach can be made to appear the living centre of all the popular religions'.[1] More recently there have been quite savage attacks on her empty 'Rhetoric of Enthusiasm' and her 'Ersatz Christianity'.[2] *Middlemarch* has been called a 'novel of religious yearning without religious object', in which traditional religious language is applied to ordinary human experience as part of a 'pseudo-religious philosophy' which mistakes the profane for the sacred.[3] My concern is not to judge George Eliot's position (though I do give a clear indication of my own estimate of its emotional appeal) but to explore it more carefully. Just as Marxist critics appreciate *Middlemarch*, in spite of its alien ideology, because it explores the disintegration of capitalist society, so Christian critics, or those with an interest in literature and religion should be able to appreciate the novel for its vivid and accurate representation of the agonies endured in the nineteenth century by those learning to live without God. It has both the advantages and disadvantages of being a 'classic realist text' on which the narrator imposes a restricted vision of 'reality'.[4]

Nowhere in George Eliot's work is the absence of God so noticeable as in *Middlemarch*. The novel is historically inaccurate in this respect, as a contemporary reviewer complained:

> That Dorothea, with her passionate enthusiasms her noble unselfish nature – Dorothea, not illustrating a Positivist thesis in 1876 [sic], but living her life more than a generation ago, in 1830 – that she should not distinctly love Christ, and, in the sorrows and disenchantment of her sad wifehood and widowhood, cast her cares on Him, is an anachronism.[5]

Mid-Victorian doubt *is* somewhat foisted upon her as a character – but the text itself is what I take to be representative of its time. It goes further than George Eliot's other novels, in which God and Christ are more prominent though very much watered down not only in the narration but in the mouths of his believers. The convert Janet Dempster, the Methodist preacher, Dinah Morris, and even the fifteenth-century Dominican, Savonarola, are made to talk in an embarrassed way about capitalised human qualities (the divinities of 'the True or Anthropological Essence of Religion'): 'Divine Love', 'Divine Sympathy', 'the Divine Sufferer' and so on. The 'Unseen Pity' also makes an invisible appearance in *The Mill on the Floss*, where it is stressed that the great devotional manual of Thomas à Kempis is to be valued as 'a lasting record of *human* needs and *human* consolations' (Book IV, Chapter 3, my italics).[6] God is reduced to a devout kind of exclamation both in *Adam Bede* and in *Daniel Deronda*. The words, 'Great God!', from Deronda's lips, come as something of a shock. He cannot surely refer to a real Being, but neither would he be irreverent. The text provides a somewhat unsatisfactory explanation:

> the words escaped Deronda in a tone so low and solemn that they seemed like a prayer become unconsciously vocal. . . . . . The old thought had come now with a new impetus of mingled feeling, and urged that exclamation in which both East and West have for ages concentrated their awe in the presence of inexorable calamity.
>
> (Chapter 17)

The narrative of *Middlemarch* avoids this kind of insincerity because it never for a moment suggests that God might exist. It is, however, a religious novel in the broad sense that it is concerned with religious need, the desire to find unity, meaning and purpose in life, in a world in which God, to use one of the key words of the novel, is a 'blank'.

Middlemarch is quite modern in its concern with the twin problems of perception and interpretation, with the way in which people look at life and attempt to invest it with meaning. It recognises the inevitability of a certain 'epistemological egoism' [7] and the need for an imaginative construction of hypothetical systems by which to interpret individual experience. But it tends to deplore those who make no attempt to modify their understanding of the world in accordance with ascertained facts. Theology, Mythology, History, Art and Science are all portrayed in the novel as ways in which men struggle to impose order on to the chaos of experience. They are all seen as necessarily subjective and the theories they construct are judged according to their awareness of this limitation and their openness to adaptation in the light of contradictory evidence. No-one, it seems, is immune from subjectivity except, perhaps, the omniscient author.

There are two very famous passages in *Middlemarch* in which George Eliot discusses the nature of this inescapable egoism of perception. The first occurs at the end of Chapter 21, after Dorothea has recognised the extent of her husband's weaknesses and limitations. It is the passage that begins:

> We are all of us born in moral stupidity taking the world as an udder to feed our supreme selves,

and goes on to discuss Dorothea's beginning to realise the 'alterity' of Casaubon. Dorothea's intuitive awareness of Casaubon's actual self, with all its self-centredness, self-distrust and self-pity, helps her to escape the worst form of egoism, which is 'moral stupidity', of the sort displayed by Rosamond Vincy, who is the immediate target of the second passage at the beginning of Chapter 27. This contains the famous image of the pier-glass on which the haphazard scratches are made to appear concentrically arranged around the light of any candle brought to it. The significance of Rosamond's affection for mirrors in contrast with Dorothea's penchant for views through windows has often been observed. This imagery, which recurs throughout the novel, reinforces the notion that progress in perception is marked by decreasing self-centredness.

The theological aspect of the problem of perception is indicated by the number of characters in the novel who believe in some form of special providence. The pier-glass passage continues with an analysis of Rosamond's 'providence of her own who had kindly made her more charming than other girls'. Her brother is also ridiculed for his primitive faith in the 'providential' nature of his uncle's gift and his astonishment when it turns out to be less than enough to meet his debts:

> What can the fitness of things mean, if not their fitness to a man's expectations? Failing this, absurdity and atheism gape behind him. (Chapter 14)

His confidence in providence is reasserted in Chapter 23 where the reader is ironically reprimanded for demanding 'a basis in external facts' for Fred's hopes in horse-swapping. It seems only natural for him 'to believe that the universal order of things would necessarily be agreeable to an agreeable young gentleman'. It is only continual disappointment, most notably in the affair of Featherstone's will, which cures Fred of his faith in 'the favour of providence' (Chapter 36).

Bulstrode's belief in Providence is more fully articulated than Fred Vincy's, more thoroughly theological. It is the kind of baptised egoism of which George Eliot read in Feuerbach and on which she wrote in her attacks on 'Evangelical Teaching: Dr Cumming' and 'Worldliness and Other-Worldliness: The Poet Young'.[8] Bulstrode's belief in Providence is most fully explored in Chapter 53, when it is first shaken by the arrival of Mr Raffles. Providence has kindly facilitated Bulstrode's purchase of Stone Court from Joshua Rigg (whose fortunes 'belonged to the unmapped regions not taken under the providential government'). Raffles, of course, enjoys calling his reappearance 'a providential thing' precisely because Bulstrode has difficulties in accommodating it to 'the divine plan' and cannot help dwelling on the possibility of disgrace, which raises all those 'egotistic fears' which he habitually clad in 'doctrinal references to superhuman ends'. For the banker's religion, analysed once more in Chapter 61, is based on fear, and 'the religion of fear remains nearly at the level of the savage'. Bulstrode is shown to have overcome his moral scruples at failing to inform his first wife of the discovery of her daughter and heir by an identification of 'God's intentions' with his own interests, which seem to have been furthered by a series of 'remarkable providences'. He is sufficiently frightened to offer Ladislaw restitution for the wrong done to his mother but continues to explain his behaviour in terms of divine rather than personal interest. He tells Lydgate, in Chapter 67, that his withdrawal from the New Hospital is a result of 'providential indications' and makes his preparations for leaving Middlemarch conditional, in the following chapter, in case 'any favourable intervention of Providence should dissipate his fears'. The fact that it is Caleb Garth to whom Raffles reveals details of his past appears to be an additional mark of providential protection (Chapter 69) as does Raffles' illness (Chapter 70). Bulstrode even manages to convince himself, when Raffles dies as a result of his failure to pass Lydgate's instructions on to his housekeeper, that it was Providence that had delivered him from his worst fears (Chapter 71).

Casaubon is another character in *Middlemarch* who is 'the centre of his own world . . . liable to think that others were providentially made for him' (Chapter 10). He makes repeated references to the providential ordering of his life, notably in his letter of proposal to Dorothea (Chapter 5) and in assuaging her feelings of guilt at the possession of too much money (Chapter 37). But it is with Dorothea's religious aspirations that the novel is most concerned. The first paragraph of Chapter 1 makes much of her reading of Pascal and Jeremy Taylor and of her passionate interest in 'the destinies of mankind'. She detracts from her attractiveness as a prospective wife by 'her insistence on regulating life according to notions' and by an ardour shared only by apostles and papists. The irony which pervades the early chapters of the novel is partly directed at Dorothea, at her qualms about riding and wearing jewelry, for instance, but more at the society which finds her religious aspirations incomprehensible. She is not portrayed as mistaken in her yearning for 'some lofty conception of the world' nor in her desire to regulate her life but rather in the inaccuracy of her early judgements about the world, in particular about Mr Casaubon. For in him we are told in the third chapter, she sees 'a living Bossuet' and 'a modern Augustine' combining knowledge and piety. In the imagery which recurs throughout the novel she imputes to him 'a whole world of which my thought is but a poor two-penny mirror' and a whole range of feelings which constitute 'a lake compared with my little pool'. The narrator makes a general point:

Signs are small measurable things, but interpretations are illimitable, and in girls of sweet, ardent nature, every sign is apt to conjure up wonder, hope, belief, vast as a sky, and coloured by a diffused thimbleful of matter in the shape of knowledge.

Dorothea, in other words, believes in Casaubon's spiritual greatness on too little evidence.

Dorothea's belief in Casaubon is described in terms analogous to religious faith. The dryness of his language after their engagement in Chapter 5 goes unremarked: 'Dorothea's faith supplied all that Mr Casaubon's words seemed to leave unsaid: what believer sees a disturbing omission or infelicity?' The final paragraph gives the Middlemarch view of her childlike reverence for her 'Protestant Pope'. Again, however, it is the judges rather than the judged who display the more limited vision. The 'symphony of hopeful dreams, admiring trust and passionate self-devotion which that learned gentleman had set playing in her soul' (Chapter 8) is indeed beautiful. It displays the riches of human nature, wasted though they are on an inadequate object. She remains in Chapter 9 incapable of seeing Casaubon's weaknesses and limitations:

She filled up all blanks with unmanifested perfections, interpreting him as she interpreted the works of Providence, and accounting for seeming discords by her own deafness to the higher harmonies.

Faith, it seems, whether in people or in God, is a matter of filling up blanks.

Contemporary reviewers complained that Dorothea's religious faith was given insufficient space. We never see her praying, they said (though in the very first chapter we are told of her praying 'fervidly' by the side of a sick labourer and in Chapter 5 she is depicted falling to her knees, 'reclining in the lap of divine consciousness', meditating and seeking 'the highest aid possible'. She has 'an impulse which if she had been alone would have turned into a prayer' in Chapter 30 and it is only in Chapter 39 that she tells Ladislaw that she 'hardly ever' prays). But we do not need more than the glimpses we are given of her devotional life to infer that her love of God reveals the same glorious qualities and glaring weaknesses examined more closely in her love of Casaubon. The text draws our attention to the same will to believe in both cases, combined with the same refusal to consider any contrary evidence.

Dorothea's religious ardour is given further treatment in Chapter 10, by which time she is already moving towards that Religion of Humanity espoused by her creator. Here there is no irony attached to the discussion of her

> eagerness for a binding theory which could bring her own life and doctrine into strict connection with that amazing past, and give the remotest sources of knowledge some bearing on her actions.

The Positivists tended to emphasise the derivation of the word 'religion' from 'religare' – to bind [9] and in her desire to regulate her life, in her sense of solidarity and continuity with Humanity in the present and in the past, and in her combination of the three activities of thinking, feeling and acting, Dorothea fulfils all the religious requirements of a model Positivist. Her sense of history, it emerges on her honeymoon, is limited. She is unable to appreciate Rome, 'the city of visible history' and 'the spiritual centre and interpreter of the world'. On her return to Lowick, too, she has a struggle to maintain 'the sense of connection with a manifold pregnant existence', a somewhat painful metaphor for that solidarity with suffering humanity that was central to the Positivist faith. She is in danger of losing all her beliefs along with her love for Casaubon:

> her religious faith was a solitary way, the struggle out of a nightmare in which every object was withering and shrinking away from her. (Chapter 28)

The 'maiden dream' has become a 'nightmare' in which the things that had mattered most appeared to have been totally unreal.

Dorothea's task is to fill the blank vacated by God, to reconstruct her world-view and to retain some kind of religion, as she tells Ladislaw in the well-known conversation in Chapter 39. In rebuking him for attempting to label her belief she insists that it is something she has found out for herself and adds, 'I have always been finding out my religion since I was a little girl'. It is unorthodox and vague and it involves a total rejection of everything Casaubon represents, so that he cannot help seeing that 'her wifely devotedness was like a penitential expiation of her unbelieving thoughts' (Chapter 42). She has to suffer the feeling of disenchantment a second time, when her faith in Ladislaw is threatened by the suspicion of his flirting with Rosamond. The language again is religious as she mourns 'her lost belief' and has to recapture a sense of belonging to a life of meaning and purpose. She is able finally to open her curtains, literally and symbolically, to look at the life outside. The light she sees is 'pearly', full of Biblical resonance. Her soul achieves the secularised heaven of solidarity:

> Far off in the bending sky was the pearly light; and she felt the largeness of the world and the manifold wakings of men to labour and endurance. She was part of that involuntary, palpitating life, and could neither look out on it from her luxurious shelter as a mere spectator, nor hide her eyes in selfish complaining. (Chapter 80)

Metaphors of light, along with those of fire, have been seen as belonging to a pattern of '"muted" apocalypse' by the critic whose dislike of her 'pseudo-religious philosophy' I quoted at the beginning of the paper.

Dorothea's religion, however, whether or not it is false, is perfectly clear. She ceases to pray to a God who no longer has any meaning, just as she ceased to believe in the husband she thought she was going to marry. She resigns herself to what cannot be altered and concentrates her energies, like a good Positivist, on those aspects of life, such as human character itself, which are modifiable. Her love for Ladislaw, her belief in him, functions in the same manner as Mary Garth's for Fred Vincy. It is a 'sort of baptism and consecration', which actually makes him behave better. Just as Ladislaw and Lydgate worship her, she strengthens her altruistic instincts by meditation on their needs, in a Positivist form of prayer. Whereas Fred Vincy incurs narrative disapproval in Chapter 24 by his failure to think of the effect on the Garths of his failure to meet his debts, 'for this exercise of the imagination on other people's needs is not common with hopeful young gentlemen', Dorothea delights the narrator by her constant exercise of her imaginative sympathies. Bored and emotionally unfulfilled by her married life in Lowick Manor she spends 'private hours' in her boudoir brooding over the imaginary sufferings of Will's grandmother. In this manner, we are told,

> the bare room had gathered within it those memories of an inward life which fill the air as with a cloud of good or bad angels, the invisible yet active forms of our spiritual falls. (Chapter 37)

The language might seem vague and obscure in its religiosity, but the significance of the angelic images is the same here as elsewhere in George Eliot's work. The invisible angels are explained in scientific terms as the physiological bearers of moral impulses.

The way in which Dorothea develops her ability to respond sympathetically to people in real situations by exercising her altruistic instincts in meditation is portrayed more clearly and more convincingly in Chapter 42. Casaubon has been shocked by Lydgate's warnings of possible heart failure and fails to respond to Dorothea's sympathetic arm. It is a seemingly trivial event but forms a crisis in their relationship which could easily turn to hatred. Dorothea retires to her boudoir, full of righteous indignation which gradually calms. After a lengthy 'meditative struggle. . . . the noble habit of the soul reasserts itself'. She realises why Casaubon must have behaved as he did. She sees an

> image of him like a shadowy monitor looking at her anger with sad remonstrance. It cost her a litany of pictured sorrows and silent cries that she might be the mercy of those sorrows. But the resolved submission did come.

She waits for him to leave the library and once more gives him her hand. The imaginative meditation has resulted in sympathetic action.

After Casaubon's death Dorothea remains emotionally 'imprisoned' at Lowick though 'her thought was going out over the lot of others' (Chapter 76). She thinks particularly of Lydgate's various trials and tribulations. And it is this imaginative participation in his troubles which enables her to help him when the opportunity arises and to overcome her personal vexation after interrupting Rosamond and Ladislaw for a second time. Her dark night of the soul gives way to a dawn of renewed altruism.

> All the active thought with which she had before been representing to herself the trials of Lydgate's lot, and this young marriage union which, like her own, seemed to have its hidden as well as evident troubles – all this vivid, sympathetic experience returned to her now as a power: it asserted itself as acquired knowledge asserts itself and will not let us see as we saw in the day of our ignorance. (Chapter 80)

Prayer and meditation have a function, it appears, even in a world from which God has disappeared.

Dorothea is not alone in her desire to construct hypothetical systems to explain the phenomena observable in the world. Lydgate too

> longed to demonstrate the more intimate relations of living structure, and help to define men's thought more accurately after the true order. (Chapter 15)

Like Dorothea, Lydgate wants to connect things, to bring them into ordered relation, to make sense of the world, though it is his weakness that he does not apply the same methods to all aspects of his life. He pursues his research into the causes of fever through disciplined imagination, 'combining and constructing with the clearest eye for probabilities and the fullest obedience to knowledge'. The role of the 'imagination' in scientific research is stressed here, as it was by George Eliot's husband, George Lewes,[10] but the mysteries it proposes are always tested against the evidence:

> he was enamoured of that arduous invention which is the very eye of research, provisionally framing its object and correcting it to more and more exactness of relation. (Chapter 16)

It is this 'exactness of relation' to which he aspires and the principle of verification on which he insists which distinguishes the Positivist approach to the problem of perception. He also venerates the scientific saints of Humanity, such as his beloved Vesalius, and meditates upon the virtues of that perfect image of womanhood, Dorothea, in the manner approved by Auguste Comte. He has been seen as a Positivist priest, who has to have a medical training and exercise with women a spiritual influence upon the temporal powers, the bankers of the community.[11]

Ladislaw is engaged in a similar use of imagination to penetrate the mysteries of the universe, to fill the ubiquitous blank, even though his approach is through the arts rather than the sciences. He is constantly depicted in terms of romantic symbols and images. He always associates Dorothea with an Aeolian Harp, the romantic symbol for divine inspiration (Chapters 9 and 21). He is likened to De Quincey in his experiments with opium (Chapter 10) while to

Brooke he appears as 'a sort of Burke with a leaven of Shelley' (Chapter 51), a comparison which is borne out by his theories of history and poetry. 'Romanticism', we are told at the beginning of Chapter 19, 'has helped to fill some dull blanks with love and knowledge.' It brings an active imagination to play on the lifeless objects of the world. But at the time in which the novel is set it is limited to 'certain long-haired German artists at Rome' and a few youths of other nationality who are brought into that 'spreading movement', including Will Ladislaw, who is conveniently at hand to explain to Dorothea the meaning of history and art.

Casaubon, it is clear, is quite unfitted to do this; all he can manage is a rehearsal of received opinion. He has no conception of the greatness of Humanity revealed in its progress through history:

> such capacity of thought and feeling as had ever been stimulated in him by the general life of mankind had long shrunk to a sort of dried preparation, a lifeless embalmment of knowledge.
>
> (Chapter 20)

When Ladislaw comes to dinner, at the beginning of Chapter 22, he is able to talk fluently about

> the very miscellaneousness of Rome, which made the mind flexible with constant comparison, and saved you from seeing the world's ages as a set of box-like partitions without vital connection . . . he confessed that Rome had given him quite a new sense of history as a whole; the fragments stimulated his imagination and made him constructive.

'Only connect', he argues, and the art-objects of Rome can acquire meaning. He attempts to tone down Dorothea's 'fanaticism of sympathy' with the miserable aspects of experience and outlines for her benefit a romantic theory of perception. The fusion of thought and feeling into a united perception of the 'vital connection' of things amounts to a faith capable of giving life meaning and of filling up the blank. When Dorothea asks him, in Chapter 39, what his religion is, by which she means 'not what you know about religion, but the belief which helps you most', his reply sounds vague: 'To love what is good and beautiful when I see it'. But it is based on a complex set of beliefs about the role of the imagination in perception. In the sense of 'binding' experience into unity, making sense of life, it is a religion, just as Caleb Garth's 'religious regard' for business, his belief in the conscientious fulfilment of contracts, is described as 'a philosophy' and 'a religion without the aid of theology' (Chapter 24).

None of the hypothetical systems constructed by the characters lay claim to objectivity. They are all self-consciously subjective, resting in some degree on the activity of the imagination, though verified by the test of experience. *Middlemarch* has been seen as an exercise in 'perspectivism', in which the narrator alone shares the perspective of all the characters and so achieves a degree of objectivity. This is certainly suggested by the metaphors of woven cloth. It is the narrator alone who can unravel the interwoven threads of human experience which make up the 'particular web' of the novel, in the famous image of the first paragraph of Chapter 15, and even he must resist 'that tempting range of relevancies called the universe'. There is an assumption, however, that the narrator is freed from the disturbing egoism of the characters and enabled to see the impartial direction of the scratches on the pier-glass. The narrator does not always resist the temptation to generalise on the nature of the experience but treats 'this particular web' as a synecdoche, a representative part from which to generalise about the whole. Just as the Western idea of history involves the investment of experience with meaning and significance, so the narrator of *Middlemarch* has been accused of assuming the role of historian which Fielding had claimed for the novelist in this opening paragraph of Chapter 15, *in spite of* the disclaimer, 'we belated historians must not linger after his example'.[12]

The narrative presence in *Middlemarch* is certainly stronger than in any of George Eliot's novels apart from *Adam Bede* where the chatty male persona is almost one of the characters. It performs, furthermore, a more important and authoritative function than it did in that novel, providing a unifying principle over and above the different cosmologies of the characters.[13] It is constantly intervening to invoke the reader's sympathy for the characters, especially for 'poor Mr Casaubon' and 'poor Dorothea'. It is 'the novel's prime builder of relations and prime restorer of order'. It is a voice of authority and comfort, benevolently avuncular, soothing the reader for the loss of an even greater and more authoritative figure.[14]

Whether the narrator of *Middlemarch* succeeds in consoling all lapsed believers for their lost faith in God is, I suspect, a matter of temperament. Most readers, in my experience, find *Middlemarch* a melancholy book. *Scribner's Monthly* reported the case of a thoughtful and sensitive young man, who rose from the perusal of *Middlemarch* with his eyes suffused with tears, exclaiming: 'My God! and is that all!'[15] George Eliot suggests that it is. The most that we can aspire to in the way of knowledge, in the words of an early review she wrote for the *Westminster*, is a 'hypothetical objectivity'[16] and, in the fields of feeling and action, the hope that our efforts will contribute in some degree to making the world a better place to live in. Many of the characters, of course, fail even in this. Dorothea, however, the latter-day Saint Theresa, with the same needs but not the same faith, is depicted in the final words of the novel as having achieved at least this. She has made no great name for herself:

> But the effect of her being on those around her was incalculably diffusive: for the growing good of the world is partly dependent on unhistoric acts; and that things are not so ill with you and me as they might have been, is half owing to the number who lived faithfully a hidden life, and rest in unvisited tombs.

It is a gloomy faith which refuses to allow itself illusory comfort. Things are only 'not so ill. . . . as they might have been'.

W. H. Mallock at the Metaphysical Society in the 1870s and A. J. Balfour at the Church Congress in 1888 posed the question, 'Is Life Worth Living?' if it is only supported by the beliefs of the Positivists in general and George Eliot in particular. What was there to celebrate, asked Balfour, in a Humanity which had sprung from 'pieces of disorganised jelly' from which

> Famine, Disease and Mutual Slaughter. . . . have gradually evolved, after infinite travail, a race with conscience enough to know that it is vile, and intelligence enough to know that it is insignificant.[17]

It apparently 'tranquillised' Henry Sidgwick in the midst of scepticism in the 1960s to feel that, 'After all, there is Positivism to fall back on'.[18] It does not seem to have tranquillised George Eliot or her readers. They were to turn by the end of the century to the less predictable and more passionate depiction of humanity offered by the great Russian novelists. George Eliot herself was to reinstate the sense of the transcendent and the mysterious in her final novel, *Daniel Deronda*, at the very least returning to the sort of compromise evident in her other novels. This uncertainty and spirit of compromise is also evident in the decisions which so annoyed the Positivists, to hold a vaguely Christian service for George Lewes at which a Unitarian minister 'half apologised for suggesting the possible immortality of some of our souls'[19] and to want for herself a burial service in Westminster Abbey. *Middlemarch* is braver and clearer than this, and for that reason almost unbearable for those with a religious temperament. It presents a world unredeemed by revelation in which religious needs must be met by entirely human means. 'Human kind', however, as George Eliot discovered and T. S. Eliot observed, 'cannot bear very much reality'. Preferring the blanks to the limited vision with which her narrator fills them, it has soon learnt to pick holes in the humanist web she wove.

NOTES

1. Richard Simpson, unsigned article, 'George Eliot's Novels', *Home and Foreign Review*, 3 (1863), 522–49, reprinted in *George Eliot: The Critical Heritage*, edited by David Carroll (London, 1971), pp. 221–50 (p. 226).
2. I. T. Ker, 'George Eliot's Rhetoric of Enthusiasm', *Essays in Criticism*, 26 (1976), 134–55 and Paul Hammond, 'George Eliot's Ersatz Christianity', *Theology*, 84 (1981), 190–6.
3. Mark Schorer, 'Fiction and the "Matrix of Analogy"', *Kenyon Review*, 2 (1949), 539–60, partially reprinted in *A Century of George Eliot Criticism*, edited by Gordon Haight (London, 1965), pp. 273–7.
4. For structuralist and post-structuralist attacks on *Middlemarch* see Colin McCabe, *James Joyce and the Revolution of the World* (London, 1978) pp. 14–22; J. Hillis Miller, 'Optic and Semiotic in *Middlemarch*', in *The Worlds of Victorian Fiction*, edited by Jerome H. Buckley (Cambridge, Mass. and London, 1975), pp. 125–45; and D. A. Miller, *Narrative and its Discontents* (Princeton, 1981), pp. 107–94. This actually contains a section entitled 'Narrative Three: God'.
5. 'George Eliot and Comtism', *London Quarterly Review*, 47 (1877), 447–71 (p. 453).
6. All references to George Eliot's novels are to the Cabinet edition (Edinburgh, 1878–85).
7. See Peter Jones, *Philosophy and the Novel* (Oxford, 1975), Chapter 1, 'Imagination and Egoism in Middlemarch'.
8. *Essays of George Eliot*, edited by Thomas Pinney (London and New York, 1963) pp. 158–89, 335–85.
9. Auguste Comte, *The Catechism of Positive Religion*, translated by Richard Congreve (London, 1858), pp. 46–51.
10. See Michael York Mason, '*Middlemarch* and Science: Problems of Life and Mind', *Review of English Studies*, n.s. 22 (1971), 151–69.
11. James F. Scott, 'George Eliot, Positivism, and the Social Vision of *Middlemarch*', *Victorian Studies*, 16 (1972) 59–67.

12. See Miller, 'Optic and Semiotic . . .' and 'Narrative and History', *Journal of English Literary History*, 41 (1974), 455–73.

13. David Carroll, 'Unity through Analogy: An Interpretation of *Middlemarch*', *Victorian Studies*, 2 (1959), 305–16.

14. U. C. Knoepflmacher, '*Middlemarch*: An Avuncular View', *Nineteenth Century Fiction*, 30 (1975), 53–81.

15. *Scribner's Monthly*, 21 (1881), p. 791 quoted in Carroll, *George Eliot: The Critical Heritage*, p. 29.

16. Pinney, *Essays*, p. 33.

17. A. J. Balfour, *The Religion of Humanity* (London, 1888), p. 24. For an account of Mallock's attacks on Positivism and George Eliot see John Lucas, 'Tilting at the Moderns: W. H. Mallock's Criticisms of the Positive Spirit', *Renaissance and Modern Studies*, 10 (1966), 88–143.

18. J. B. Scheewind, *Sidgwick's Ethics and Victorian Moral Philosophy* (Oxford, 1977), p. 23.

19. F. Locker-Lampson, *My Confidences* (London, 1896), pp. 314–16.

9 'Heaven's Lidger Here': Herbert's *Temple* and Seventeenth-century Devotion

Helen Wilcox

The influence of George Herbert's posthumous volume of lyrics, *The Temple* (1633), on seventeenth-century readers, poets and preachers was widespread and profound. Herbert's popularity may be discerned in a great variety of forms and expressions from sources across the range of political, religious and literary positions in that most divided and turbulent century. When David Lloyd wrote in 1668 that 'all are ravished' by Herbert's poems, his 'all' was appropriately inclusive and his 'ravished' a suitably unspecific metaphor, encompassing at least didactic, literary and devotional delight in reading *The Temple*.[1] From the mass of evidence of reactions to Herbert among his early readers, this paper will examine two major elements in devotional response; these indicate that Herbert's admirers came to rely upon his example and his work in a way closely resembling Herbert's own attitude to the Bible. *The Temple*, regarded by modern readers as a triumph of the literary imagination, was perceived in its own day as primarily a source of religious inspiration and a model for practical devotion. It became no ordinary devotional text but, it seems, a kind of seventeenth-century Scripture.

It is important to recall that *The Temple* itself originated on the borders of literature and devotion. Immensely gifted as a poet, Herbert was fearful of indulging his talent, of 'weaving' himself rather than God into 'the sense' of his art.[2] Walton's *Life* asserts that

Herbert's only reason for passing on his 'little Book' was its didactic value; the work should be burnt, unless it might 'turn to the advantage of any dejected pour Soul'.[3] The purpose and the manner of the poems were to be the exalting of holiness. Herbert's belief – expressed with disarming wit and skill – was that a 'true Hymne' required love more than rhyme:

> The finenesse which a hymne or psalme affords,
> Is, when the soul unto the lines accords.[4]

In his prose handbook for the complete country parson, Herbert again stressed piety above style:

> The character of his Sermon is Holiness;
> he is not witty, or learned, or eloquent, but Holy.[5]

Not surprisingly, the deepest influence on Herbert's own work was not strictly literary – though traces of Sidney, Campion and Donne may be found – but the 'book of books', the Bible (p. 228). In its combination of the practical and the visionary, the complex and the challengingly simple, *The Temple* was much indebted to Holy Scripture.

In his sonnets celebrating the Bible – God's written word, the meeting point of the religious and the literary – Herbert revealed the special power and delight which he found in scripture. The first sonnet in particular expresses its glories:

> Oh Book! infinite sweetnesse! let my heart
>> Suck ev'ry letter, and a hony gain,
>> Precious for any grief in any part;
> To cleare the breast, to mollifie all pain.
> Thou art all health, health thriving till it make
>> A full eternitie: thou art a masse
>> Of strange delights, where we may wish & take.
> Ladies, look here; this is the thankful glasse,
> That mends the lookers eyes: this is the well
>> That washed what it shows. Who can indeare
>> Thy praise too much? thou art heav'ns Lidger here,
> Working against the states of death and hell.
>> Thou art joyes handsell: heav'n lies flat in thee,
>> Subject to ev'ry mounters bended knee.
>>> ('The H. Scriptures' (I), p. 58)

Two features of the Bible dominate here: the work as representative of heaven (a 'handsell' of eternal joy, a map of heaven itself which 'lies flat' in its words) and as a store of 'sweetnesse', source of 'all health' and a 'masse of strange delights'. Typically, Herbert stressed both the closeness of heaven (that 'easie quick accesse'[6] of man to God) and the benevolence of God's book, which is no 'dead thing'[7] but alive and efficacious.

These two central qualities of the Bible – what it represents and what it offers – are combined in the punning phrase, 'Heav'ns Lidger here'. The primary meaning of 'Lidger' is an ambassador;[8] the Bible is God's envoy on earth, actively combating the 'states' of 'death and hell'. But implied within 'Lidger' is also the variant 'ledger', the Bible as a book in which are recorded God's trans-actions with man. With precision characteristic of Herbert's rhetorical skill, the double thrust of his positive responses to the Bible is contained in this unusual word. And just as Herbert discerned a dual function in Scripture – active but comforting, specific yet inclusive – so it seems that Herbert's followers reacted to him with a similar pattern of devotional response. Herbert himself, as poet and priest, was seen as an ambassador of God, combating evil in his verse and in his life; and *The Temple* offered a record of Herbert's experience with God from which others might gain instruction and joy. As both 'Lidger' and 'ledger', Herbert entered the devotional lives of his seventeenth-century readers.

The autobiographical tenor of *The Temple*, set alongside the pious rules of *A Priest to the Temple* and, later, Walton's *Life* (1670), ensured that the devotional pattern set by Herbert was more than merely literary. He himself, poet and priest, became a didactic 'type', a man whose 'Character, and Rule of Holy Life'[9] made him a 'Lidger' of God. As early as 1642, Thomas Fuller modelled his character of a 'faithfull Minister' on Herbert,[10] and during the century several other handbooks on priesthood and preaching cited his example.[11] The response to Herbert as active divine envoy was also, in itself, practical; Bishop Thomas Ken shaped his life and ministry round Herbert's example, from the writing and singing of poems to the sharing of Sunday lunch with the poor in his parish.[12] The philosopher-poet John Norris of Bemerton went so far as to take the same living as Herbert to keep the spiritual succession alive.[13]

Every age appears to need its new typology, and none more so than the century in England after the Reformation. The creation of typology, as Herbert himself was aware, is a continuing process of reading and acting:

> For as the Jews of Old by Gods command
> 　　　Travell'd, and saw no town;
> So now each Christian hath his journeys spann'd:
> 　　　Their storie pennes and sets us down.
>
> 　　　　　　　('The Bunch of Grapes', p. 128)

Herbert's 'story' – his life and writing – 'penned' his readers' lives
for them to understand, in the pattern of typological tradition.
Herbert became a near-contemporary ideal of the poet-parson,
from the reading of whose art and life others might gain insight into
the nature of God.

　As well as pointing to the present in this way, Herbert was seen by
his readers to be taking them back to less tainted days. Though this
often recalled recent memories of Anglican piety before the Civil
War, to Walton and others, Herbert's life was also a timeless
'pattern' of 'primitive piety'.[14] His holiness was unquestioned. A
mid-century Puritan reader referred to him as 'blessed Herbert';[15]
to a late-century Presbyterian he was 'Divine Herbert'.[16] James
Duport, the Restoration Cambridge divine, expressed the desire to
canonise Herbert but, as a true Anglican (and indeed following
Herbert's own restraint in 'To all Angels and Saints'), he discreetly
held back from this questionable Catholic honour.[17] But as early as
1638, Robert Codrington had no doubts about Herbert's worthiness
of a saintly title:

> View a true Poet, whose bare lines
> Include more goodnesse than some shrines.
> Wee'le canonize him, and what er
> Befalls, style him heavens Chorister.[18]

Other writers offered more specific parallels in Church tradition.
While one distinguished Herbert as '*Prophet*, and *Apostle*',[19] a more
colourful Englishman of the 1640s claimed that

> [Herbert's] pious Life and Death have converted me to a full
> beleefe that there is a *St. George*.[20]

In view of the closeness of *The Temple* to the mood of the Psalms, it
is perhaps not surprising that Herbert was most frequently compared with David, the Biblical singer of poems; thus Herbert
became 'our sweet Psalmist', another 'Royall Prophet'.[21] Barnabus

Oley, Herbert's early biographer, pointed out the significance of the title of his collection of lyrics in calling Herbert the 'sweet singer of the Temple'.[22] The non-conformist Oliver Heywood later expanded this phrase, with the poignancy of his own personal exile, into 'the incomparable sweet singer of our *Israel*'.[23] Samuel Woodford wrote in 1670 that Herbert had known the 'Chords' of David's harp 'More perfectly, than any Child of Verse below';[24] and Ralph Knevet, the Norfolk parson who was one of Herbert's early poetic imitators, stressed that it was only Herbert who 'rightly knew to touch Davids Harpe'.[25]

Knevet was also one of a number of Herbert's seventeenth-century followers who, almost blasphemously, identified him with Christ. He took the trouble, for example, to explain that Herbert's surname meant 'Bright Lord' (p. 279). Cardell Goodman, a poet much inspired by Herbert in the 1640s, wrote of him as his 'Leader',[26] and others referred to him as their 'Master', the term reserved by Herbert for Christ himself.[27] John Dunton, as late as 1694, described 'dearest Herbert' as

> O *more* than *Man*! O *All-divine*!
> *Jesus* thy *Master* was, and *thou* art *mine*.[28]

An even more explicit divine parallel is found in Daniel Baker's poem, 'On Mr. George Herbert's Sacred Poems, called The Temple', in which the three traditional roles of Christ – prophet, priest and king – are, as it were, lent to Herbert.

> Hail, heav'nly Bard, to whom great LOVE has giv'n
>   (His mighty Kindness to express)
> To bear his Three mysterious Offices;
> Prophet, and Priest on Earth thou wast, and now
>   a King in Heav'n.
>   There thou dost reign, and there
>   Thy Bus'ness is the same 'twas here,
> And thine old Songs thou singest o'er agen:
>   The Angels and the Heav'nly Quire
>   Gaze on thee, and admire
> To hear such Anthems from an earthly Lyre,
> Their own Hymns almost equall'd by an human Pen.[29]

Here, indeed, Herbert's function as divine ambassador is of deep significance, comparable even with the roles, other than sacrificial, of Christ himself.

Why was Herbert so especially appealing as a devotional type, a holy 'Lidger' on earth? As Baker points out earlier in his epic celebration of Herbert's poems, 'mighty *Herbert*' had with 'holy Zeal' rescued poetry (and, of course, his own career) from the grip of the profane world (p. 84). In doing so, he returned verse to its original sacred purpose, and reasserted its Biblical function. Even the most determinedly literary of Herbert's seventeenth-century commentators noted that *The Temple* represented more than a new poetic style: it struck the reader with the freshness of its spiritual intent. Thus major followers of Herbert, such as Vaughan and Knevet, changed not only their poetic manner as a result of reading *The Temple*, but also their subject-matter; they became 'converts' to devotional poetry. Vaughan hailed Herbert as

> the first, that with any effectual success attempted a *diversion* of this foul and over flowing *stream* [of 'lascivious fictions'] . . . the blessed man, *Mr. George Herbert*, whose holy *life* and *verse* gained many pious *Converts* (of whom I am the least) . . .[30]

Herbert had, it seemed, succeeded in making poetry into 'lawful bait' for spiritual purposes, as graphically explained by Joshua Poole in 1657:

> Many have been, which Pulpits did eschew,
> Converted from the Poets reading pew,
> And those that seldome do salute the porch
> Of Solomon, will come to Herbert's Church;
> For as that English Lyrick sweetly sings,
> Whilst angels danc'd upon his trembling strings,
> A Verse may find him who a Sermon flies,
> And turn delight into a Sacrifice.
> Then let the poet use his lawfull bait,
> To make men swallow what they else would hate.[31]

The two lines quoted here by Poole from Herbert's 'Church-porch' formed the most popular single quotation from *The Temple* in the seventeenth century. Herbert's devotional niche was as the saintly writer of a work which, as one admirer put it, 'gain'd more Souls to God' than any other prose or verse except, presumably, the Bible.[32]

The Temple was thus fulfilling an active missionary role, combining delight in reading with practical religious results.

This scriptural function of *The Temple* leads us to the second major element of Herbert's devotional influence – his book as a new heavenly 'Ledger'. The evidence suggests that seventeenth-century readers found in *The Temple* a book parallel to the Bible as a written record of an individual's 'spiritual Conflicts'.[33] Richard Baxter wrote of *The Temple* that '*Heart-work* and *Heaven-work* make up his Books'.[34] What better summary could there be of the Biblical interplay between human will and divine purposes? Baxter, a moderate non-conformist, was not alone in finding a Biblical level of inspiration in *The Temple*. James Duport, orthodox Restoration Anglican, praised *The Temple* as second only to the Bible, on the grounds that no other book, 'God's Word apart, is so sacred or good'.[35] At the other extreme of political and religious attitudes, the mystic Peter Sterry, chaplain to Cromwell, recommended that his wayward son should read the Bible and 'Mr. Herbert'.[36]

It was common for *The Temple* to be placed alongside the Bible as catechistical reading for seventeenth-century children and servants, and it appeared in Downing's *Young Christians Library* as late as 1710.[37] These recommendations implied that Herbert's writing combined simplicity with profundity, in an acceptable, indeed Biblical way. At the other end of the intellectual scale, Herbert's *Temple* was read with the same scholarly care as was afforded to Holy Scripture. Archbishop Robert Leighton's copy of *The Temple* contains handwritten marginal notes from the Church Fathers,[38] and in 1715 Herbert's poems were treated to a full Biblical-style commentary by George Ryley.[39] His 'discourse upon each poem' not only offered a breakdown of the structure and paraphrase of the meaning, but – exactly as in seventeenth-century Biblical commentaries – a practical devotional response. Herbert's poems were also adapted towards the end of the century for use as congregational hymns;[40] as were the Psalms of the first David; like the Bible, *The Temple* became the property, as it were, of all the faithful.

The title of *The Temple* invited Biblical comparisons. Donne referred to Scripture as 'Gods fairest Temple',[41] and Robert Boyle wrote of the Bible in 1663 as

a Matchless Temple, where I delight to be, to contemplate the Beauty, the Symmetry, and the Magnificence of the Structure, and to Encrease my Awe, and Excite my Devotion to the Deity there Preached and Ador'd.[42]

It was also crucially important to the popularity of *The Temple* during this divided century that its title metaphor – and its contents – allowed various interpretations appropriate to a range of religious beliefs and practices. The Cornishman John Polwhele, for example, had a vividly Laudian impression of *The Temple*:

> Statelye thy Pillers bee,
> Westwards the Crosse, the Quier and
>   thine Alter Eastward Stande,
>   where Is most Catholique Confrmitie . . .[43]

Herbert's Puritan readers, on the other hand, identified closely with his personal religion, his intimate friendship with Christ. *The Temple* represented to them the individual soul where, St Paul asserted, 'the Spirit of God dwelleth' (I Corinthians 3.16). Hence selective readings and interpretation made *The Temple*, like the Bible, available to justify and enrich a variety of devotional approaches.

The attitude of seventeenth-century readers of *The Temple* was thus similar in outline to the contemporary combination of freedom and reverence in respect of the Bible. The parallel, however, continues in the detail of specific responses; *The Temple* was used – or abused – by its earlier readers as a source of the four spiritual aids which Herbert found in the Bible. As he wrote of the country parson,

> The chief and top of his knowledge consists in the book of books, the storehouse and magazene of life and comfort, the holy Scriptures. There he sucks, and lives. In the Scriptures hee findes four things; Precepts for life, Doctrines for knowledge, Examples for illustration, and Promises for comfort: These he hath digested severally.[44]

While Herbert found 'precepts for life' in the pages of the Bible, his own readers extracted them from the poems of *The Temple*. In printed books and commonplace notebooks throughout the century, there appear lists of 'precepts' taken from 'Mr. Herbert'.[45] Among the many designed for young people was an 'A to Z' of couplets from *The Temple* entitled 'Youth's Alphabet: or, Herbert's

Morals'.[46] Herbert's 'precepts' also appeared, like Scriptural verses, on a wall-tablet in at least one seventeenth-century home. John Ferrar, brother of Nicholas Ferrar of Little Gidding, advised his son in 1648 to remember daily

> those tow Divine verses of your Unkells Most Deare Freind [Herbert] . . . And I shall leave you a Table to be hunge up in the house where in these Verses shalbe written.[47]

It had evidently become clear by 1656 that *The Temple* was also being read as a 'storehouse' of 'doctrines for knowledge', since the edition of that year appeared with an 'Alphabeticall Table for ready finding-out of places'.[48] The index is based on theological subjects and suggests that *The Temple* was being regarded, and used, as a spiritual reference book. Some readers discerned the substance of doctrine and controversy in *The Temple*. Barnabus Oley wrote that those who read 'attendingly' would find

> not onely the excellencies of Scripture Divinite, & choice passages of the Fathers bound up in Meetre; but the Doctrine of *Rome* also finely and strongly confuted.[49]

The many writers, too, who imitated Herbert's style and doctrines used occasional lines from his poems as received knowledge, the spiritual truth towards which their own art was leading them.

In this way, Herbert's work also supplied, like the Bible, 'examples for illustration'. Seventeenth-century prose writers frequently turned to Herbert to round off an argument or a treatise. This is common not only among the nonconformists, such as Heywood and Baxter, but also in works not overtly spiritual, such as Walton's *Complete Angler*:

> But Sir, lest this Discourse may seem tedious, I shall give it a sweet conclusion out of that holy Poet Mr. *George Herbert*, his divine Contemplation on God's Providence.[50]

Herbert's weighty sayings were cited in the same way as Biblical authority, to prove a point in a sermon or other morally serious work. The nonconformist divine Matthew Henry even gave examples from *The Temple* in his 'Friendly Admonition to Drunkards and Tipplers'.[51] And in using *The Temple* for both doctrines and examples – however strange the context! – seventeenth-century readers and writers absorbed Herbert's distinctive style as well as the spiritual ideas and experiences described. As is the case with Biblical language, the devotional usage of a text very easily becomes a literary influence on the user.

In the end, it is impossible to separate these literary and devotional aspects, since *The Temple*, like the Bible, was a 'masse of strange delights' to its readers, who would hardly have wished to distinguish between aesthetic and spiritual delight. The 'promises for comfort' which the poems undoubtedly offered to their readers, were comforting in their expression as well as their doctrinal 'promise'. When he first received the manuscript of *The Temple*, Nicholas Ferrar welcomed it for its beauty and its truth, in terms appropriate to the Bible itself:

> The wch when [he] had many and many a time read over, and embraced and kissed again and again, he sayd, he could not sufficiently admire it, as a rich Jewell, and most worthy to be in ye hands and hearts of all true Christians . . .[52]

The Preface to the Authorised version of the Bible referred to Scripture as a treasury of 'precious things', 'good gold' and 'true pearle'.[53]

When Ferrar released to the public, in 1633, the book which he so much admired, it won similarly ecstatic praise, again reminiscent of responses to the Bible, for its heavenly promise and comfort. In 1647, John Legate enthused,

> *Herbert!* whóm when I read
> I stoop at Stars that shine below my head.[54]

In his second sonnet to 'The H. Scriptures', Herbert wrote of the Bible as a glorious 'Constellation', a 'book of starres' which 'lights to eternall blisse'.[55] Thus Legate saw *The Temple* as a new scripture, a new heavenly constellation comfortingly in our midst. And the last great expression of devotional response to *The Temple* in the seventeenth-century manner – a poem by John Reynolds published in 1725 – echoed Herbert's inclusive description of the Bible as a 'magazene of life and comfort'.[56] He praised *The Temple* as

> Rich magazine of health! Where's found
> Specific balm for ev'ry wound![57]

Devotional texts were required to heal as well as to inspire.

Thus the model for the devotional use of *The Temple* in the seventeenth century appears to correspond, in almost every detail, with Herbert's own response to the Bible. *The Temple* was a heavenly 'Ledger' to its early readers, in all the ways in which Herbert described God's own record-book; and Herbert himself acted as a new type of piety, a poetic ambassador or 'Lidger' representing God in earthly deeds and words. The two senses of Herbert's pivot word are in fact united by the preservation of the memory of Herbert the man, in the words of his own celebrated works. Though Walton's *Life* coloured the legend (after 1670), it was Herbert's holiness and experience as expressed in his art which formed the basis of devotional responses to Herbert the man. That man was, after all, the 'sweet singer'[58] who renewed the spirituality and Biblical purpose of poetry. When Codrington wrote in 1638 that Herbert should be canonised, he was the source of his saintliness in 'his bare lines' (see note 18); Herbert's 'shrine' contained not bones but words. His piety might have been 'primitive', but his entry into devotional tradition was new in its association with his book rather than any miraculous acts. In the creation of a non-Catholic tradition of devotion, the efficacy of Herbert's words, alongside those of Holy Scripture, was clearly of vital importance. As Cranmer had written a century earlier, the words of the Bible formed the 'most holy relic that remaineth upon earth'.[59]

The consequence of such practical, Biblical-style admiration for *The Temple* was that Herbert's readers made the work very much their own – by selective reading, by quotation, adaptation, even absorption into their own works and spiritual lives. In fact, their initial response appears to have depended upon their finding themselves expressed in Herbert's work. As Reynolds commented on *The Temple*,

> Strange! how each fellow-saint's surpris'd
> To see himself anatomiz'd!
> The *Sion*'s mourner breathes thy strains,
> Sighs thee, & in thy notes complains;
> Amaz'd, & yet refresh'd to see
> His wounds, drawn to the life, in thee![60]

Herbert's words were an 'anatomy' of every Christian's experience; his language set the reader in a refreshingly new perspective.

Herbert found a similarly mutual experience of learning in the reading of the Bible. In 'The H. Scriptures' (II) he wrote of finding and understanding his own 'secrets' in the doubleness of Biblical texts:

> Such are thy secrets, which my life makes good,
> 		And comments on thee: for in ev'ry thing
> 		Thy words do find me out, and parallels bring,
> And in another make me understood.
>
> 								(p. 58)

Reader and text offer a gloss on each other; devotional reading, whether of the Bible or *The Temple*, becomes a partnership, a process of mutual learning.

This method of reading *The Temple* is expressed most fully in Vaughan's poem 'The Match', in which he not only praises Herbert's poems in profoundly Biblical terms, but undertakes to 'join hands' with him in a shared spiritual endeavour:

> Dear friend! whose holy, ever-living lines
> 		Have done much good
> 	To many, and have checkt my blood,
> My fierce, wild blood that still heaves, and inclines,
> 		But is still tam'd
> 	By those bright fires which thee inflam'd;
> Here I joyn hands, and thrust my stubborn heart
> 		Into thy *Deed*,
> 	There from no *Duties* to be freed,
> And if hereafter *youth*, or *folly* thwart
> 		And claim their share,
> 	Here I renounce the pois'nous ware. [61]

The range of seventeenth-century devotional attitudes to Herbert is found compressed in this poem. Vaughan addresses Herbert using the endearment reserved by Herbert for Christ; *The Temple* is described in terms ('holy, ever-living lines') appropriate to God's word in the Bible. The result is an association by the reader, Vaughan, with the work, *The Temple*, in a partnership of devotion. Vaughan sees himself in the perspective offered by Herbert's writing, and endeavours to share in the spiritual intention of *The Temple*. Vaughan's intensely creative response epitomises the method of devotional reading common among Herbert's seventeenth-century admirers.

The devotional use of *The Temple* is revealing, in all its detail, of seventeenth-century Protestant needs and attitudes, as well as of qualities in Herbert's verse often overlooked by modern literary criticism. It also raises important critical questions about the process of reading and inspiration, which are highlighted in the way in which Herbert's early followers made use of their reading of *The Temple*. Herbert's poetry, as a kind of new Scripture, was absorbed not only into his readers' experience, their moral understanding and their private devotions, but into their commonplace books, diaries, sermons, treatises and poems. Herbert himself had found that 'sweetnesse' was 'readie penn'd' in God's word, waiting to be copied out (p. 103); Cardell Goodman, and many other followers of Herbert, found their 'Coppy' in *The Temple*.[62] The hand which guided Herbert to hold his 'quill' was God's;[63] Christopher Harvey and other imitators felt the 'hand' of Herbert directing their writing.[64] When a writer – such as Herbert himself – draws heavily upon Biblical inspiration, it is regarded as a legitimate part of an individual imaginative act. But when a writer finds inspiration – stylistic and spiritual – in *The Temple* and uses its phrases and features in his own work, then it is perhaps regarded as a sign of lack of original imagination, or indeed as plagiarism.

This literary judgement of Herbert's followers brings into focus the difficulties associated with devotional literature. The reading of a literary text, *The Temple*, in the manner of a devotional response to Scripture challenges our sense of literary imagination, the clear distinction of text from reader; devotional reading becomes a kind of spiritual and linguistic partnership. The absorption of elements of a pseudo-Biblical text like *The Temple* into a new work challenges our sense of literary individuality, the clear distinction of text from text; devotion breaks down the barriers of ownership of created material. As Herbert wrote of The Bible,

> heav'n lies flat in thee,
> Subject to ev'ry mounters bended knee.
>
> (p. 58)

The Temple offers 'heavenly' material which , though approached in devotion, on 'bended knee', is yet vulnerable, 'subject to' the reader who uses the book as a means to mount to that heavenly end. The seventeenth-century devotional use of *The Temple* as a contemporary Scripture thus raises the status of the literary work – suggests that it is divine – and at the same time challenges its inviolability as an individual imaginative creation. In a fascinating inversion of the central Christian paradox, the book is exalted in order to make it the more accessible.

NOTES

1. David Lloyd, *Memoires* (London, 1668), p. 619.
2. 'Jordan' (II), *The Works of George Herbert*, edited by F. E. Hutchinson (Oxford, 1941), pp. 102–3. All Herbert references are to this edition.
3. Izaak Walton, *The Life of Mr. George Herbert* (London, 1670), p. 74.
4. 'A tree Hymne', p. 168.
5. Herbert, p. 233.
6. 'Prayer' (II), p. 103.
7. John Milton, *Areopagitica, Complete Prose Works*, edited by D. M. Wolfe *et al.* (New Haven, 1953–4), II, 492.
8. *OED* 'ledger', definitions 6 and 7.
9. Herbert, p. 223.
10. Thomas Fuller, *The Holy State* (London, 1642), II, 83–7.
11. Jeremy Collier, *Miscellanies* (London, 1694), pp. 40, 42; John Edwards *The Preacher* (London, 1705), p. 202.
12. W. Hawkins, *Life of . . . Thomas Ken* (London, 1713), pp. 5, 14–15, 24.
13. F. J. Powicke, *A Dissertation on John Norris of Bemerton* (Liverpool, 1894), pp. 20–1.
14. Izaak Walton, *Lives* (London, 1670), dedicatory epistle, A3^v.
15. Giles Firmin, *Stabilising against Quaking* (London, 1656), pp. 14–15.
16. John Bryan, *Dwelling with God* (London, 1670), p. 274.
17. James Duport, *Musae Subsecivae* (Cambridge, 1676), p. 372.
18. Robert Codrington, poetic fragment in Bodleian MS Eng. poet. f 27, p. 296.
19. Anonymous commendatory poem, *The Temple* (10th edition, London, 1674), T2^r.
20. Philo-Dicaeus, *The Standard of Equalitie* (London, 1647), dedicatory epistle, A3^v.
21. Daniel Baker, *Poems upon Several Occasions* (London, 1697), p. 86; George Daniel of Beswick, *Selected Poems*, edited by Thomas B. Stroup (Lexington, Kentucky, 1959), pp. 66–7.
22. Barnabus Oley, 'A Prefatory View of the Life and Vertues of the Authour', *Herbert's Remains* (London, 1652), a 11^v.
23. Oliver Heywood, *The Sure Mercies of David* (London, 1672) p. 119.
24. Samuel Woodford, commendatory poem to Walton's *Life of Mr. George Herbert* (London, 1670), A3^r.
25. Ralph Knevet, *Shorter Poems*, edited by Amy M. Charles (Ohio, 1966), p. 281.
26. Cardell Goodman, *Beawty in Raggs*, edited by R. J. Roberts (Reading, 1958), xiv.

27. Herbert, p. 4.
28. *The Athenian Mercury*, 6 January 1694.
29. Baker, *Poems*, pp. 87–8.
30. Henry Vaughan, *Works*, edited by L. C. Martin (Oxford, 1957), p. 391.
31. Joshua Poole, *The English Parnassus* (London, 1657), A7ᵛ; lines 7–8 of this extract are lines 5–6 of Herbert's 'Church-porch'.
32. Anonymous commendatory poem, *The Temple* (10th edition, London, 1674), T3ᵛ.
33. Walton, *Life*, p. 74.
34. Richard Baxter, *Poetical Fragments* (London, 1681), A7ᵛ.
35. Duport, *Musae Subsecivae*, p. 358: 'Nec sanctior alter,/Nec melior mihi, post Biblia Sacra, Liber'.
36. Letter from Peter Sterry, in Emmanuel College, Cambridge, MS 290, p. 43.
37. Joseph Downing, *The Young Christian's Library* (London, 1710), p. 15.
38. The volume, which appears to have been missing for over a hundred years, is described in A. B. Grosart's edition of *The Poetical Works of George Herbert* (Blackburn, 1874), II, cxxxiv.
39. George Ryley, *Mr. Herbert's Temple and Church Militant Explained and Improved* (1714/5), in Bodleian MS Rawlinson D199.
40. See, for example, *Select Hymns Taken Out of Mr. Herbert's Temple* (London, 1697).
41. John Donne, *Essays in Divinity*, edited by Evelyn M. Simpson (Oxford, 1952), p. 40.
42. Robert Boyle, *Some Considerations Touching the Style of the Holy Scriptures* (London, 1663), p. 78.
43. John Polwhele, 'On Mr. Herbert's Devine poeme the church', Bodleian MS Eng. poet f16, fol. 11ʳ.
44. Herbert, p. 228.
45. See, for example, the commonplace book of Dame Sarah Cowper (c. 1700), in Hertfordshire Record Office MS D/EP F44, p. 348.
46. Thomas White, *A Little Book for Little Children* (London, 1671?), pp. 91–3.
47. *The Ferrar Papers*, edited by B. Blackstone (Cambridge, 1938), p. 303.
48. *The Temple* (7th edition, London, 1656), I1ʳ–K6ʳ.
49. Oley, 'Prefatory View', b1ᵛ–b2ʳ.
50. Izaak Walton, *The Complete Angler* (2nd edition, London, 1655), p. 43.
51. Matthew Henry, *Works* (London, 1726), p. 371.
52. *The Ferrar Papers*, p. 59.
53. *The Holy Bible* (1611), B4ᵛ, B2ʳ, B2ᵛ.
54. Commendatory poem in Christopher Harvey, *The Synagogue* (2nd edition, London, 1647), p. 88.
55. Herbert, p. 58.
56. Ibid., p. 228.
57. John Reynolds, *A View of Death* . . . (London, 1725), p. 112.
58. Oley, 'Prefatory View', a 11ᵛ.
59. Harold R. Willoughby, *The First Authorized English Bible and the Cranmer Preface* (Chicago, 1942), p. 45. I am grateful to members of the Conference seminar, particularly the Revd. Ben de la Mare, for stimulating discussion on this point.
60. Reynolds, *A View of Death* . . . , p. 111.

61. Vaughan, *Works*, pp. 434–5. The 'deed' refers to Herbert's 'Obedience'.
62. Goodman, *Beawty in Raggs*, xiv.
63. Herbert, p. 116.
64. Harvey, *The Synagogue*, A1ᵛ.

10 Exegesis: Literary and Divine

Dominic Baker-Smith

Whenever we talk about inspiration or imagination, or what Sir Thomas Elyot calls with a certain Anglo-Saxon embarrassment, 'celestial instinction', we imply the intervention into material life of some mental 'set' or vision which illuminates; and any discussion of these themes faces us with questions about the relationship between human intentions and their physical expression in time. This holds true for a sacrament as much as for the art of writing. Indeed the ambiguity of my title can be taken as a hermeneutic parable for the tormented battleground between letter and spirit; it points to a cluster of possible interests but gives little direct indication of its aim.

In the year 1022 we hear of certain heretics burnt at Orleans, in part because of their disparaging remarks about the qualifications of the examining clergy. This may strike any professional academic as a wholly reasonable outcome, but the case points beyond outraged self-esteem to a darker problem. The heretics rejected the arguments of their judges as human fabrications 'written on the skins of animals', in contrast to 'the law written in the inner man by the Holy Spirit'. Now that derogatory formula about animal skins appears in a number of medieval contexts: there is a nice example in the clash over Investitures between Henry I and Anselm when the royal supporters choose to dismiss an inconvenient letter of Pope Paschal II with a *reductio ad litteram*. What was it in fact but 'the skins of ewes blackened with ink and weighted with a little lump of lead'? It does not leave much scope for hermeneutics.[1]

These medieval episodes are extreme illustrations of that tension between human utterance and its physical medium which is as fully recognised in II Corinthians 3. 3–6, as it is in Plato's *Phaedrus*. In a conference on inspiration I need not remind you of St Paul's distinction between letter and spirit, but it may be useful to recall Socrates' complaint that:

> once a thing is put in writing, the composition . . . drifts all over the place, getting into the hands not only of those who understand it, but equally of those who have no business with it; it doesn't know how to address the right people and not address the wrong. And when it is ill-treated and unfairly abused it always needs its parent to come to its help, being unable to defend or help itself.
>
> (*Phaedrus*, 275 d–e)

Obviously this has relevance to modern concern about authorial control, and Henry I's supporters preferred oral testimony to that papal letter. But the feature that marks out Socrates from the traditional image of the sage is his recognition that wisdom is something sought after rather than possessed; it is not resident in signs or formulae or even sages but is accessible in the moment of interpretation. His admission of his own ignorance extends into his distrust of written language, since it is only in confrontation with a reality outside ourselves, in the recognition of a context that we no longer wholly control, that meaning can be generated or wisdom achieved. Writing is orphaned speech and like all orphans it is vulnerable.

Before interpretation can occur authority must be established and that is one reason why Socrates' complaint may be said to anticipate the doubts of the pre-Reformation church about the vernacular Bible. It is not wholly facetious to adapt Whitehead's famous dictum about Plato and claim that the history of the Christian *Church* is a series of footnotes to the drama of biblical translation. As Northrop Frye has recently reminded us, Christianity is uniquely dependent on translation.[2] Christ is shown in the Gospels as an interpreter of the Scriptures, while in *Acts* his life and death are controlling symbols which render the Scriptures in a new language (Acts 2. 22–31). Paul Ricoeur formulated the principle clearly when he wrote that 'Religion . . . is the place where the manifestation of the Spirit and the death of its representation may be seen'.[3] The rending of the Temple veil in Matthew's account of the crucifixion marks the death of a representative scheme which has ceased to be manifest and has become a dead end, an idol. The rather hostile semantic load which we now give to the phrase 'institutional religion' can reasonably be compared to T. E. Hulme's definition of prose as 'a museum of metaphor'. Indeed that definition is the shaping principle adopted with remorseless detail by Rabelais in his anti-Roman *Quart Livre* when Pantagruel visits Papimanie and enters the shrine of the Decretals. It is no accident that anti-papal satire, from Erasmus to John Donne, tends to depict the Roman vision of Catholicism as that of a self-contained system which no longer needs God, a signifier that has lost its signification. The simile of the canonists, 'quasi Deus in terra', is made a literal truth.

The key point that concerns me here is the manner in which revolt against such late medieval religious legalism (or literalism) is deeply marked by the figure of St Augustine. I am thinking here not of the Augustine of Original Sin, but the ex-professor of rhetoric who brought to the Scriptures a sense of language and signification trained in the encounter with a mature secular literature. In the *De Doctrina Christiana* Augustine enumerates the skills necessary for the exegete but he subordinates these to the reference frame or mental set which enables us to discern the spiritual sense in material things,

> Thus in this mortal life, wandering from God, if we wish to return to our native country where we can be blessed we should *use* this world and not *enjoy* it, so that the 'invisible things' of God 'being understood by the things that are made' (Rom. 1. 20) may be seen – that is, so that by means of corporal and temporal things we may comprehend the eternal and spiritual.
>
> (I, iv, 4)

The theme of wandering has its special significance here, a platonic nostalgia, but it is eased by discerning a higher reference as we distinguish between *things* – wood, stone, cattle – and *signs* – the wood that Moses cast into the bitter waters, the stone Jacob placed at his head, the ram substituted for Isaac (*De Doctrina*, I, ii, 2). Things become types or signs when they lead us out of a single event and refer us to the metatext of divine action. As words are to thought, says Augustine, so Christ's body relates to his divinity. Writing can reveal a voice, and reading takes on the character of a sacrament.

Augustine's exegesis, in which Christian liberty is the proper interpretation of signs, provides the basis for a mode of reading which is at once more concrete and historical than platonic allegory and yet at the same time bound like that allegory to a world of

invisible things, of universals. The dramatic intervention in Book
VIII of *The Confessions* when Augustine hears the child chanting,
'Tolle, lege', is a classic moment in the history of hermeneutics.
Petrarch recognised this when, at the top of Mount Ventoux, he
pulled out his copy of *The Confessions* and was struck to the heart by
the words he read:

> And men go to admire the high mountains, the vast floods of the
> sea, the huge streams of the rivers, the circumference of the ocean
> and the revolutions of the stars – and desert themselves. [4]

The Confessions are a manifesto for the inner life, a struggle for self-
definition set in the memory, but they are also a way into the inner
life dense with references to that most intimately available of all
texts, the Psalms. Augustine's fusion of the particular sign with a
type or role makes possible the imaginative play by which letter
becomes spirit and the private moment reveals a concrete universal.
That expansion of the self which confrontation with a text implies
becomes to the Augustinian interpreter participation in sacral
history, in the Incarnation. The concept has been expressed
memorably by von Hügel.

> [Christ's] character and teaching require for an ever fuller yet
> never complete understanding, the varying study, and different
> experiments and applications, embodiments and unrollings of all
> the races and civilisations, of all the individual and corporate, the
> simultaneous and successive experiences of the human race to the
> end of time. [5]

It has been said of Petrarch that his corpus represents a major
manifestation of the switch from objective to subjective modes of
thought. This assessment underestimates his debt to classical
rhetoric, which he absorbed as much through his obsessive
relationship with Augustine as through Cicero. But we can certainly
accept Charles Trinkaus' assertion that the doctrine of the primacy
of the will, always a feature of rhetorical culture, 'was necessarily a
powerful stimulus to the rise of a poetic and rhetorical spirituality
and to the decline of philosophical and metaphysical theology'. [6]
The dominant concern of humanist scholarship, from Petrarch to
Erasmus, is to restore an Augustinian exegesis which is directed to
religious feeling rather than the intellect. Words do not so much

support definitions as relationships. The implications of this for the emergence of modern literature are immense.

In many respects this subjective exegesis marked a return to the older monastic habits of reading which have been described by Jean Leclercq. The text is not treated as a store of isolated *dicta* suited to syllogistic elaboration but as a personal encounter which unfolds naturally as prayer and what can best be called imaginative participation. In consequence of this alertness to the nature of the text seen within its total context, the highly formalised four-fold exegesis of late medieval commentators gives way to a number of variants on what Jacques Lefèvre d'Etaples in his *Quincuplex Psalterium* of 1509 calls the *true* literal sense. In his preface to this pioneer work Lefèvre mentions that he has been struck by the depression suffered by certain monks who adhered to the merely literal or historic sense. They are, indeed, imprisoned by the letter. Seeking guidance from the Apostles and Prophets, Lefèvre has discovered 'another sense of Scripture: the intention of the prophet and of the Holy Spirit speaking in him. This I call 'literal' sense, but a literal sense which coincides with the Spirit'.[7] What Lefèvre was looking for was something very like E. D. Hirsch's concept of authorial intention as intrinsic genre. What he does achieve is a middle course between historic literalism on the one hand and allegorical indulgence on the other. His spiritual-literal sense is derived from a christocentric reading of the Old Testament, one which allows also for the direct involvement of the reader's projected self. Letter and Spirit are reconciled by the Incarnation, which mediates the sense to every believer. The result is an affective exegesis which works through imaginative response to establish a dramatic confrontation with the text.

Such an exegesis extends Revelation to include the interpretative act of the reader. It is only through the mediation of the reader that 'things' become 'signs'; and to Lefèvre the 'things' include events in history as well as marks on parchment. In the spiritual drama of the individual these are reanimated and their meaning extended. Now this mode of 'humanist' exegesis clashes with the textual assumptions which underlie the scholastic theology of men like Petrus Sutor, a vigorous opponent of both Erasmus and Lefèvre precisely because they deny the finality of the Vulgate. Not only is the Vulgate text the foundation for traditional theology but Sutor sees it as inspired even to the letter. The Hebrew and Greek texts are irrelevant, by-passed, and in any case polluted by apostasy and schism. Clearly there is no room here for any sense of the cultural medium of revelation, the text is frozen and institutionalised. Sutor's attack on Erasmus in 1520 not only condemns the presumption of a new version of the New Testament, it attacks the affective habit of exegesis outlined in the *Ratio Perveniendi ad Veram Theologicam* that Erasmus had published with the 1518 edition of his New Testament. Behind this key work one can sense that pervasive model of humanism, the orator: its image of the theologian is Cicero in a surplice, 'professio theologica magis constat affectibus quam argumentis'. The aspiring theologian must be trained not only in the three tongues but in all the arts of language and the wiles of criticism. The *Ratio* is, in fact, an important text in the development of hermeneutics and reveals an alertness to the complexities of language quite beyond the semantic range of the Paris Theological Faculty. It is clear from the Faculty's condemnation of Lefèvre that its members either cannot or do not want to grasp figurative language, but then even St Thomas criticised Plato for using words figuratively. The affective bias of Erasmus' hermeneutic is not directed at emotion for its own sake, it need hardly be said, but at releasing the text from the constraints of the historical letter to promote personal application. It aims to disclose the world within the work and relate that dynamically to the world of the reader. The Bible is thus a repertory of roles that must be acted out in the individual's life.

Erasmus encourages the reader to make a library of Christ in his own breast. By using that profoundly Augustinian faculty, the memory, it is possible to recognise signs in one's own experience, to make a constant application. This development of hermeneutics into an inner drama is an important consequence of humanist exegesis and it is very fully developed, for example, in John Donne's reading of the Bible. To him the memory is (in St Bernard's phrase) 'stomachus animae', the Holy Ghost's pulpit, a picture-gallery or a book in which a man 'may reade many a history of God's goodnesse to him'.[8] In this very private space it is possible to interpret all history; to find our life in the Scriptures:

> But draw the Scripture to thine owne heart, and to thine owne acts, and thou shalt finde it made for that; all the promises of the Old Testament made, and accomplished in the New Testament, for the salvation of thy soul hereafter, and for thy consolation in the present application of them.
>
> (*Sermons*, II, 308)

It is the application that is crucial, and Donne puts this vividly in his Christmas sermon for 1621.

> This is *scrutari scripturas*, to search the Scriptures, not as though thou wouldest make a concordance, but an application; as thou wouldest search a wardrobe, not to make an *Inventory* of it, but to finde in it something fit for thy wearing.
>
> (*Sermons*, III, 367)

That is precisely the distinction between Sutor's mode of exegesis and that of Erasmus; on the one hand an inventory, on the other garments 'fit for thy wearing'. The close relationship between this kind of religious experience and literary experience is clear; religious experience results from a willingness to adopt a particular frame of reference which, in its turn, structures the content of perception. Such a response, or mediation, is essentially creative. An apt example is Archbishop Laud's scaffold speech in 1644 when, as he prepares for the axe, he makes a suitably 'metaphysical' connection between his plight and the Israelites' passage through the Red Sea.

> I have prayed as my Saviour taught me, and exampled me, *Ut transiret calix ista*, That this Cup of Red Wine might passe away from me, but since it is not that my will may, his will be done; and I shall willingly drinke of this Cup as deep as he pleases and enter into this Sea, age and passe through it, in the way he shall be pleased to lead me.[9]

– Into the Promised Land, in fact. Type and antitype, Red Sea and Calvary, are relived for a moment on Tower Hill. By appropriation physical fear and defeat are transformed.

This typological habit of self-projection is a necessary condition for Donne's finest literary achievements, in the occasional poems such as 'Goodfriday' and in the sermons, where the domineering *persona* of the early poems is broadened out into the collective *persona* of Christian experience. It is in *The Devotions*, in particular, that religion is treated as a repertory of roles to be enacted in a world demanding constant interpretation – nothing is itself alone.

> The *stile* of thy *works*, the *phrase* of thine *Actions*, is *Metaphorical*. The *institution* of thy whole *worship* in the *old Law*, was a continuall

Allegory; types & *figures* overspread all; and *figures* flowed into *figures*, and powered themselves out into further figures . . .[10]

As with Laud, events constitute a language.

This wit of application reflected an exegesis alert to the experience of secular literature. It seems equally valid to see the impact of such exegesis in the status accorded to fiction in, for example, Sidney's *Apology for Poetry* (1795). Sidney's work is, in essence, a defence of fiction and should be read in terms of a specific convention, that of the anti-scholastic polemic. This genre, typified by Erasmus' *Antibarbari*, is concerned with warring views of language, stressing the occult resonance of words against the merely definitive language theory of the scholastics. Like Erasmus, Sidney stresses the imaginative element necessary in true education, justifying fiction by its power to touch the roots of human motive and guide it. Thus the philosopher with his jargon of 'genus and difference' may fill the memory with doctrines

which, notwithstanding lie dark before the imaginative and judging power, if they be not illuminated or figured forth by the speaking picture of poesy.[11]

Christ's use of parables, for example, ensured that his teaching 'would more constantly . . . inhabit both the memory and the judgement'. The highly spatial terms Sidney uses are reminiscent of Augustine's account of the cave of memory in the *Confessions*.

It is Sidney's use of the theologically coloured terms 'erected wit' and 'infected will' which is especially suggestive. The golden world of art is seen as in a moral sense contagious, allowing some traffic between the projections of idealising imagination and the limping efforts of fallen man. The imagination performs, in effect, a moral alchemy. It is on this basis of imaginative engagement or vicarious experience that Milton in the *Areopagitica* (1644) can esteem 'our sage and serious Poet *Spencer*, whom I dare be known to think a better teacher than *Scotus* or *Aquinas*'. Scotus and Aquinas are rated lower not because they are Catholics (not primarily at least) but because they are schoolmen; *Areopagitica*, too, belongs in the anti-scholastic polemical convention. The approval of Spenser is based on his creation in Guyon's journey through Mammon's Cave of a type to be appropriated by 'the imaginative and judging power'. Milton's brief apology for poetry points to its own convention in its clear echoes of Melanchthon's *Encomium Eloquentiae*, the inaugural of Protestant rhetoric.

When Samuel Johnson told Boswell over breakfast, 'I do not approve of figurative expressions in addressing the Supreme Being', he reveals in religious terms the same kind of restriction which blocked his reading of 'Lycidas'. It is a restriction that can be traced to a theology of edification and reasonable piety, the product of that 'unenlivened generalizing Understanding' which Coleridge associates with Lockian philosophy. Coleridge, by way of contrast, notes that 'Donne's poetry must be sought in his prose', a recognition that the prose religious writings are the fullest expression of Donne's imaginative power. Coleridge's alertness to the older hermeneutics underlies his important remarks on imagination and the Bible in *The Statesman's Manual* (1816). Imagination is described as the 'reconciling and mediatory power' which incorporates the reason in images of the senses, and thus 'gives birth to a system of symbols, harmonious in themselves, and consubstantial with the truths, of which they are the *conductors*'. Where 'the present age' can see no link between literal and metaphorical, the Bible reveals

the stream of time continuous as Life and a symbol of Eternity, inasmuch as the Past and the Future are virtually contained in the Present. According therefore to our relative position on its banks the Sacred History becomes prophetic, the Sacred Prophecies historical, while the power and substance of both inhere in its Laws, its Promises and its Comminations. In the Scriptures therefore both Facts and Persons must of necessity have a two-fold significance, a past and a future, a temporary and a perpetual, a particular and a universal application. They must be at once Portraits and Ideals.[12]

This matches the strategy of Donne's *Devotions*, and it is not difficult to see how Coleridge's grasp of affective exegesis leads him to his conception of the literary symbol as a 'concrete universal'. The status accorded to poetry by Coleridge and by Wordsworth (whose *Prelude* can be read as an Augustinian 'recollection') was possible because of the way in which, unlike the less permeable surface of naturalistic prose fiction, it had maintained the functions of personal 'placing' which an older tradition practised on the Bible.

All this suggests the importance of incarnational exegesis or *applicatio* for the emergence of reading habits and thus of literary possibilities. Hermeneutics may by now have been secularised, but that does not affect its religious roots. Jonathan Culler has written how,

> By offering sequences and combinations which escape our accustomed grasp, by subjecting language to a dislocation which fragments the ordinary signs of our world, literature challenges the limits we set to the self as a device of order and allows us, painfully or joyfully to accede to an expansion of self.[13]

Augustine would recognise the point of such an ascesis. As readers we use our familiar prejudices in order to escape from them; in the dialogue between text and reader our sense of possibility is continually reanimated, the idol of self discarded. If, as Nicholas Lash has argued,[14] the theologian has as much to learn from the literary circle as the philosopher, that is partly because the critic remains something of a theologian in disguise.

NOTES

1. The medieval examples are described in M. T. Clanchy, *From Memory to Written Record* (London, 1979), p. 210.
2. Northrop Frye, *The Great Code* (London, 1982), p. 3.
3. 'Biblical Hermeutics', *Semeia*, 4 (1975), 29–148 (p. 141).
4. *Confessions*, X, 8, 15. Petrarca, *Le Familiari*, IV, 1, 27–8.
5. Friedrich von Hügel, *The Mystical Element in Religion* (London, 1923), I, 26.
6. Charles Trinkaus, *The Poet as Philosopher* (New Haven/London, 1979), p. 113.
7. *Quincuplex Psalterium* (Paris, 1509), sig., translated in H. O. Oberman, *Forerunners of the Reformation* (London, 1967), pp. 297–301.
8. *The Sermons*, ed. G. R. Potter and E. M. Simpson (Berkeley, 1953–61), VIII, 261. Bracket references are to this edition.
9. *The Archbishop of Canterbury's Speech* (London, Peter Cole, 1644), p. 7.
10. John Donne, *Devotions Upon Emergent Occasions*, ed. A. Raspa (Montreal/London, 1975), p. 100.
11. *An Apology for Poetry*, ed. G. Shepherd (London, 1965), p. 107.
12. S. T. Coleridge, *Lay Sermons*, ed. R. J. White (London, 1972), pp. 28–30.
13. J. Culler, *Structuralist Poetics* (London, 1975), p. 130.
14. N. Lash, *Theology on Dover Beach* (London, 1979), p. 20.

11 Story: Towards a Christian Theory of Narrative

Michael Edwards

There are many ways in which Christians may explore narrative, nearly all of them useful. If a theory of narrative is to be developed, however, the one question which needs to be asked, surely, and asked again, is the most basic and also the most vulnerable: what is story, why does it exist? The question stands further back than the enquiry into, say, the religious vision of this writer, or biblical themes in that work, so as to focus, not on the possible Christian bearing of any particular story or set of stories, but on the Christian bearing of story in general – that is, the meaning of story in a world created by God, fallen, and some time to be recreated. It also goes deeper than the more familiar theoretical questions, about the nature of epic, of romance, of the novel, of the folk tale; it leaves aside the forms which narrative assumes, to confront narrative itself. And it extends beyond narrative as a genre, since it can be referred to drama, or to poetry or, for that matter, to jokes.

Story, indeed, is quite mysterious, and certainly not to be taken for granted. We might, rather, be surprised that we tell each other tales, and write them down, obsessively, from country to country and from generation to generation: that we delight in engaging our minds with hypothetical situations and notional persons, with happenings that did not happen, in a world not exactly ours. This is a singular determination, to involve ourselves in fiction, but we begin to understand it, I suggest, when we consider the fact that we cannot imagine stories in Eden. There could certainly be the recounting of events, so as to pass on information or communicate a

179

response; but the events would be received as in no way different from reality, and if the recounting was felt as having a form, the form would be that which reality continually displayed – a small instance of the Cosmos. There would be no need for stories in which event is imagined and form is created. Nor would there be any need for invented characters, or for invented place or time. Since evil and death would be unknown, one presumes that being would be undivided, the present would be presence, and the real would be enough. According to the old adage, a happy people has no history; it also has no story.

The need for story comes with the exile from Eden. And this is so whether or not Eden actually existed. It suffices that we know that, in either case, we are not living there now. Whatever our beliefs or lack of them, a flaming sword 'turns every way' between our notion of what a Garden of perfection would be and our experience of what the world is. The oneness of Eden excludes story; when evil enters to corrupt that oneness – whether as an event in history or an event in our consciousness – story is born, as another world to be reached for out of this fallen one. Necessity is the mother of invention, as they say, and need is the mother of story.

We tell stories in a fallen world. By their matter they may lament and counter that fall, as is supremely the case when their import is tragic or comic. The strange power of story, however, is also to achieve those ends simply by being itself. Whatever its 'content', it opens a story-world, where everything coheres infrangibly and is impeccably. That world may well be as fallen as the one we inhabit daily; it may even be more terrifying or more grotesque. Yet as a narrated world it represents a desirable otherness. Story quits a world that does not, seemingly, have a story – or whose only story: 'There was a fall from Eden', may be repeated but cannot be finished – for a world that, within the consciousness of the tale, does. We tell stories because we desire a world with a story.

Story offers an otherness, of unity and purposive sequence. It also offers, in particular, beginnings and ends. The search for beginnings is, naturally, a fundamental enterprise, in cosmogonies, genealogies, histories. The specific of story is that it appeals to the desire for a new beginning. We may come to story with any version of the idea that a first beginning, if there was one, has gone deeply wrong, that universal, individual or social Creation has been succeeded by Fall, and that evil needs to be removed in a fresh start.

The start of story is so fresh that it occurs in another dimension, which replaces ours in the twinkling of an opening sentence. Into the dead present of Ecclesiastes: 'The thing that hath been, it is that which shall be; and that which is done is that which shall be done: and there is no new thing under the sun' (1.9), it intrudes the magic departure of 'Once upon a time'; it responds to the Preacher's question: 'Is there any thing whereof it may be said, See, this is new?' (1.10), by presenting itself. It provides, in the seeming safety of narrative, an aesthetic version of St Paul's *kainē ktisis* (2 Corinthians 5.17), a 'new creation' that promises an irresistibly unfolding story ahead.

An end is equally a form of salvation, substituting, for mere addition, finality and climax, and concentrating time into a shape. It may also be another kind of beginning. It is so, though irresponsibly, in popular narratives – which are likely to manifest more clearly than others the latent design of story – whenever any version of the formula 'and they lived happily ever after' in-augurates a future of undemanding and quasi-infinite hope. The characters do not so much 'quit the story', as Raymond Queneau phrases it, [1] as enter a further dimension of the story-world so secure that it does not even need to be told.

As story is a response to fallen history, so it responds to a fallen physical universe. Again, this need not imply that it transforms the latter's 'vanity' and 'corruption' (in St Paul's words) into order and newness, since the change operates in terms not of the universe to which story alludes but of the manner of existence of that universe. The most chaotic, alien physicality will inevitably be a locus of narrative, a story-place, invulnerable before the forces by which real place is undermined.

The time of story also is different from our time. One sign of this among many is that while story-time is usually articulated by the past tense of the verb, the pastness of the tense has been strangely removed. The verb does not refer to the past of the writer or of the reader, nor does it refer to the past of the world – even in stories located in history. Within the tale, their past is no more historical than that of stories occurring in the present, or even in the future: if we discover in Sir Walter Scott that Edward Waverley took leave of his family sixty years ago, we also learn, on opening Orwell's most famous book that 'It was a bright cold day in April' 1984. The function of the tense is to proclaim itself the tense of narrative: it is less the past historic than the past storic. It 'signals an art' (according to Roland Barthes in *Writing Degree Zero*[2]), and eases our passage into the story world.

Most importantly, personae in story live charmed lives in comparison with persons in reality. As we want the world to have a story, so we should like our life to be a tale, its moments caught up into significance and its whole governed by the logic of final causes. The characters of fiction (I use the word 'characters' for want of a less loaded term), even if they see themselves as amorphous, and even if they are presented as such, have already achieved that privilege. However 'true to life' they may be, and however they may suffer within the tale, their salvation lies in the fact that they are narrated. Although they may, referentially, be denizens of our own, fallen world, they also inhabit the glory of form. Their story may be read over and over again, and can never be damaged.

Modern narrative and reflection on narrative have familiarised us to a certain extent with the notion of the possible otherness of the story world. This otherness, however, this fictionality of fiction, is not a feature of one type of story only, to the exclusion of others. In *Le livre à venir*,[3] Maurice Blanchot describes what he calls the *récit* as treating of 'an exceptional event which escapes the forms of quotidian time and the world of habitual truth', so as to distinguish it from the *roman*, which is 'an entirely human story', founded on human time and human passions (pp. 11–13). Yet, no matter how far a narrative may be from a concern with the exceptional and the inhabitual, no matter how meticulously it may set about a plausible and exact rendering of what it assumes to be the real, by the very nature of story its events happen elsewhere, in another time, and differently. The world of the most dogged *roman*, of the most realist of Victorian novels, is a world essentially narrated.

The same is true of what seems to be the natural conclusion of the foregoing: that the navigation of story is supremely towards itself. Again, Blanchot says of the *récit* that it 'is not the relation of the event but the event itself, the approach to the event, the place where the event is called on to occur: an event still to come and through whose drawing power the *récit* also can hope to materialize' (p. 13). Yet here too, even when narrative pretends, as it usually does, that its events have occurred already, prior to their being written about, it is nevertheless the story which produces them – they can only occur, in fact, as they are narrated, and even real events change in narration and occur in a new guise – and which, by the same act, produces itself. What story recounts is its own recounting; it tells its own possibility. It is naturally reflexive, not only within the scope of modernism but under any historical conditions.

Not all stories, of course, are aware of themselves in these terms. Very many are, however: in a surprising array of major works, the self-telling is essential and explicit. I should like briefly to consider several such works, not for the purpose of illustrating a theory but so as to meditate it from a number of different points of view, and in a way to allow the writers – all great storytellers – to speak for themselves.

Consider, first, Boccaccio's *Decameron*. It begins by describing the Black Death of 1348 at a length and with an insistence that have been found puzzling. Why does Boccaccio dwell so much on the plague when he only needs to indicate, apparently, that it was the reason why the ten young people left the city together? Is he merely taking the opportunity of expressing compassion, horror, indignation at the cruelty and foolishness of the citizens? Or is he establishing the plague as the source of the subsequent hundred stories? In terms of mimesis, seven young women and three young men escape from plague-ridden Florence to a carefree estate on the slopes of a nearby hill; in terms of narrative self-reflection, future storytellers flee from a fallen world, 'in quest of health',[4] to a world of stories.

Through the particulars on which the narrative focuses, moreover, the Black Death resembles original sin. It spreads from the East, passes from person to person through far slighter contact than contagious diseases usually demand, and affects not only humans but all living creatures. There is also a suggestion that the storytellers escape from the wrath to come: the narrator speculates that although the pestilence may have been disseminated by the influence of the celestial bodies, it may also have been 'sent upon us mortals by God in His just wrath by way of retribution for our iniquities'.[5] And the place where the storytellers assemble to tell their stories is Paradise. There are strong hints of this in the description of the domain in which they spend the first two days; it becomes explicit when they move to another domain. They enter a walled garden, are 'wonder-struck', smell odours of 'all the spices that ever grew in the East', and conclude that no beauty could be added to it and that no 'other form could be given to Paradise, if it were to be planted on earth'.[6]

Their journey to this further story-world is also carefully plotted in terms of the Christian dialectic, of life, death and rebirth. They leave one place of health, travel over a Friday and Saturday during which they remain silent and story-less, in memory of Easter Friday on which 'He who died for us bore His passion', and enter a more splendid Paradise on a Sunday of resurrection.

The Decameron is exemplary in that it causes the significance of story to declare itself. It tells the story of characters whose main occupation is to tell stories, thereby suggesting that story's intrinsic concern is itself. It places story-telling in the context of death and a fallen world on the one hand and paradise on the other. It defines the site where narrative occurs. If that site is paradisal and resurrectional, moreover, one also realises that the plague brings the narrative domain back, as it were, to earth. It qualifies the paradise of story, as being not an achieved salvation from the world's ills but a glimpse, a metaphor of that salvation.

Chaucer's *Canterbury Tales* also tells of people telling stories, and indicates the narrative status of its world. It is a kind of voyage through tales: the characters travel both towards Canterbury and towards heaven – towards St Thomas the 'hooly blisful martir' – and they do so by making their way along a road of stories. The first line of the very first tale: 'Whilom, as olde stories tellen us', even declares that one is about to enter, not a tale but the tale of a tale; it draws its hearers, and also its reader, into more than one narrative depth. The *Tales* are themselves a pilgrimage, and where they lead is into a story-world.

They refer to the fact that they are being related; and they also refer, on one brief occasion, to the person who is relating them. I am thinking of the Prologue to Sir Thopas, whose function is not only (if at all) to provide a now famous description of the real-life Chaucer, but to summon the author out of hiding:

> And thanne at erst [our host] looked upon me,
> And seyde thus, 'What man artow?' quod he;
> 'Thou lookest as thou woldest fynde an hare,
> For evere upon the ground I se thee stare'.[7]

It is not merely that the Host turns for a story to 'Chaucer' the pilgrim. The person staring intently downwards may well be Chaucer the pilgrim taking notes, but he is also Chaucer the writer, who is scrutinising the page on which he is in the process of writing those very lines. The Host looks both within the poem and out from the poem, to detect his author and to mock him. He even calls him a 'popet', as if punning on 'poet'. As the author's master of the tale-telling, he addresses the only actual tale-teller, by piercing his disguise as narrator-pilgrim, and asks him for a tale. It is a vertiginous moment, and an extremely sophisticated one.

The sudden shift from the story-world to the room of the storyteller, by occurring in the middle of the book, brings to our attention the fact that the entire work through which we are making our way, however prolifically, pleasurably and instructively 'real', is a huge and single Tale, the invention of a particular writer. It invites the reader not to lose himself in the story but to find himself there, by measuring one against the other the fiction and his sense of fact. The Host may even be addressing the reader directly, since he too is looking down. In that case, the work springs him out of the story-world even more drastically, makes him aware of the activity in which he is engaged, and forces him to relate to the story-world before returning to it.

Furthermore, as it discloses the writer behind the narrator, so the Host's gaze puts Chaucer himself on the spot. I suggested that we should like our lives to be tales and ourselves to be characters; Chaucer has achieved that ambition, by placing 'Chaucer' among the pilgrims and so entering his own tale thinly camouflaged. He is aware, however, of the problematic nature of that move. By causing his Host – a real character – to banter him back into his study, he makes clear the merely fictive, ludic status of himself-as-character. And by having the Host pose that most searching of questions: 'What man artow?' he reveals even more of a deep personal exploration in the *Tales* and acknowledges, in a marvellously swift piece of comedy, that if the writer sounds himself and the world through his work, the work also sounds him. I take it that only as the *Tales* come to an end is the question beginning to be answered.

Sir Thomas Malory's *Tale of the Sankgreal* also refers to itself as narrative, and is in some ways even more unexpected. It tells the story of a story-world, not simply in the sense that its medieval knight-errantry is romance, but in the sense that the events of the story are described, over and over again, as 'adventures'. What happens in the story is story. It also moves forward to a point from which it can look back on itself, and exhibit its own concluding:

And when they had eaten, the king made great clerks to come afore him, that they should chronicle of the high adventures of the good knights. When Bors had told him of the adventures of the

Sangrail, such as had befall him and his three fellows, that was Launcelot, Percival, Galahad, and himself, there Launcelot told the adventures of the Sangrail that he had seen. All this was made in great books, and put up in almeries at Salisbury.[8]

The adventures attain their end by being told; and they are gathered finally into a book, which, at a number of removes, is the book that we have just been reading.

One thinks of Proust. The most celebrated of modern quest narratives, his *A la recherche du temps perdu*,[9] is also a search for story, as much as for lost time, since Marcel turns his experience of involuntary memory, and the adventurous moments of pure time which it procures, into the possibility of writing. He is only about to begin writing as the novel closes, but, as in Malory and Malory's source, the book to which he refers at the end is nevertheless the book that we have already read. *A la recherche* is another story questing for itself. Its modernity lies partly in the fact that it is now the narrator who searches for narrative, partly in the extra degree of explicitness – indeed, in the obviousness – of the reference to that search.

The Tale of the Sankgreal recounts the means by which it became itself. The special interest of the tale, however, from the point of view adopted here, is that its characters are also endeavouring to become, precisely, characters in a tale. In seeking the Grail they seek 'adventures', which, as the etymology suggests, will come to them, and take control of them in real life (as it were) just as stories control characters in a book. Accordingly, a voice says to Galahad, Perceval and Bors: 'Lords and fellows, tomorrow at the hour of prime, ye three shall depart every each from other, till the aventure bring you to the Maimed King';[10] while the white knight tells Galahad, in what is both a command and a promise: 'go where the aventures shall lead thee'.[11] Whereas Boccaccio's characters re-count stories in paradise, Malory's characters desire actually to enter the paradise of story.

Malory also isolates, however, a higher level of story and declares it alone to be genuinely paradisal. Not all knights, nor even all 'adventures', have access to it. Before being adopted by the higher level, Galahad and Lancelot find 'many straunge adventures and peryllous', but since they do not concern the Grail they remain unrecounted: 'the tale maketh here no mention thereof'.[12] Other knights, refused entry, find that even ordinary adventures have abandoned them. Gawain rides 'long without any adventure', and meets the equally luckless Ector, who tells of twenty other knights in the same distress.[13] They ask a hermit why they no longer meet with adventures as before, and are told that they are unfit for the story which has superseded all others, for it is 'the adventure of the Sangrail which be in shewing now'. This is partly a matter of self-explaining literary choice: certain knights and certain events are required for the particular story to be written, while others are not. Relations are also established, however, between the story-world and our world. It is because of real, human failures that knights are excluded from the Grail story: Gawain and Ector for their 'evil faith' and 'poor belief', Lancelot for his 'old sin'. Those who succeed do so because of real qualities.

The *Tale* is again placing story, like *The Decameron*, in terms of Fall and Paradise. The knights travel through this 'unsyker' or unstable world, compounded of a variety of evils, and what they seek is simultaneously the Grail and adventures, as if the heavenly vision, or the road towards it, were to be understood as a narrative – as if, story being a kind of paradise, paradise were also a kind of story. Some knights fail both of the Grail and of adventure; their lot is not only sorrow but, more pointedly, 'disadventure' or 'misadventure'. Some become the heroes of ordinary adventures, and enter the fiction of a redeemed world; they enjoy finality, significance, looming eventfulness. Some few are accepted for the adventure of the Grail, and are, simply, redeemed.

Each of these works, as it happens, is a compilation of tales, and two indicate as much by their title. This type of narrative seems particularly significant: it attests a desire for story after story, and for story within story, and suggests that we can never have enough stories. The *Thousand and One Nights* also belongs here, with Ovid's *Metamorphoses* and Dante's *Commedia*, as do numerous and various works of episodic fiction from the *Odyssey* to picaresque novels. So, tellingly, does a short and tightly organised narrative like Mme. de La Fayette's *La Princesse de Clèves*, with its several 'digressions'.

In their showing of the need for story and of the ease with which story becomes self-aware, however, works that are not overtly tales at all are even more suggestive. Take, for example, the plays of Shakespeare, considered not as dramas or dramatic poems but as dramatic narratives. Many realise their status as stories at the moment of their completion. In the final scene of *Romeo and Juliet*, Friar Laurence resumes the events for the benefit of the Prince in a

long and circumstantial 'tale', whose technical purpose seems to be
to reiterate as story what the audience has been experiencing as
theatre. The audience perceives the whole play now as a single
narrated sequence, and is even invited by the Prince in the
concluding couplet to compare it with others of a similar nature:
'For never was a story of more woe/Than this of Juliet and her
Romeo'. There is a kind of literary withdrawal from the events of
the play, comparable to the moment when the stories in Malory are
chronicled and 'made into books'. A similar effect is produced when
plays finish by having their characters retire, perhaps to an abbey or
a cell and with a circle of listeners, to recount and to hear the 'story'
or 'discourse' of all that has been performed (*The Comedy of Errors,
The Two Gentlemen of Verona, The Tempest*); or when they are
prolonged into a fictive future by the promise of a good tale of more
limited scope (*The Merchant of Venice, Much Ado About Nothing, All's
Well that Ends Well, Pericles*).

The writer may also be revealed. The Chorus at the end of
Henry V, in the lines, 'Thus far, with rough and all-unable pen,/Our
bending author hath pursu'd the story', replaces play, players and
playhouse by story, writer and study. Interestingly, the expression,
'bending author', reminds one both of Chaucer's sudden appearance and of his physical posture. Characters too may become
literarily self-aware, at the end of the play and of their life, by
perceiving their life as narrative. Hamlet, for instance, appeals to
Horatio to tell his 'story', and much is made of the fact, with Horatio
giving Fortinbras a kind of foretaste of the tale ('carnal, bloody, and
unnatural acts . . .'), and Fortinbras responding by gathering a
circle of hearers and calling 'the noblest to the audience'.

The most remarkable of such cases is Othello's. About to kill
himself, he tells Lodovico what to write about him:

> I pray you, in your letters
> When you shall these unlucky deeds relate
> Speak of me as I am . . .
> Of one that lov'd not wisely but too well;
>   . . . of one whose hand,
> Like the base Indian, threw a pearl away
> Richer than all his tribe; of one whose subdu'd eyes
> Albeit unused to the melting mood,
> Drop tears as fast as the Arabian trees
> Their med'cinable gum.

(Act V. ii. 342–53)

Not only does Othello foresee his life become narrative at some
future date: he himself transforms it into narrative by recounting it
with the conventional signs of the past tense and the third person.
The sudden move into the present tense – 'Drop' – shows, moreover,
that he is also apprehending the present as story; and with almost his
last words and his last action he causes the two temporal dimensions
to merge:

> Set you down this;
> And say besides, that in Aleppo once,
> Where a malignant and a turban'd Turk
> Beat a Venetian and traduc'd the state,
> I took by the throat the circumcised dog,
> And smote him thus.
>
> (ii. 353–8)

He returns to the narrative past, but he continues to live the
narration in the present. His stabbing himself may be 'a superb *coup de
théâtre*'[14] – it also brings the time of story into the time of his life (at
the stroke of death). In the dizzy time-shift between 'smote' and
'thus' Othello becomes, even more self-consciously than the Grail
knights, the hero of a story. It is left to Lodovico, in the final lines, to
distance himself from the play and from the place, and to gather the
deed into more customary narrative: 'Myself will straight aboard,
and to the state/This heavy act with heavy heart relate'.

When they have run their course, Shakespeare's plays achieve
various ends, as tragic fulfilment, or comic marriage. They also
achieve story. A happy train of events is likely to brim over into tale;
an unhappy, by being perceived as a tale, may transpose its *misère*
into the otherness of story. Characters may even be aware of that
otherness. Once again, works uninfluenced by modern theories of
fiction bring to their surface their quest for narrative. One wonders,
indeed, if the idea of 'story' was not as important for Shakespeare as
the more familiar idea of 'theatre'.

To identify story as a response to the Fall, as the fiction of a fallen
world remade, offers a possible beginning, it seems to me, for a
Christian theory of narrative. It immediately opens two further
lines of enquiry. One would concern itself with the relation between
the fiction of story and, shall we say, the other fiction that we call
fact; it would meditate in particular the inclination of story, by
reason of its otherness, to devalue and maybe lose the world in a
flight towards story for story's sake. The second would explore the

relation between our stories and the one Story, or history, of the world – a story both controlled and narrated by God; and especially the story of Jesus, along with its interestingly multiple narrating in the Gospels. Such a radical beginning, moreover, would also seem a guide towards an equally radical beginning for a Christian theory of all writing. This might well be grounded on questions even more steep and extravagant than the one posed at the start of this chapter: what is literature?, why is there literature?, what and why is language?

NOTES

1. Raymond Queneau, *Une histoire modèle* (Paris, 1966).
2. Roland Barthes, *Writing Degree Zero* (London, 1967).
3. Maurice Blanchot, *Le livre à venir* (Paris, 1959).
4. Boccaccio, *The Decameron*, translated by J. M. Rigg (London, 1930) p. 15.
5. *Decameron*, pp. 4–5.
6. *Decameron*, p. 154.
7. Chaucer, *The Canterbury Tales*, F. N. Robinson (ed.), Second Edition (Oxford, 1957), p. 164, lines 691–4.
8. Malory, *Le Morte D'Arthur*, Janet Cowen (ed.) (Harmondsworth, 1969), Vol. 2, p. 371.
9. Marcel Proust, *A la recherche du temps perdu* (Paris, 1913–27).
10. *Le Morte D'Arthur*, p. 350.
11. *Le Morte D'Arthur*, p. 354.
12. *Le Morte D'Arthur*, p. 353.
13. *Le Morte D'Arthur*, p. 301.
14. F. R. Leavis, *The Common Pursuit* (London, 1952), p. 152.

Index